JOSEPH WAMBAUGH

FIRE LOVER

A True Story

WILLIAM MORROW

An Imprint of HarperCollins*Publishers*

HarperCollins books may be purchased for educational, business, or sales promotional use. For information please write: Special Markets Department, HarperCollins Publishers Inc., 10 East 53rd Street, New York, NY 10022.

FIRST EDITION

Designed by Nicola Ferguson

Printed on acid-free paper

Library of Congress Cataloging-in-Publication Data

Wambaugh, Joseph.
Fire lover / by Joseph Wambaugh.—1st ed.
p.   cm.
ISBN 0-06-009527-X
1. Arson—California—Case studies. 2. Pyromania—California—Case studies. 3. Orr
John Leonard. I. Title.

HV6638.5.U6 W36 2002
364.16'4—dc21   2002020139

02 03 04 05 06 RRD 10 9 8 7 6 5 4 3 2 1

For Mike Matassa

CONTENTS

ACKNOWLEDGMENTS

There are many people to thank for the interviews and for providing thousands of pages of documents, reports, and court transcripts. In alphabetical order, these include: Jim Allen, Karl Anglin, Chris Blancett, Walter Brown, Mike Cabral, Mike Camello, April Carroll, Marvin Casey, Ken Croke, Rich Edwards, Carl Faller, Sandra Flannery, Chuck Galyan, Gus Gary, Peter Giannini, Pat Hanly, John Herzfeld, Tom Kuczynski, Joe Lopez, Glen Lucero, Mike Matassa, Douglas McCann, Steve Patterson, Edward Rucker, Walt Scheuerell, and Stefan Stein.

My interviews with John Leonard Orr and the permission to use his unpublished autobiography were invaluable as well.

Hopefully, those depicted in this book will find their portrayals to be fair.

This Is a True Story

FIRE
LOVER

PROLOGUE

I t wasn't until January of 2002 that an episode in Los Angeles finally closed the book on a unique criminal investigation and prosecution. This massive inquiry involved a person whom a U.S. government serial-arson profiler at the FBI's National Center for the Analysis of Violent Crimes had dubbed "probably the most prolific American arsonist of the twentieth century."

California arson investigators would concur that this case was like nothing seen before, transforming the methods of those who scan fire scenes for that elusive "point of origin." Arson sleuths were forced to consider certain possibilities that had seemed unthinkable prior to an unprecedented series of incendiary fires that blazed across Central and Southern California for many years. The flames would never be damped for those who had been psychically seared by the inferno.

Perhaps an arbitrary point of origin for this story might be found in the quiet old Los Angeles suburb of South Pasadena, on the evening of October 10, 1984, during the World Series.

I

CALAMITY

South Pasadena is a small city of some twenty thousand residents who live within three square miles of mostly aging homes and limited commercial property. Many of the houses were built in the 1920s, the heyday of California mission architecture, before the Great Depression stifled home building. Neighboring Pasadena, host to the famous Rose Parade, continued building luxury homes well into the 1930s, some of them gems of California style, all in need of periodic renovation. A good place for homeowners to buy materials to refurbish those old houses was Ole's Home Center on Fair Oaks Avenue, an eighteen-thousand-square-foot building in a strip mall, three blocks from the town's only fire station.

At 7:30 P.M. that October evening, a middle-aged couple, Billy and Ada Deal, and their two-and-a-half-year-old grandson, Matthew William Troidl, arrived in Ole's parking lot. Matthew immediately spotted the neighboring Baskin-Robbins and wanted ice cream. His grandfather promised him they would have their treat after they finished shopping, and they walked through the entry door.

Working in the housewares department that evening was seventeen-year-old Jimmy Cetina. He was a high-school senior and a talented athlete. In fact, this varsity center fielder was being scouted by the Chicago Cubs to play double A ball. He had Latino good looks, and had recently entered a Bullock's department store modeling competition and won it. Doubtlessly, he would rather have been at some other place than Ole's Home Center on that October evening, especially during the World Series, but there were seven children in his family who had to look for empty bottles and cans to exchange for deposits if they wanted to buy sports equipment. He needed this job.

Billy and Ada Deal knew that the near-empty store was about to close, so they decided to split up and shop separately to save time. Billy wanted to buy some cheap two-by-fours, so he headed for the lumber display, which was between the north and south fire doors. Ada said she was going to the paint department.

Carolyn Krause was working in the paint department that evening, so she may well have seen the fifty-year-old grandmother pushing her grandson Matthew William in a shopping cart. Carolyn Krause was married to an LAPD lieutenant and had two young children of her own. She may have heard Matthew asking when he was going to get his ice cream. And someone else who was in that store may have heard him too. Or perhaps not. This issue would be later debated in courts of law.

It had been a long shift for Jim Obdam. The young clerk had been working in the hardware department all day and into the evening. Just after 8:00 P.M. he heard something over the PA system, but couldn't make out what had been said. He was headed for the front of the store, toward the south aisle, and there he was astonished to see a column of dark smoke rising from a display rack, all the way to the ceiling.

Jim Obdam hurried toward the west end of the store, looking for customers. He saw people heading toward the exits, but still was not alarmed when he arrived at the paint department.

"Are there any more people in your section?" he asked Carolyn Krause.

She answered, "I'll check my area!" And then she rushed through the hardware department looking for stragglers.

Still, nobody was alarmed. Nobody had seen any fire, just that column of dark smoke. In fact, Jim Obdam found two people browsing in hardware, looking at tools. He told them to leave the store at once.

And then he encountered a middle-aged woman with a small child in a shopping cart. Ada Deal was looking at merchandise on an end cap at the foot of the aisle.

"We've got to leave the store," Jim Obdam told her. "But don't be alarmed."

Ada Deal put some merchandise into the cart behind her grandson, Matthew. Jim Obdam walked hurriedly down the north aisle toward the main part of the store, but when he looked around, Ada Deal hadn't started to follow, so he went back.

"You should probably leave the cart here," he said, more forcefully. "Take the child and let's go!"

And then he headed toward the front of the store, assuming that Ada Deal and her grandson were following behind him. He was near the north fire door, about two aisles away, when he looked back toward that column of smoke. But it was no longer a cloud. It was a *wall of flame*. It was bright orange and *raging*. Then he noticed the north fire door had closed. That steel door had dropped down.

When he turned to look for the woman and child he heard a popping noise and the lights went out. And Jim Obdam suddenly felt alone and *trapped*.

A bell chimed in the lumber area: *"Ting ting ting."* That's how Billy Deal described it. And there was an unintelligible announcement. He thought that the store was closing so he looked at his watch. It was 8:05 P.M. Yes, it must be a closing announcement, he thought.

But then a peculiar thing happened. A young man on a forklift jumped off the vehicle and cried, "My God, it's a fire!" And he took off running.

Billy looked around. He couldn't see what the young man was getting excited about. There was nothing. But suddenly some people ran through the fire door and yelled, "Get outta here! There's a fire!"

Billy peered through that door, that fireproof barricade, toward the
west side of the store, and he saw a big cloud of smoke in the center of the
space. He ran toward the south fire door searching for Ada and Matthew,
and when he got there the cloud behind him had turned into a wall, a
wall of very black smoke.

Billy Deal screamed, "Ada!"

He ran toward the entrance doors that he and his wife and grandson
had passed through a half hour before, and saw that a fire engine was
arriving.

In the darkness, Jim Obdam battled panic. He was all alone in the smoke
and heat. He knew there were steps to an emergency exit in the back
stockroom. He couldn't see, and hoped he could feel the steps, but his
thoughts were fragmenting, and he began praying. Then he remembered
there was a fire exit in the hardware department in the far northwest corner, if he could only *find* the far northwest corner.

He staggered to the back wall and duck-walked his way along, feeling
the wall and feeling merchandise, feeling anything to guide him. He was
holding his breath, low to the floor, and he dropped even lower, desperate
for the same oxygen that the fire craved.

He was just about to give up. He couldn't go any farther. When he
suddenly realized he was six *feet* from the emergency exit, he felt an energy
rush and he lunged, pushing the bars, activating the alarm. And he was *out*.

But though the hungry flames couldn't reach him, the trailing heat
did. He was outside, but he felt as though he were still inside. It was hot
and he was burning. His arms, neck, and ears all suffered second- and
third-degree burns.

Jim Obdam, covered head to foot with soot, ran toward the front of
the store, anxious to call his parents to tell them he was all right, but
when he touched his hand to his burning wrist, the flesh fell off onto the
pavement.

An employee in the electrical department, Anthony Colantuano, had
been at his workbench at 8:04 P.M. when a voice screamed "Fire!" He

spotted a fellow employee and a few customers rushing down an aisle toward the south fire door and he stopped them, herding them toward the fire exit in the electrical department.

"Come with me!" he yelled. "The door is over here!"

As they exited the store, he looked back and it was like wading through surf when a mountainous breaker is roiling toward you. But this wave was made of fire. It was heaving and cresting and roaring.

When he later described it he said, "It was coming, coming fast toward us. The flame. The fire. *Everything.*"

They were literally blown outside by a flashover, the instant burn of gasses and smoke, when the carbon that *is* smoke burns hotter than one thousand degrees and the entire contents of a room erupt in flame and no living thing survives. People, smoke, flames, merchandise, *everything,* were blasted through the door into the cool autumn night.

The six men of Engine Company 81 had been just settling in front of the TV, waiting for the start of the World Series game between the San Diego Padres and Detroit Tigers, when they heard the police dispatch a "possible 904," the police term for a fire. They were still sliding the pole when the alarm bell went off and they figured it was more than a "possible."

Since Ole's Home Center was only three blocks from the station the fire company arrived in a few minutes. The fire captain in charge, William Eisele, didn't think there'd be much to this one. There was no glow or header of smoke above the roof line indicating a major structure fire. All he saw was some haze in the air. He thought it might be a trash Dumpster or maybe a vehicle fire.

But when the firefighters leaped from their engine Captain Eisele saw flames rolling out the southwest door. When he got close to that door the fire actually hissed at him. The flames emitted very little smoke and had a bluish-green tint from the merchandise—polyurethane foam, they would later learn—that produced a strange sound, the hissing.

The firefighters prepared to attack those flames, only three feet off the floor but lapping out the door, hungry for oxygen, lunging against the overhanging facade, climbing up.

Never in his fifty-four years had Billy Deal been so thirsty. He was parched. "Just like I was in a desert," he would later say.

Maybe Ada and Matthew had gotten out some other way, he kept telling himself. He actually made an attempt to enter the building again before being driven back. Then he joined the gathering crowd of onlookers as neighboring engine companies neared, honking and wailing.

Billy plodded on, trying to avoid the helmeted firefighters in turnout gear who were pulling hose and adjusting their breathing apparatus. But he couldn't bear it another moment, the incredible thirst. He staggered into a nearby restaurant and asked for a drink of water, but he was told that they didn't give free drinks; he'd have to buy something. So Billy bought a Coke and poured it down his throat.

And then he spotted young Jim Obdam, carbon covered, running in front of the store, toward other huddled employees in the parking lot who shouted to him, overjoyed to see him *alive.*

And Billy thought, Well, *he* got out, didn't he? Maybe Ada and Matthew did too. Maybe.

Billy ran to the fire captain and cried out that he had escaped but his wife and grandson were trapped, maybe only ten feet inside the door.

"Did the fire doors roll down?" the fire captain yelled.

Billy didn't know what a fire door was, but he said, "No, I didn't see any doors close."

Eisele later reported that he had all the confidence in the world that if somebody was only ten feet inside that door he could go in and get them out, so he said to Billy, "Don't worry, we'll take care of that!"

And then Eisele gathered his firefighters for a rescue attack. He ordered that they pull three folds of two-and-a-half-inch hose, each fold being fifty feet long, in a try to make a quick knockdown and rescue. They charged the line with water and made their approach.

The fog nozzle was like a giant shower head designed to break up water particles and consume BTUs, drawing the heat from a fire. Because fire needs oxygen, heat, and fuel to survive, the fog nozzle was meant to disrupt the fire triangle by turning heat into steam, in effect, shooting steam at the fire to lower the temperature. It was all logical, very logical.

So after sending his sixth firefighter to find and shut down utilities, especially natural gas, the captain and his men entered through the southwest door, where suddenly they were looking into a blinding orange *inferno.*

They tried to attack under those flames, vivid orange but with a weird blue-green tint, but they only got a few feet inside. The fire had obviously flashed over. There were no aisles, there were no people, there was nothing but fire. *Everything* was aflame. But now came an eerie sound commingled with the hiss of the burning foam. The battery-powered display smoke detectors were going off, one after another. And the firefighters could hear high-pitched squeals within the flames, like animals burning alive.

Captain Eisele yelled at the nozzle man to hit the Celotex ceiling tiles, but the 225-gallon nozzle created so much steam in the superheated air, emitted so much nozzle pressure, that it blasted the firefighters back out the door.

While other engines were still racing to Ole's Home Center, Eisele ordered a one-and-three-fourths-inch attack line to be brought to another entry, but learned that the fire doors had in fact rolled down and could not be pried open. The captain sent a man up to ventilate the roof because the fire had not burned through yet. When the firefighter cut the hole, flames shot into the sky, pulling heat with them in a chimney effect, but it was too little, too late. It was about seven minutes into the fire and the entire roof was perilously threatened, so Eisele had to order his firefighter back down.

And where in the hell was Engine 41, he wondered, yelling into the radio. And why did he hear an engine being radio-dispatched in the *wrong* direction?

What Captain Eisele didn't know at the time was that there was another, nearly simultaneous fire at Von's Market, only blocks from Ole's Home Center. He would later say that it was unheard of: *two* South Pasadena fires in close proximity? In retail establishments, during business hours? Unheard of!

It was indeed a bizarre evening for firefighters in that part of the San Gabriel Valley. Prior to the Ole's fire and the fire at Von's Market, there had been a fire in nearby Pasadena, at Albertson's Market on East Sierra Madre Boulevard, about seven miles from Ole's. Arson investigator Scott

McClure had arrived at Albertson's at 6:45 P.M. and met with a battalion chief for a quick briefing.

McClure had found the point of origin easily enough, in the grocery racks piled high with bags of potato chips. At 7:45 P.M. McClure called dispatch and requested that they send arson investigator John Orr from nearby Glendale Fire Department, probably the most accomplished arson sleuth within the several fire departments that rendered mutual aid in the area.

John Orr showed up very quickly, and he explained to McClure about the volatility of potato chips, that the oils in the chips and the bag material are highly combustible, a sack of solid fuel. John Orr told McClure that in his opinion, the Albertson's fire was deliberately set, as is usually the case with fires in retail stores during business hours when customers are present. When McClure later finished his investigation and returned to his car, he heard radio reports of the disaster that was unfolding seven miles away at Ole's Home Center and he sped toward the scene.

When he arrived at Ole's John Orr was already there.

After he'd ordered his firefighter off the roof of Ole's, and after the interior attack was aborted, Captain Eisele found John Orr standing at the rear of his engine carrying a thirty-five-millimeter camera.

"John! What're you doing here?" Eisele asked.

"Passing by," John Orr said. "Do you mind if I shoot some pictures?"

Eisele wished that Orr had turnout gear in his car, but since the arson investigator was in civilian clothes and hadn't offered to help, the fire captain assumed he did not.

"Help yourself, I've got work to do," Eisele said.

And while Eisele awaited the arrival of engine companies, and while Jim Obdam was led to the back of an ambulance, and while Billy Deal stood in front of Ole's Home Center, where he would remain for twenty-two hours, and while John Orr shot film of the conflagration, the roof caved in and a geyser of flame and sparks exploded high into the night.

In the parking lot of Ole's, the sister-in-law of Carolyn Krause, who was a community-service officer for the Glendale Police Department, saw a blue Dodge that belonged to the Glendale arson unit, and standing by the car were John Orr and his partner, police officer Dennis Wilson.

After checking in vain at the triage area for her missing sister-in-law, Karen Krause approached the arson investigators and told them that Carolyn Krause was missing.

John Orr told her that they would keep an eye out for Carolyn, but that until the fire was suppressed nobody could get near the building except the firefighters—the implication being that a search for bodies would be hours away.

Karen Krause stayed as the rest of the family arrived, and they remained for several hours. Waiting.

The fire chief of South Pasadena was at a fire-prevention class in Los Angeles when he learned of the disaster at Ole's. Chief Gene Murry excused himself, jumped in his staff car, and sped to South Pasadena, arriving close to 8:30 P.M.

He saw that one of the crews was attempting to breach an exterior wall in order to penetrate it with heavy "master stream poles," an appliance that could deliver more than five hundred gallons of water per minute. While Chief Murry was assuming command, he learned of the fire in progress at Von's Market on the same street, just a few minutes away. He couldn't believe it.

Chief Murry spotted John Orr snapping photos, and asked if he would assist by going to Von's to conduct an investigation. It wouldn't be until midnight that the fire chief could declare that 125 firefighters had the Ole's blaze under control.

Moments before the smoke was observed in the housewares department, Patricia Parham, the mother of Carolyn Krause, had gone to Ole's Home Center to see her only daughter. Patricia Parham was with Carolyn's two children: her son, age three, and her two-year-old daughter. Mrs. Parham picked up her daughter's house keys so that she could take the grandchildren home and put them to bed.

Back at Carolyn's house, Mrs. Parham received three phone calls in quick succession, one from Carolyn's father-in-law, one from Carolyn's sister-in-law, and one from Carolyn's brother. When Mrs. Parham raced back to Ole's parking lot, the building was engulfed, and she never saw her daughter again.

Sometime after 8:00 P.M. the phone rang in the Cetina residence. Luis, Jimmy's older brother, picked it up and a family friend said, "How's your brother? Is he home?"

She seemed upset, so Luis said, "Why?"

And she said, "Because there's a fire where he works."

Luis's mother asked him in Spanish what was wrong, but Luis answered, nothing. Then he ran out to his car and drove to Ole's.

Fair Oaks was cordoned off by police cars, so he had to detour and take Orange Grove Avenue, finally parking in a handicapped zone near Ole's. He jumped from the car, leaving the lights on and his keys inside, and just started to run, until a cop stopped him and said, "You can't leave your car there."

Luis turned to him and cried, "My brother works there!"

The cop hesitated, but let him go.

When Luis reached the flaming building he spotted an employee whose name he couldn't remember, and he yelled, "Where's my brother?"

The young man said, "I don't know!" Then he added, "I think he *might* still be in the building!"

Luis Cetina then ran to the north side of the building and entered an open area, splashing through four inches of water where the sprinklers had activated.

Another Ole's employee whom he recognized was standing there watching, and Luis shouted, "Where's my brother?"

The young man said to him, "I saw him a little while ago! He went back inside!"

"Back *inside*?" Luis cried.

"Yeah, there were people banging on the door! One of those fire doors that dropped down!"

Then Luis Cetina, not knowing *where* to run, circled around to the back, to the door through which Jim Obdam had escaped. The door was open now, but impassable. Luis returned back the other way to the fire door that had previously served as the main entrance to a Thrifty Drug Store that formerly occupied a space in the strip mall.

Luis stayed right there, where there also used to be a Laundromat at which the children would wait while their mother washed the family's clothes. Their dad would sometimes buy them an ice cream there at Thrifty's, when he could afford it.

It was two o'clock in the morning before he went home to face his mother with the truth.

Matthew Troidl was at home with his wife, Kim, and their five-year-old daughter, Bethany. Matthew William, his two-and-a-half-year-old son, was with his grandparents, and while Matthew Troidl's wife was speaking on the phone, there was an emergency breakthrough on the line. It came from one of her brothers, who said that Billy Deal had called about a fire at Ole's, and that Billy couldn't find Ada and Matthew William.

While en route to Ole's, Matthew Troidl and his wife kept reassuring each other that it was probably a small fire, maybe a trash can or Dumpster, and that it had just caused some confusion. That's all it was. Confusion.

But when they arrived, they saw the ventilated roof shooting flames one hundred feet in the air. And there were police cars, and fire engines, and ambulances, and *chaos*. But they managed to find Billy Deal in all that pandemonium and he told them the worst.

Matthew Troidl said later that he had all kinds of crazy thoughts. Maybe they'd gotten out a back door! Maybe they'd been hurt and were already at a hospital! Maybe they'd crawled up in the air-conditioning vent and were okay! Maybe. So many of them just kept thinking, *maybe*.

The man designated to lead a six-man investigative team the next morning was Sergeant Jack Palmer, a twenty-five-year law-enforcement veteran assigned to the Los Angeles County Sheriff's Department arson-and-explosives detail. He had investigated nearly five thousand fires in his twelve years as an arson cop, and had the resources of the county of

Los Angeles on which to draw. The tiny South Pasadena Fire Department needed vast assistance for this major disaster, and the LASD in their green jumpsuits—the Lean Green Machine—were there in force.

Sergeant Palmer immediately did his walk-around of the ravaged structure, looking for the fire's point of origin. The west portion of Ole's was destroyed, and the east side showed heat and water damage from the sprinklers that had gone off.

Skip loaders and bulldozers were already moving debris while the investigators, armed with shovels and wheelbarrows, tried to find the bodies of the four missing victims. Each time a skip loader would snare a load, investigators had to look inside for remnants of charred human beings.

Sergeant Palmer saw the crane remove twisted steel beams from the center of the building where the roof had collapsed, and talked with an employee who had been called to the scene. Palmer was told that plastic products had been on display, but he was not told that there were racks full of polyurethane foam products, which, he would later say, "go like wildfire."

After his hour-and-a-half investigation, the arson cop decided that he was unable to eliminate as a fire cause the possibility of electrical shorting in the attic area. He later said that this fire was very hard to read because there was so much potential fuel in the store, and that overhead burning, which caused ceiling material to drop and start secondary fires, could have ignited numerous hot spots.

Jim Obdam was interviewed by Sergeant Palmer, and he did tell the investigator that he'd observed a column of dark smoke nearly two feet in diameter in the southeast part of the store, by the housewares section. But Palmer never interviewed Anthony Colantuano, the employee who had seen not only smoke in that area, but fire burning in the racks, an amazingly fast fire that chased him and created a draft of its own, blowing him out the door.

And employee James Cuellar later said that he had been only thirty feet from the southwest fire door when the starting point of the fire was still the entire length of the store away. Yet he had barely escaped without injury. The fire was on him just that *fast*. He was not interviewed.

But Sergeant Palmer did learn that there were two other retail-store fires in the area on that terrible evening, and that they had both been deemed arson fires, but Palmer decided that since they were set in potato chip racks and not polyfoam, they were probably unconnected to the Ole's blaze.

Soon, in the northern portion of the ruined building, far from where Jim Obdam and Anthony Colantuano had seen the first column of smoke, searchers found human remains.

Another fire investigator, who arrived on the scene at 7:00 A.M., was a supervisor with the arson-bomb unit of the California State Fire Marshal's Office, where he'd worked for sixteen years.

Jim Allen, like any arson investigator, was looking for signs of the fire's direction. Normally, fire moves upward through a heat-transfer process, and as it hits a surface—a wall, a ceiling—it follows the path of least resistance, spreading out in a V pattern, upward and outward. The V or convex pattern reveals the point of origin in a simple fire, but the Ole's disaster had not been simple.

Allen noted that it was in the center of the building that the roof had collapsed. In addition, after temperatures in the location reached 160 degrees and melted the doors' fusible links, both north and south steel fire doors had rolled down as they were designed to do. The assumption was that a major fire would occur after hours when no one was in the store, but the speed and heat of this fire had been astonishing, and those doors had sealed egress quickly, very quickly.

Allen stayed about seven hours, a lot longer than Sergeant Palmer, and after three or four of the aisles had been dug out, he prowled through the southeast corner with John Orr, a friend and colleague who had also arrived on the scene.

Jim Allen was of the opinion that the investigation, like the fire, was moving too fast. This fire had caught up with people trying to outrun it, so there had to have been a large load of fuel. Of course, he knew that polyurethane foam is a hydrocarbon fuel that comes from a petroleum product, with the burn characteristic of petroleum, but he did not learn of its presence, not that day.

Allen didn't like the speed with which Sergeant Palmer's conclusions were being offered, and he said so to John Orr, but his colleague failed to tell Allen that there had been two *other* retail-store fires in the area the night before. And he never mentioned that he had been at the scene of one of them to consult, and was the official investigator on the other. Three such fires might indicate an arson *series,* and play a significant role in determining the nature of the Ole's fire.

During the early afternoon, Jim Allen, John Orr, and other arson investigators were ordered out of the area by a tall sheriff's department lieutenant who said, "We're going into body recovery now."

When Allen protested, the tall lieutenant said, "You can leave, or run the risk of being arrested for interfering."

In addition to never learning about the polyfoam in the southeast quadrant of the building, Allen was curtailed by the LASD investigators, who said that all witnesses would be interviewed by *them.*

At a meeting that then took place there in Ole's shopping center, at a Winchell's doughnut shop, Sergeant Palmer said to the huddle of fire investigators, "I can't eliminate an electrical problem in the concealed space between the false ceiling and the roof."

"We haven't come up with a point of origin," Jim Allen offered. "Let's keep going."

"We should be unified with our conclusion," Sergeant Palmer said, but Allen replied, "I'm writing up my report that it's an undetermined fire. I don't know for sure if it started in the attic or *where* it started."

Ultimately, Palmer believed it had been a "drop-down" attic fire probably caused by faulty electrical wiring. There was no spirited debate. The dozen or so arson investigators who had shoveled through the debris, and watched the recovery of four bodies, ate their Winchell's doughnuts, drank their coffee, and by their silence acquiesced to Sergeant Jack Palmer's conclusion.

In order to understand the compliance of so many trained arson specialists at the fire scene one must understand the hierarchy and class structure that divides the profession. First, there are arson investigators who have been drawn from the firefighting ranks. Although they have peace-officer status, carry firearms, and effect the arrests of fire-setting criminals, they are and always will be, to the *other* class, just gun-toting firemen who, if they depart from arson investigation, will go back to the firehouse to scrub fire hose and polish chrome. The *other* arson investigators, those who come from the ranks of the police service, are first and foremost *cops.* They are law-enforcement officers assigned to arson investigation and will be law-enforcement officers after leaving the arson ranks. Their K-9 symbol is the German shepherd police dog, the true descendant of the wolf, not some white-and-black bag of spots that chases a fire truck.

Also, Sergeant Jack Palmer was not a cop from a town like South Pasadena or any of the other little cities that make up the foothills area and the San Gabriel Valley. He was with an agency that numbered in the *thousands*, the Los Angeles County Sheriff's Department, which, along with the Los Angeles Police Department, was one of the major police entities in California. The Lean Green Machine sometimes was called by critics the *Mean* Green Machine.

Fire investigator Jim Allen, who had, early in his adult life, been a San Joaquin deputy sheriff, knew who wins in a pissing contest between cops and firemen. So, when Sergeant Palmer essentially called it an accidental fire, there was not much argument. In fact, people never did speak publicly of their differing opinions, not for a long time. They all knew who the Big Dog was.

John Orr was especially angered by Sergeant Palmer's meeting and placed a call late that morning to Dennis Foote, a fellow arson investigator for the city of Los Angeles Fire Department. He asked Foote if he or some other member of the mutual aid force, the Foothill Arson Task Force Group, could respond to assist with the Ole's inquiry.

John Orr also wanted to see a file that Foote had been compiling, a file dealing with a fire series that had been occurring in Los Angeles and the vicinity for about four years. Some of those fires involved the ignition of potato chips, others involved combustible materials such as polyfoam. What they had in common was their occurrence in retail establishments during business hours, usually in the afternoon or early evening.

On one of those investigations Dennis Foote had collected a delay device that was different from most cigarette-matchbook devices. This one, or what was left of it, was a Marlboro cigarette with three paper matches attached to it by a rubber band. Such a device provided up to fifteen minutes or more for an arsonist to leave a store before the burning cigarette ignited the matches, which in turn ignited flammable material around them.

When Foote arrived at Ole's, Orr told him that there had been other fires in the area the night before, and that possibly a delay device had been used to start them. Dennis Foote put on his helmet and his rubber boots and entered Ole's with Orr, but that area of the building was just about totally destroyed and the sheriff's investigators were already finishing up. Before he left, Foote gave his file—he called it "The Potato Chip File"— to John Orr.

Then, a few days later, a peculiar thing happened: a fire erupted in Builder's Emporium in North Hollywood. It was in the polyfoam section, like so many of the others. Foote wanted another look at Ole's, another chance to determine if the Ole's fire could have been ignited in polyfoam products that burn *violently*. But it was too late. A wrecking company had cleared almost all debris from the building space.

Matthew Troidl had tried to call his parents, who lived in the Bay Area, but when his father answered, the son couldn't speak. Troidl's wife, Kim, had to take the phone and tell the older man that his grandson was dead. And Matthew Troidl couldn't personally make the funeral arrangements for his son. He just sat in the house and rocked back and forth.

They decided to bury the two of them in the same casket, Ada Deal cradling her grandson in her arms.

The *Pasadena Star-News* reported that more than twelve hundred people packed the church for the funeral of Jimmy Cetina. The monsignor had decided to have the mass during school hours and the classrooms emptied. The police had to block traffic for miles down San Gabriel Boulevard for the two hundred cars that drove to the cemetery.

Jimmy Cetina had applied for the job at Ole's to help out the family with the purchase of a used white Volkswagen. They couldn't afford insurance yet, so nobody had driven the car. It was parked in the backyard, and Jimmy had liked to sit in it and tell his family what he was going to do to fix it up. But Jimmy never got to drive it. His brother drove it behind Jimmy's hearse in the funeral cortege. Later they sold it. His father couldn't bear to have that white car around anymore.

If dalmatians deferred to police dogs that day at the scene of the Ole's calamity, there were other canine cousins on the prowl, sniffing and panting and baying at the possibilities. And these could outsmell any tracking dog, or bomb dog, or dope dog, or cadaver dog that ever lived. These could simply point a nose at a headline, then raise up and smell it in the air: grief, misery, death! They were contingency-driven trial lawyers.

When all was said and done, everybody would be sued: Ole's, its parent company, electrical contractors, subcontractors, anybody who might be willing to fork over some big bucks either through their insurance carriers or from their own pockets, or from Grandma's sugar bowl. When the Ole's Home Center investigation had officially concluded, with the finding of probable electrical malfunction in the attic space, the trial lawyers and the defendants settled out of court for four million dollars, costs that usually get passed on to consumers.

A few days after her sister-in-law's funeral, John Orr spoke to Karen Krause at the Glendale PD, and said how disappointed he was that the fire had been called accidental. He told her of other such fires in home-improvement companies, specifically mentioning Builder's Emporium in North Hollywood, where a fire had been started in a polypropylene mattress but, luckily, got extinguished by the sprinkler system, and had left behind remnants of a delay device.

"There should've been investigators present at the autopsies of the victims," he told her. "Polypropylene may have left particles in the victim's lungs or in their tracheas. Or there may have been gases present that were absorbed by the bodies, and it might've come out in a proper autopsy."

If there had been investigators there knowing what to look for. But there were not, and now no one would ever know.

Two months after the Ole's calamity in South Pasadena, another disaster nearly befell that unfortunate company. The Ole's Home Center on Colorado Boulevard in Pasadena barely escaped a similar fate. A partially burned incendiary device was found by an employee.

Arson investigators called it a "signature device": the cigarette, the three paper matches, and a rubber band. It was found in a partially burned stack of polyfoam that had been scorched but hadn't fully ignited. This signature device was known only to local arson investigators, who hadn't publicized it—therefore, it couldn't be a copycat. Some wondered if the fire setter had graduated from potato chips to bigger targets.

Another possibility would not be considered for some time to come: by attacking the second Ole's store, perhaps a fire setter was making a statement to the entire arson-investigating community—that they had got it *wrong* the first time.

2

THE WANNA-BE

John Leonard Orr described in a memoir how two events early in his life may have foretold his future as a prominent Southern California arson investigator. The first involved a residential blaze that could have been fatal to three classmates who set fire to a sofa in their home. John and his two brothers stood in a rainstorm and watched while firefighters battled in vain to save the house.

Then, some weeks later, he had occasion to observe another fire, this one in an alley, a trash fire that had ignited a telephone pole. One of his friends had called the Los Angeles Fire Department, and they all watched Engine 55, a bullet-nosed Seagrave, coming to the rescue, red lights blinking, the old-fashioned "growler" siren moaning quietly when the rig stopped, waiting. Waiting for *what*? Young John began yelling that the pole was on fire! Still, the engine wouldn't budge.

Years later, after he was firefighter, he understood that Engine 55 was waiting for a "first-in" report from the other engine before committing itself as the second. But it was painfully frustrating, waiting for that engine to thunder forward and *attack*. John never forgot how the ash spilled from the cardboard box that was the fire's point of origin. He described how he searched up and down the alley that day for evidence of who may have started it.

As the years passed, the boy developed a love of hunting. He hunted with bows or guns, stalking small animals in the foothills. Once, when he and his pals were out near the western side of Mount Washington, desperate for action, they spotted a skunk shambling through the brush on a hillside trail. John let fly with a barbed hunting arrow that fatally penetrated the creature's throat.

The skunk emitted its horrendous reek as it died, and the young hunter wondered: Why did I kill it? I can't eat it. A skunk was certainly not a trophy kill. It wasn't even a game animal. And now he had to retrieve his costly arrow, and his young friends thought his impulsive skunking was hilarious. He was always impulsive and he was always hunting, for one thing or another.

Whenever John Orr had to take preemployment or prepromotion psychological exams during his career as a civil servant—whenever an examiner asked him to summarize his childhood in the 1950s and 1960s—he would always say, "It was all *Ozzie and Harriet*," conjuring images of that happy, middle-class, bygone television family.

His father had owned a sporting-goods store on York Boulevard in the old northeastern corner of metropolitan Los Angeles known as Highland Park. His business failed, as did the next, but they got by. The Orrs' two-bedroom, wood-frame house was behind the home of John's grandparents in a neighborhood where the Orrs had lived for more than forty years.

When he was sixteen, John's Ozzie-and-Harriet world imploded with no explanation or warning. His mother left home without telling anyone where she was going, only that she would call in a few days. John's eldest brother had already moved away, and his other brother was in the navy. Now he was alone with his father, and began to have morbid fears that his dad just might be so grief stricken that he'd take down one of the hunting rifles. But his mother did call after several days to say that she'd gone to her childhood home in Missouri, so father and son learned to cope. He didn't see her again for nearly three years, and she never returned to his father when she came back to L.A.

When one of the recent high-school graduates was killed in Vietnam, John Orr realized his options were college, Canada, or military service.

On career day, when he was a senior, he talked to an L.A. Fire Department captain who told him that fire-fighting experience in the military was as good as a degree in fire science. The navy wouldn't work for him because, strangely enough for a California boy, he couldn't swim, and he didn't like the machismo of the marines, so he joined the air force, leaving on his eighteenth birthday, April 26, 1967, for Amarillo Air Force Base.

After basic training he was assigned to a jet mechanic's school at Chanute Air Force Base in Illinois, but soon managed to transfer to fire-fighting school, where he learned such skills as how to operate pumps and shoot chemical foam from turrets onto training fires.

By 1968, the young airman married his high-school girlfriend, Jody, and after a big Italian wedding paid for by her family, they shipped out for Seville, Spain, where he was assigned to an air base near the commercial airport. However, during his two-year tour in Spain he only got to respond to two air crashes.

In the winter of 1970, John and Jody were transferred to Great Falls, Montana, where the only real fire he ever got was a minor off-duty blaze. His military fire-fighting life was exceedingly uneventful, and he was honorably discharged on his twenty-second birthday in April 1971, when Jody was seven months pregnant.

As he later recalled it, John was very resentful of authority after leaving the military. He affected a cocky demeanor—compensating, he said, for repressed feelings of insecurity. But he was eager for a career. Though there were many applicants and few positions available at that time, he applied to the Los Angeles Police Department, the Los Angeles County Sheriff's Department, the City of Los Angeles Fire Department, and the Los Angeles County Fire Department. And he waited to be called.

Then his daughter Carrie Lyn was born in June, at a time when he was "catching up on high-school antics" that he'd missed. That meant street racing in muscle cars, beer drinking, and after getting off work from his job at Sparkletts Bottled Water Company at 11:00 P.M., heading for the bars until 2:00 A.M.

The marriage was already shaky. He admitted to others that he was "a typical sexist prick." He also admitted that he lacked "insight." That had always been a problem for him, insight.

In 1971, the Los Angeles Police Department, arguably the best and certainly the most glamorous police agency in America at the time, sent John
a letter inviting him to test.

He passed the written test, the physical agility test, the oral interview,
and the medical exam. He was given a date when he'd be starting the
police academy and he was ecstatic. Except that there was a second part
to the medical exam—psychological testing.

He later described the 550-question MMPI self-inventory test as
"comical," and said there were questions such as "I enjoy the ballet more
than loading a truck." Well, who wouldn't?

He gathered up as much maturity as he could muster and plunged
into the Rorschach with gusto.

"I actually started seeing some pretty cool images," he reported.
"Dancers, drummers around a bonfire, a ship moored in a foggy lagoon,
butterflies. Then the examiner played the sex card."

The one where everybody sees a vagina but nobody admits it. John
said he was afraid to be labeled a sex fiend so he told the guy that he saw
a map of Italy instead of a woman's snatch.

He received a rejection letter some weeks later based upon the psychological evaluation. The letter said that he was "unsuitable."

He was shattered. Unsuitable? Then he was outraged. He followed the
procedure outlined in the rejection letter, and consulted with a psychologist whose name he got from the Yellow Pages. The hired gun quickly
found him "suitable," and John made an appointment with the LAPD
psychologist, armed with his second opinion.

The doctor was a congenial fellow in the manner of his profession, but
he informed the former candidate that he could not reveal specific reasons for the rejection other than that the test revealed passivity, and police
officers need to be assertive.

"Some people actually learn test taking," the shrink told him, "as a
way of passing these exams."

"That would be cheating," John said, resenting the implication.

"That's a good spontaneous answer," replied the psychologist.

Then the shrink did a surprising thing. He placed John's file on the
desk, and announced that he needed a cup of coffee.

"Be back in five minutes, son," he said to the astonished former
candidate.

John carefully opened the file and found the name of a Sparkletts co-worker who had been interviewed by the LAPD background investigator. The worker had told the cop that John Orr was lazy and resentful of the other man's promotion over him. He described how John had been late on two occasions, and he thought the candidate would have trouble adapting to police work.

John was bewildered. Was *that* it? A jealous coworker? Or was it that he'd confessed to stealing a beer from a former employer? He'd revealed this trivial peccadillo because he feared that if they gave a polygraph it might disclose deception when they asked "Have you ever stolen from an employer?" Well, he'd eventually paid for the beer. Was *that* it? Finally, the evaluation stated that he needed a few years to mature and examine his life before reapplying.

Weeks later, the heartbroken air force vet quit Sparkletts and entered the management program at Jack in the Box restaurants. But he quickly left there for a job at Kentucky Fried Chicken, and toward the end of 1973, despite a raise and bonuses and Jody's protests, he gave notice again.

About the failed psychological exam, he later said that maybe the LAPD didn't want people to see dancers and butterflies and sleepy lagoons in those ink blots. Maybe, he said, he should have given the LAPD "spiders and snakes and lightning bolts."

He *would've* been a good cop, he thought, but if it wasn't in the cards, he'd be a great firefighter. He applied and was accepted by the Los Angeles Fire Department. He was a firefighter now. Almost. He still had to get through the fire academy. But he hadn't prepared himself physically for the academy rigors, figuring that his years as an air force firefighter should be enough for them. Two days before he was to enter the LAFD academy, John decided to play his first game of racquetball with another fire recruit. He ended up with painful foot blisters and also learned that his stamina was not so good.

In November, on Friday the thirteenth, he was called into the captain's office at the LAFD academy in North Hollywood and told that he hadn't scored well on a written test, nor on two rope-and-ladder exams. John offered an excuse about sore feet, and the captain listened politely. Then he told the recruit that he could resign quietly now or wait for the next exams, which, if also yielding poor results, might result in his being *fired*.

Stunned, John said he wanted to take the exams with renewed dedication.

In the U.S. Air Force, getting onto a roof was a cinch, and almost anybody could muscle their lightweight aluminum ladders. But the LAFD academy used wooden ladders, *heavy* wooden ladders. How it was placed, even the angle, was critical. Lots of the other recruits had gathered to practice ladder-carries on their off-duty days. And they'd quizzed each other from the books and training manuals, but not John Orr.

His attitude was, "I've *been* a firefighter for four years in the air force. Surely I can tie a bow knot and throw a ladder."

In the air force, yes, but not to the satisfaction of the L.A. Fire Department. He was released on Monday morning and went home and wept. He described it as "paralyzing."

The Christmas of 1973 was bleak. His marriage was nearly in ruins, and the only work he'd found was with a kindly neighbor who renovated gas pumps at service stations. And by now he had *two* infant daughters to support. In desperation, he applied, in January 1974, to the Glendale Fire Department, which was near the bottom of the pay scale for the fifty-five fire agencies in Los Angeles County.

Glendale was a city of 160,000 and encompassed 32 square miles. There were 9 fire stations and 160 firefighters, and it bordered that area of Los Angeles where he'd been raised. He knew Glendale, and he would gladly settle, if they'd take him.

He breezed through the written exam and was called for the oral interview, very fearful of explaining his rejection by LAPD for psychological reasons, and his washing out of the LAFD academy.

He sucked it up and boldly told the oral board that the L.A. Fire Department's academy was "rigid," but diplomatically added that he should have adjusted to their rigidity. He then explained that his failing marriage had been disrupting his focus and draining his energy while he'd been at the academy.

The oral-board members seemed to appreciate that he had been a U.S. Air Force firefighter, and they actually counseled him on his marital problems. He later claimed that he was more open to these men than he ever had been with the woman he had married. He soon received a letter of congratulations upon being accepted as a recruit in Glendale's first formal fire-academy class.

On March 1, 1974, John Orr, number one on the hiring list, began his training, and eight weeks later, he and twelve others graduated. He was sent to Station 6 as a full-fledged fireman. Job hunting had ended. A real career had begun at last.

It will never be known if the LAPD psychologist had left that file open to mollify the distraught applicant, and it's uncertain if his diagnosis was even in the file at the time, but if it was, the applicant never admitted to seeing it:

> Non-acceptable applicant. Reason for rejection based upon his past history and test results. Currently having marital problems with separation. Recently walked off a job, gave no notice. Supervisors gave him poor evaluation, described him as goof-off, know-it-all, irresponsible and immature. The testing reemphasizes this. Rorschach showed him passive, indecisive, with problems with women and sex. The MMPI confirmed this and showed a schizoid person who is withdrawn from people and may have sexual confusion in his orientation. Very non-objective.
>
> Diagnosis: Personality trait disturbance. Emotionally unstable personality.

After his final examination, in February 1975, John Orr was no longer a probationary rookie. He was one of them, an unconditional firefighter, and nobody could ever again say he was "unsuitable." He grew a mustache during the decade when cops and firemen wore fiercer "stashes" than Turkish hammer throwers. Winning his spurs hadn't happened a moment too soon. He was sick of training manuals and knot tying.

On his off-duty days, hearth and home bored him silly, so he took a part-time job working as a clerk at a 7-Eleven Store. With the extra bucks he bought an old Ford pickup with a camper shell for his hunting and camping excursions. At the 7-Eleven, he worked with another restless employee, who was on her third unhappy marriage. And the two young people impulsively decided to get out of dreary wedlock and take an apartment in Glendale as platonic, rent-sharing housemates.

Like his mother before him, John just got up one morning, left a note for Jody, and bugged out. The next day he drove to the Department of Public Social Services and asked how much child support he should pay for his two young daughters. And after they set up housekeeping, he reported that the platonic relationship "lasted about twenty minutes."

He began taking college classes in fire science on his G.I. Bill allowance, and despite his stated dislike of cops, with their machismo and bullying ways—cops, he felt, never showed the proper respect for fire-fighters—he also took police science courses. He said it was because he wanted to "explore the conflicts" between the two emergency services, but also for the report-writing experience. Firemen wrote little, cops wrote all the time, and he had a knack for writing. And while working as a 7-Eleven clerk he found that he had a knack for something else: spotting shoplifters.

The boredom at 7-Eleven had been getting intolerable until one day when the young firefighter started watching the kids who stopped to buy junk food on their way home from school. It was the too-cool body language. He started grabbing them in the act, making them empty pockets and backpacks. His boss was impressed. John Orr had a *gift*.

Pretty soon the firefighter was spotting shoplifters everywhere. In 1976, while shopping at the Eagle Rock Plaza, he saw a guy running toward a car with an armload of men's suits from Montgomery Ward's. He chased the thief, tackled him, and with the help of a store security officer, held him for the cops, who came and hauled him to jail.

That was a seminal moment, a significant piece of police work. He spoke with one of the security people, a woman whose husband was a Glendale police detective, and asked her what his chances would be of getting hired as a part-time security employee.

She said they only hired off-duty cops, not firemen. He was disappointed, but admitted he was "hooked on this new shoplifting game." And that same day, while shopping at the Sears store, he spotted a geezer boosting a few hand tools. He went to the cashier and asked her to call security, and they nailed the guy, who had lots more merchandise in his pockets.

Once again, John asked about part-time work as a security employee and was once again told that the night shift was full of off-duty Glendale cops.

But then, he was asked, "Could you work day shift?" They couldn't get cops to work the day shift. The look on his face was enough and the security boss said, "When can you start?"

He gave notice at 7-Eleven and started at Sears the next week.

John Orr was a crime crusader. In his first few months at Sears, he caught thirty people for the police, and an additional twenty whom he admonished and sent on their way. He also nailed one dishonest employee and two car burglars. The arrest of a husband-and-wife shoplifting team led to the recovery of thirty thousand dollars' worth of Sears property.

"I found that I had a cop's sixth sense" is how he explained the change that had come over him. "For those off-duty cops it was just a job, for me it was like hunting. I *loved* going to work." He would have done the job for free.

Lots of the merchandise boosters were addicts. Some carried knives and a few had guns in their cars. John Orr wasn't just making more arrests than anyone, he was in more foot pursuits, risky foot pursuits. The police chief's administrative assistant also worked off duty at Sears, and he helped the new employee to get a concealed-weapon permit, one of only six issued for the entire city.

Now he could legally carry a gun, and he began hanging out at bars where cops gathered, entering into all the cop talk, as badge-heavy as any of them, with a noticeable swagger. And soon, around the fire department *and* the police department, John Orr became known as a "cop wanna-be."

After a few months the wanna-be took a few days off from fire fighting and shoplifters, loaded his car with camping gear and his lady, and headed for a weekend in the desert. And since they were in the desert anyway, and so close to Las Vegas . . . It was on a "whim," he said. They got married: his second, her fourth.

So, what does a wanna-be who packs a piece do when he's back to a fire-fighting job that doesn't challenge him? He requested and got assigned to the hill patrol, driving a Chevy three-quarter-ton pickup that carried a pump and water tank, doing fire inspection and prevention. It beat lying around the fire station, tits up, staring at the tube, waiting for second-alarm fires. When you came right down to it, the hill patrol was more like police work: cruising alone, watching, always watching. Ready for action.

———

During the 1970s there was an arson series in Glendale; two of the fires were at Webb's Department Store. The local news media harped on the failure of both the fire and police investigators to come up with a likely suspect. Then one Friday night, Webb's Department Store experienced its third and final arson fire. The point of origin was in a pile of luggage and boxed items, and it was set during business hours, near closing time. John happened to be working one block away at the Sears store that evening. And he happened to be on his way home, he said, when he spotted the flames. He went into action and fought the fire along with several engine companies, for two hours. The entire building was destroyed. The serial arsonist was never caught.

John Orr knew he was creating too much work for the Glendale cops with his stalking of Sears shoplifters, but he could not stop. One of the reasons he was so good at the security detail was his appearance. People always described him as an "average-looking" guy. Ordinary. Not tall, five foot nine, maybe twenty pounds overweight, most of it around the middle and starting to round out his face. His slate-blue eyes were a bit narrow and almost lashless, making one think that as he aged, puffiness might tend to make those eyes look a bit amphibian. He had very straight, dark hair just starting to recede, and uneven pointed teeth. He wasn't good-looking, he wasn't bad-looking. He was just *ordinary-looking*. But he had a very pleasing voice and excellent diction, like one of those mellow radio announcers who played cool jazz.

Such an ordinary-looking guy could easily melt into the background at Sears, lurking in clothing racks, peering under, over, and around, like Peter Sellers as Inspector Clouseau. In fact, Glendale cops called him "Clouseau." Let them, he thought. He'd never worked at anything he enjoyed as much as this.

Maybe it was that radio voice and the sense of humor and a certain cleverness, whatever it was, he *did* seem to net more than his share of babes. One of his harshest critics said, "Well, you throw your line in the water often enough . . ."

His wife didn't like the hours he was keeping with fellow firefighter Don Yeager. The duo did a lot of hunting together, and both worked at

Sears, enjoying generous employee discounts that helped with those hunting trips.

John described their "hunting" trips to the desert as diversions where they'd end up at hot spring spas surrounded by "desert flora, fauna, and females." Not surprisingly, he divorced his second wife and moved into a two-bedroom cottage in Glendale, close enough to Engine 6 to ride to work on a bike, and close to his two favorite saloons.

This was when John began his writing career in earnest. He rewrote a manual for fire-patrol procedures because the old one was outdated, and that extra effort alienated him from colleagues who didn't want their responsibilities so tidily delineated. He said that this served to enhance his image as an "eccentric," which is how he described himself. The Glendale cops and firefighters who were not his fans replied that every neurotic thought of himself as "eccentric."

His patrol responsibilities widened. The fire patrol had to inspect one thousand vacant lots, many of them on hillsides in residential areas where a brush fire driven by Santa Ana winds could be catastrophic. The fire patrol's job was to locate the property owners, write warning notices, and instruct them to clear their property of dry brush. And there were pesky fire-alarm boxes that the kids liked to pull on their way home from school.

John began to use what he called his "shoplifting skills" to bag the little bastards. He'd park his Chevy patrol truck, which, like all of the Glendale fire rigs, was painted a god-awful lime yellow, and he'd "hide in plain sight," by just blending into backgrounds they were used to seeing. He bagged so many kids on his alarm-box surveillances that the other firefighters increased the moniker file to include "Officer Orr," "Dirty Harry Jr.," and more.

And he even snared some young firebugs, kids who liked to set trash fires. Many times he'd con them with the "phantom witness" gag, as in: "Son, a lady down the street told me you were right *by* that trash fire when it started. Did you maybe drop a match and it struck the edge of the trash can, and you didn't *mean* to do it?"

He had a way about him, he said, like a priest in confession. But as the 1980s approached, he needed bigger game. Nailing shoplifters was getting too easy; grabbing juvie fire setters was getting boring. He was sick

and tired of shooting arrows at skunks, as it were. He wanted the real thing. He wanted to detect and arrest *real* arsonists.

It was rumored that the Glendale Fire Department was going to hire a full-time arson investigator. This person would work directly for the head of the fire-prevention bureau. He wanted it badly, but nobody else did. As a measure of how most firefighters feel about work that resembles police work, John was the only applicant at the time.

He almost got killed during a shoplifting shift at Sears on a day when he was not wearing a .38 in his ankle holster, but carrying a *big* gun, a .45-caliber semiautomatic. He got a page from an employee at the Sears automotive garage about a guy who tried to "pick up a car" that the employee suspected didn't belong to him. The man had been turned away and was last seen crossing the parking lot and getting into a Mustang.

John quickly located the Mustang and saw a wire in the thief's hand, who was too busy hot-wiring the Mustang to even notice him. This was a *real* felony and he drew his gun.

John yelled, "Give it up, asshole!"

But the guy got the Mustang started, jammed it into reverse, and floored it. John couldn't jump fast enough, and got clipped by the front fender, flopping onto the pavement and rolling out of the way. The Mustang crashed into two parked cars and stalled.

Then the Sears sleuth was on him, but there was a problem. John Orr had all the moxie in the world, but not the training. He didn't know the law. The bastard had hit him with a car. Did he have the *legal* right to dump him?

The car thief got the Mustang started again, with John yelling, "Move an inch and I'll drop the hammer, you son of a bitch!"

For emphasis, he actually cocked the hammer, and now he was a few pounds of trigger pull away from a fatal shooting. But did he have the right and the authority?

"I had the *balls* to cap the asshole," he later said, but he just wasn't sure that he was legally justified.

His dilemma was resolved by a Glendale motor cop who'd been drinking coffee at a hamburger joint across the street. The cop hadn't heard the crash, but heard John hollering and cussing, so he moseyed over, coffee cup in hand, to have a look. And the car thief saw the motor cop and surrendered meekly.

Why had the guy refused to give it up to John, even when he was about to be dropped by a goddamn .45? Why had he cried uncle the second he laid eyes on a *real* cop? John pondered it as he drove to the police department for the arrest reports, and decided that a real cop would've dropped the hammer.

What was it? Was there something the dirtbag read in his face? That he wasn't a real cop? That he was just a wanna-be? Was *that* it?

His next caper actually got in the newspaper. It happened on a warm winter afternoon when the Santa Ana winds were blowing in from the desert. While he was on his fire patrol he spotted a couple of Latino homeboys wearing those trademark long-sleeved Pendleton shirts that cover track marks and those shitty "BORN TO LOSE" jailhouse tats, sitting at a bus bench. He said they "lighthoused" him, but it's hard to understand why, in that most *vatos* couldn't care less about a fireman in a lime-yellow pickup truck. But that's how he saw it, and his reporting was just a tad lurid: "Behind my sunglasses I locked onto them like the guidance system on a cruise missile. My sixth sense was functioning. Heart racing, my grip tightened on the steering wheel. If I was a German shepherd I'd be growling and pulling at my chain."

John circled the block, parked, pulled out his binoculars, and watched. He didn't dare call for a police unit because if it turned out to be nothing, he'd catch *tons* of crap from those assholes. But he knew the fire dispatcher on duty that day at Verdugo Dispatch Center, so he keyed his mike and said, "Verdugo, patrol twenty-one. Can you contact GPD and see if they have any cars near Glenoaks and Idlewood?"

"Patrol two-one," the dispatcher answered. "Are you *requesting* a police unit?"

"Not yet," John responded. "Not yet."

"Ten-four," the dispatcher said, and then came back a moment later to say that there did not seem to be any police units on patrol in that area.

John fired up that ugly lime-yellow beast of a pickup and headed down the street after one of the dudes began walking toward an alley. He turned the pickup around and rumbled through an alley parallel to the *vatos.* Then he got out and sneaked up on foot, spotting one of them standing beside a blue Toyota with its trunk open.

He jumped back in the truck, fired it up, and in a minute or two the yellow pickup and the blue Toyota were heading toward each other, passing in the alley. He looked down into the Toyota and spotted a small TV, a blender, and several shopping bags. On top of one of the shopping bags were a camera and a clock, and those hadn't come from any supermarket! And if that weren't enough, the dude on the passenger side held a ten-inch kitchen knife by his left leg. *That* did it.

He keyed the mike and said, "Verdugo, patrol two-one. Go to tac two."

"Go ahead, John," the dispatcher responded on tac two, the less formal channel.

And while the dispatcher's mike was open, John could hear another dispatcher laughing an "Oh shit! What now?" laugh.

The dispatchers got their answer on the open radio mike when they heard the yellow truck's engine rev and the tires squeal as it made a screaming U-turn and peeled out of the alley.

"Residential burglars!" John yelled into the mike. "Blue Toyota, no plates, two male Latinos, twenty to twenty-five years!"

Shit! The Toyota spotted him closing in, then it hung a U-ee, rubber smoking, and wheeled off onto a side street. But when the ugly yellow fire truck clattered after them, the Toyota whipped it around again and roared right at him.

He scarcely had time to jerk the wheel and get out of the way. His truck bounced and clattered over a curb with all kinds of gear crashing around the truck bed, and the Toyota's passenger *laughed* as they sped by. And flipped him off.

Nobody was scared of a fireman driving something that looked like a Tijuana taxi. Well, they didn't know *this* fireman. He flicked on the red lights, and the chase was on, with his overloaded rig sliding and skidding and clanging around corners, and everybody on the street wondering what in hell the fireman was up to.

"Verdugo!" he yelled into the mike, pulling out all the stops now. "They're running! Eastbound on Glenoaks! No . . . *southbound* now!"

"Patrol twenty-one, patrol twenty-one," the dispatcher said. "Are you in pursuit?"

It was unbelievable! A cop-style pursuit? Of burglars? By a fireman in a ratty yellow truck?

John was still afraid to officially announce a cop-style pursuit. So he said, "No! I'm not in pursuit. I'm just following. *Real* fast!"

Except that when he got to a busy intersection and had to pop the siren, the dispatcher heard it over the open mike and came back with, "Patrol twenty-one. Will advise Glendale PD that you're *not* in pursuit. Just following real fast. Riiiiiight."

The Toyota jerked a hard left into another alley, and the driver jumped on the brakes, seemingly ready to bail out.

John thought about that big knife as he chugged in behind them. He reached for the bag next to him. His .38 was unloaded, but he'd also stashed a .22 automatic in there. He grabbed both guns, but the burglars didn't bail. The Toyota took off again.

After another block or two of crazed driving the Toyota went into a wheel-locking slide right into the Greyhound bus depot. The doors blew open and they were *gone.*

One guy headed for an industrial park and got away. The other hot-footed down a residential street, the asshole that had flipped him the bird, so John racked a round into the chamber of the .22 and lit out after him, with two police units, sirens howling, headed his way.

After rounding a corner, the burglar, who was in worse shape than the overweight fireman, had had enough. He made a halfhearted attempt to climb a block wall, but gave up.

It was a neighboring Burbank Police Department motor cop who got there first. He looked at the prone burglar, then at the Glendale fireman, then at the little .22 pistol in the fireman's hand, and he said in disbelief, "Is that your fire truck back there?"

"Yes," John responded. "Don't make me explain right now, 'cause I don't feel too . . ." Then he threw up. He tossed his cookies all over the burglar, who by now couldn't believe any of this shit, nor could the Burbank motor cop.

It turned out that the addicts had burgled an apartment, and their Toyota was loaded with a few thousand bucks' worth of loot. John made a self-effacing claim to his colleagues that though the pursuit was undeniably exciting, he "didn't want any attention for it."

And their answer to that was the same given by the Verdugo dispatcher: "Riiiiight."

When they gave him the Deputy Dawg horseshit again, he said, "If I was a straight police officer this caper would've been chalked up as a righteous bust." He was absolutely right. He added, "But because I'm a half-breed wanna-be I'm a target of ridicule." And he was absolutely right about that too.

The *Glendale News-Press* grabbed the story and published it the next day, and every fire station in the city and beyond heard about the swashbuckling fireman who ended up getting a commendation from the city council for his derring-do. The fire marshal gave him thirty merit points in his personnel file, but took back fifty for the offense of carrying a firearm in a fire department vehicle.

It was getting hard for the fire marshal to decide what to *do* with this guy.

John said that the next time he went to one of those cop bars, a young officer who actually seemed to get a kick out of the Glendale fireman's reputation sent the wanna-be a half-pitcher of margaritas. Now *that* was a bit of recognition, coming as it did from a *real* cop.

John Orr enjoyed it immensely, and drank the pitcher dry, and played his favorites on the jukebox: Neal Diamond and the Doors. And of course, everybody loved the Doors' signature song: "Come on baby light my fire!"

3

THE BIG SHOW

During the early eighties John Orr enrolled in a few more fire-investigation courses with his firefighter colleague Don Yeager and a Glendale cop, Detective Dennis Wilson, who attended because the police were still handling the arson cases for the city of Glendale. Arson, according to the cops, was part of "the garbage detail," not like handling homicides or robberies.

There was one aspect of those training sessions that John found fascinating. It was the staged fires where furnished rooms were set alight and allowed to burn. They got to watch the ignition and progression, and to examine the aftermath. He said it was a "privilege" to observe the before and after of a fire scene, something many firefighters never got a chance to see.

When the training was finished, the fire marshal, only too aware of John's job enthusiasm, approved of his being called out after hours on unusual fires. John Orr was becoming a de facto arson investigator even though the responsibility still resided with the police department. His primary task still lay in inspecting vacant property for brush and weed abatement, and issuing citations to recalcitrant property owners, which wasn't always easy.

He said it *would* have been if he were a six-foot-three-inch cop in a blue uniform, carrying a six-inch Magnum, wearing mirrored shades. But no, he was just a five-foot-nine-inch fireman in a pale blue work shirt, like a "towel guy at a car wash."

A case in point was the wealthy real-estate broker who had been avoiding costly weed abatement by listing post office boxes on property deeds in order to hide his true address. One of his properties was an abandoned and derelict duplex apartment. Kids would hang out there and the property was window high with weeds.

The fire marshal had sent five notices, but got no response. John obtained the miscreant's home address but couldn't catch him there, so he staked out several real-estate offices that the broker owned until he spotted the guy entering one of them. He sneaked up to the door, doing, as he described, "a low crawl."

John knocked at the door, calling out. "Hellooooo! Is this Dr. Beauchamp? I have a delivery for the office manager!"

The elusive broker peeked out but couldn't see the creeping fireman, and yelled, "You have the wrong address. I am *not* Dr. Beauchamp."

John knocked again and said, "Well, my package has this address on it and I've been instructed to leave it here!"

The broker opened the door then, and said, "Look, buddy, I told you . . ."

But there he was, staring into the grinning face of a fireman, and not just *any* fireman, as he would soon discover.

"I think you're the guy I'm looking for," John said.

"He was my *target*" is how John later described him.

But even after all that, the "target" denied his true identity as owner of the property in fire-code violation, until John said, "Come on, gimme your identification and let's get this over with." And he stepped inside.

The target was *outraged*. He ordered the fireman out. The fireman refused. He shoved the fireman. The fireman shoved back.

John Orr later said, "If I was a *real* cop the confrontation would never have progressed. The dude woulda taken his licks."

And when the fireman picked up his radio to call for a *real* cop, the target said, "What're you doing?" and snatched it away. And he shoved John again, causing the radio to clatter to the floor. They wrestled and the radio was kicked outside. They crashed into the door, and it slammed shut. The target broke free and ran for his desk, jerking open a drawer, rummaging for . . .

A gun! John thought. He dove across the desk and pulled the guy's hand out. They grappled on the desktop.

And then, as John Orr later maintained, "For the first time in my entire life I threw a punch."

It turned out to be a dweeby little skittering punch, and did nothing but piss off the broker even more.

But the broker was no Bruce Lee, and John managed to get him in a choke hold and drag him out the front door and down to the ground, where he kept the guy's neck in the crook of his arm and grabbed the damaged radio with the other hand.

While John was calling for help, the broker wriggled around enough to slide his mouth down and sink his fangs into the fireman's forearm, and the fireman yelled "Yoooooowwwww!" into the radio.

But the son of a bitch wouldn't let go! He just hung on like a fucking alligator, so John shouted his location and "Help!" into the radio, and threw only the *second* wimpy punch of his entire life, smacking the guy in the back of the head. And breaking his own finger.

By and by, the nearest engine company showed up along with a bunch of cops, and nobody was shocked to see who it was sitting there on the stoop of the real-estate office, nursing his chomped arm and broken pinkie, while the real-estate broker wheezed.

And then, to John's surprise, out of the office walked the guy's ten-year-old stepson. He'd been in one of the other rooms during the entire donnybrook, afraid to come out. The broker screamed that this wack-job fireman had come to his door demanding identification, and that when he momentarily refused because of the overbearing attitude, the fireman had hauled off and punched him in the chops! And the ten-year-old kid nodded yes, and swore to it.

The broker was quite a big shot around Glendale and had friends. He threatened to sue the city for a million bucks and did. But there was some horse trading done, the city quashed the citation that John had written and the broker settled his million-dollar lawsuit out of court for five hundred bucks. John Orr was informed that he'd been lucky because some of the city bigwigs had considered filing assault charges against *him*!

With everyone around him getting exhausted by his antics, John

decided that there might be something wrong with his approach to citation writing, and maybe he needed to learn how *real* cops did it, so he
asked permission to do ride-alongs with the Glendale police, and was
told, yes yes, *anything* to prevent future punch-outs and lawsuits. So he
rode several times with a Glendale cop who, John said, was "ferocious on
the job." That cop's ferocity was irresistible and intoxicating. He almost
fell in love with her.

It was during this time that Glendale hillsides were frequently being set
on fire, especially near the affluent homes in Chevy Chase Canyon.
Nobody ever caught anyone, but the arsons were forcing Chevy Chase
property owners to do their part in brush and weed abatement.

John devised a scheme where he would phone up a brush-clearance
company that would work without front money, and posing as the
owner, he'd make appointments for the properties to be cleared.

He would say "Bill me, please," giving the owner's address or the P.O.
box that he'd ferreted out.

And it worked, but it wasn't easy because the goddamn post office
wouldn't show him the box applications as they would for a *real* cop. The
way he solved that problem was by dating a not-so-hot-looking letter
carrier who introduced him to a postal inspector at a party, and from then
on, the post office was *his*.

He later portrayed how he loved tracking down these miscreants and
ticketing them:

> The violators I dealt with were minor bandits, but their evasion
> tactics were better than some career criminals'. I found it challeng-
> ing to conduct the "hunt" using any tracking abilities I had to find
> them and make the "kill"—writing a citation or getting the hazard
> eliminated—as the "trophy head." A bit like my pursuit of women
> during my days as a single man.

The zealousness of Glendale's fire-prevention guy struck some of the
firefighters as quite peculiar. John not only responded to all brush fires
while on duty, but he'd even show up off duty. He said it was to study
"fire-fighting tactics and fire behavior." And why should he worry about

what a bunch of guys thought, guys who spent so much firehouse time on their backs that he felt like drawing a chalk line around the whole station.

Everyone knew that 80 percent of brush fires were set deliberately, and this was at a time when John longed for Glendale to form a real arson unit. He was doing a kind of "arson profiling," before the profiling of serial criminals by the FBI had been given much publicity. And since almost all the brush fires were roadside starts, he said he "put himself in the arsonist's car, and in the arsonist's head." He began looking at traffic patterns, searching for homes or landmarks from which a fire starter could be spotted gazing at his handiwork.

While poring over old reports, one conclusion became inescapable: the past arson investigations were inadequate. He found places where fire setters must have parked to admire their fires, yet so-called arson cops had never thought to head for the high ground or other locations where an arsonist would likely sit and observe.

And then he discovered his first incendiary device. It was at a small hillside brush fire, and he'd traced the fire path to a blasted chaparral bush where the damage fanned out as if from an explosion. The battalion chief had ordered his firefighters to turn off their lines so as not to interfere with John Orr's investigation, and in the middle of the chaparral he found the remnants of a cigarette-and-matchbook delay device. They never found the arsonist, but John got an attaboy for finding the evidence.

In April he bagged his first serial arsonist. A cluster of small nuisance fires had been set around the grounds of a convalescent facility, and it didn't take a Miss Marple to deduce that the fire setter was probably one of the codgers who lived there. John Orr spotted the arsonist right away.

He noticed that the first two fire scenes could easily be seen from a certain cottage, and a biddy was peeking at him from behind her curtains. He knocked on her door and used the phantom witness gag. And she bought it, confessing to setting the fires, whereupon the loony lady was transported to a more secure mental facility and she became the first of many serial arsonists John would catch in his career. The others, he hoped, would bring a bit more glory.

The next one came in the same week, when he did some follow-up work on a VW bus that had been stolen and torched. The ignition had been popped and hot-wired, and a witness had seen a guy with a shoulder-length shag and a hand wrapped in a bloodstained bandage. John was only supposed to collect arson evidence, but that would be like asking a bear to only take a sniff of that old honey tree. He cruised through the streets of Glendale scoping out every longhair he saw. All the dudes with hands in their pockets got the hawkish stare from the fireman in the ugly yellow truck.

He did a lot of paper shuffling and snooping through police reports until he found a report of a longhair living in a vacant apartment house who had accidentally started a fire while attempting to keep warm. John sped over there and found the guy, who, sure enough, had a bandaged hand. But the hand carried a brick in it. The wacko was hammered or stoned or both, and threatened to bash the fireman's fucking head in. But after his recent experiences, John didn't draw the gun he was forbidden to carry. Instead, he keyed his mike and called for real cops while he tried to persuade the guy that he was a friend, and didn't everybody like firemen?

Cops arrived and the ding was charged with auto theft, burglary, and two counts of arson; ergo, John could say that he was the only employee of Glendale, cop or fireman, who had ever busted two serial arsonists in one week. The fire marshal told him that there would soon be a selection process for the newly created job of arson investigator, and that he had the edge. By then, seven firefighters had applied for the job, two of them former cops.

But the other firefighters said, well, maybe the fire marshal bought into all the super sleuthing, but what had John Orr caught? A poor old loony tune from a rest home and a certifiable head case who was probably just trying to roast some wienies he'd boosted from a 7-Eleven store.

When you came right down to it, it was something like shooting skunks.

Meanwhile, he was still busy womanizing, having given up on his second marriage. He'd been dating a divorcée from Sears who had three kids. He won her heart while on a camping trip to a cabin that she owned in the Angeles National Forest. But in July, his professional life took a dive when he tried to issue a citation to a property owner who'd neglected to clear his property even after several visits by an engine company.

The property was in an upmarket neighborhood, and though the grounds could have used a flatbed full of stoop laborers, the house was big, beautiful, and impressive. When the lady of the house answered the knock she may as well have been gawking at Bigfoot. "I know who *you* are!" she cried. "I know what you did to the real-estate broker!"

When he tried to get her to calm down and accept a citation, she refused, saying, "I'm calling my husband right now!"

"You can't refuse," he told her. "Your name's on the tax roll with his."

With that, she slammed the door in his face. He called for backup, and a police unit got dispatched. In a few minutes that ferocious female cop pulled up in her black-and-white, heard his story, and said, "What's the problem? So write the bitch up and if she refuses the ticket, she goes to the slam."

However, as he later reported, "The lady of the house called her husband who called the mayor who called the fire chief who called the fire marshal, saying, 'Get out there and find out what Orr's up to *this* time.'"

Later that day, John was called into the office of the fire marshal, who said, "John, the guy's on the planning commission. You gotta be more *careful* with these people."

"These people? These people?" John sputtered.

And then he launched into a tirade about *these people* who were no better than ordinary citizens like himself. And he demanded to know if this was how it would be if they formed the arson unit. Was this how he'd have to treat *criminals* if they had money and influence and lived in a big goddamned house?

"Cool down, John," the fire marshal advised.

So he cooled down and requested a couple of days off, dropped his citation book on the desk, and left the office with red and watery eyes.

He went camping with the only person he was truly comfortable with, himself, and tried to analyze his recent controversies. Sure, at times he'd been a bit undiplomatic and pissed off some people, but in the end, he believed he was fundamentally right. So he cleared the campsite and headed home to visit the girlfriend from Sears and get some feedback.

The next day he drove to work and dropped a note on the fire marshal's desk that read: "Please remove my name from consideration for the arson investigator position. I am no longer interested."

He decided to go back to being an ordinary firefighter. More than ever he thought of himself as an "eccentric," and he wouldn't have it any other way. So if they didn't understand and appreciate what he could do, fuck 'em all.

During his self-imposed exile there seemed to be increased arson activity in Glendale, including foothill brush fires and a series of car fires. Then, toward the end of the year, the fire chief prepared to select an arson investigator from the seven applicants, and that included John Orr's camping friend, Don Yeager, whom John considered argumentative, aggressive, condescending, and inflexible. In short, coplike.

The fire chief called John in and asked him to reconsider applying. He was told that the new position would mean that the man selected would be a real investigator with peace-officer authority, able to carry a firearm full-time.

It took John about a nanosecond to reconsider. Within a week he took a psychological exam that once again included the MMPI self-inventory, but this time he passed it. And he was selected to be the Glendale Fire Department's first arson investigator. Don Yeager told him he hadn't really wanted the job anyway, not liking the eight-to-five hours.

John was teamed up with Glendale police detective Dennis Wilson, and they were the arson team. No more fire prevention, no more fighting fires, this was The Big Show.

Lots of good things happened in the early 1980s. John's fire department, one of the lowest paid in the L.A. basin, became one of the highest paid after the members hooked up with organized labor. And now that he was an arson sleuth he started picking up cop habits, like parking on the wrong side of the street when there was plenty of room to do it legally.

He said, "To a cop it's a form of marking territory. To show that this is my turf."

But he *wasn't* a cop, and he wrote of his feelings:

There was never total approval. An arson investigator wasn't totally a firefighter or totally a cop. We were bastard children, especially to real cops. But I had news for them. I wasn't a wanna-be. I was a cop whether they wanted to believe it or accept it. Full-time arson investigators in the state of California are defined, in penal code section 830.37, as law-enforcement officers.

So the *real* cops could just get over it. He wore an ankle holster and a Walther PPKS .380 semiautomatic, and his little investigative unit was considered low maintenance and brought in several thousand bucks a year in restitution. But he didn't catch any of the arsonists setting those brush fires.

John and his senior partner, Dennis Wilson, were given a tiny office in the old headquarters fire station, but had to scrounge their own desks, typewriter, and file box. Their car was a Ford with a red spotlight, a radio, and eighty thousand hard miles on it. Wilson was a big, fifteen-year Glendale cop with graying hair and a macho cop mustache. The detective was, according to his partner, gruff, irritable, and nonverbal, a family man and a recreational bowler. He intimidated John with his "standard-issue cop attitude."

This was in evidence on one of their first assignments. Glendale police personnel were required to pack a gun at all times, but no fireman, not even the brand-new arson investigator, was allowed to pack while riding in a fire truck. But after a call-out, John climbed aboard a five-ton GMC to drive it to a suspicious fire explosion, and Dennis Wilson *made* his partner take off the .357 Magnum and stow it in the trunk of the arson car, which Wilson drove to the blaze. That was the first humiliation.

John decided to tie the knot in April with number three. He figured that maybe the third time was the charm. He felt that her daughters got along well with his, and they'd all get together for Ozzie-and-Harriet weekends.

John thought he saw felons everywhere, and sometimes he did. While on a weekend jaunt to a swap meet in Santa Clarita with fellow firefighter Don Yeager, they parked Yeager's Chevy Blazer by a busy highway while they moseyed among open-air stalls. When John happened to glance toward the Blazer he saw somebody sitting inside and it wasn't Yeager, who was talking to some chick at one of the stalls.

Next thing you know, John Orr and a car thief were out there on the highway, in asphalt-melting one-hundred-degree heat, thrashing around and grappling for choke holds. A California Highway Patrol unit happened to be cruising the other way on the highway, spotted the donnybrook, spun a U-ee, and, in that moment, while John was sweating, breathless, scared of being pancaked by a passing eighteen-wheeler, what did he think of when he saw the CHiP running toward him, gun drawn?

"I theorized it wouldn't carry much weight to shout, 'I'm a fireman, don't shoot.' Knowing cop attitudes toward wanna-bes, it might lead him to the wrong conclusion."

So, using cop jargon for "grand theft auto," he yelled, "I'm a cop! This guy's a GTA suspect!"

The traffic cop couldn't possibly have cared if the citizen fighting the dirtbag was a fireman, a cop, or a plum picker from Modesto, yet John Orr was obsessing about cop attitudes toward wanna-bes.

John Orr bagged his first pyromaniac when a landlord reported a series of small fires in an apartment complex. On the last one a "bystander" shouted a warning to residents and escorted some of them out before the engine company arrived. He was the same guy who had recently spotted a purse snatching and captured the thief after a foot pursuit.

John immediately suspected the bystander hero. He wrote, "This guy sounded like *me*. He even looked like me right down to the mustache."

Then the hero was a bystander once too often and tried fighting a fire with a garden hose, but got overcome by smoke and ended up in an ER with an IV in his arm. He had to give the address of his employer for the hospital records, and he did, but the address belonged to the Glendale Police Department, a clue to the hospital staff that the guy just might be a head case.

John went to see the fellow and got incriminating admissions, filing not only arson charges against him but also bigamy, after the firebug's estranged wife admitted that he hadn't bothered to divorce his first wife when they got married.

He thought that pyros were interesting. He learned that they made up less than 5 percent of arson suspects and that typically they were loners.

John wrote: "The fire becomes a friend they can relate to. Their fires bring attention, friends, admiration as heroes, and self-esteem. Like a drug addict, one good score leads to the desire for another."

In the August 1982 issue of *American Fire Journal,* a Glendale battalion chief wrote about his new Arson/Explosives Unit.

> During the first thirteen months, 153 incidents were investi-
> gated by the unit: 78 cases were cleared, 25 arrests were made, 23
> cases were filed, resulting in 11 convictions. In addition, 29 cases
> were referred for inter-agency counseling. Cases cleared by the
> unit were approximately 21 percent above the national average.
> Additionally, incidents involving arson dropped to 31 percent
> within the first year. When news media carried the stories it had an
> immediate effect on those who may have had arson in mind.

So it seemed to everyone that the "marriage" of cop and firefighter was working. But, as with the other unions in John Orr's life, this one was shaky. He suffered a truly humiliating experience.

"Dennis treated me like a training officer," he reported. "With his rookie on a leash, he belittled me publicly because one night I wore a gun while processing a fire scene. A reporter showed up and asked Dennis how the unit was working out, and he responded, 'John still has to work out his *wanna-be* image. He's in there now digging around a fire scene wearing a gun. What's he need a pistol for? It's a fire scene and we're the only ones around.' "

The quote appeared in the *Glendale News-Press* the very next day, and of course, the horse laughs could be heard in every firehouse in town. John Orr said that his partnership with Dennis Wilson henceforth looked like "a marriage of convenience."

And the other one wasn't doing too hot either. He and his wife of one year could have a three-hour debate about how long to cook a meat loaf.

Of course, there was nothing that infuriated a real cop more than to have a fireman solve his cases for him. And John Orr did solve a few, including one involving a stolen and torched Mercedes convertible that was used by a pair of residential burglars to haul away loot, including guns and jewelry.

It was a no-suspects case, but he and his partner started to canvass the neighborhood, several blocks in every direction from the Mercedes dump

site, and they came up with a few rumors about some neighborhood bad
guys. Then they put on Public Service Department shirts, knocked on
doors, and made cold calls on the phone, posing as employees of the
Water and Power Department.

Finally they ended up at the house of a local thug who'd been in a lot
of trouble in his life, and when John Orr learned that the dude happened
to be out of town, he went undercover for the first time, playing the part
of an old jailhouse cellmate. He wangled a recent snapshot of the guy, and
learned that he'd been at a recent party given by the burglary victim.

One burglar got state prison time and the other was put on probation,
and, any way you cut it, some good police work was done by the wanna-
be and his partner.

He sent his writing to *American Fire Journal*. After he submitted a piece
about training burns of abandoned houses, the editor asked for more. So
he wrote another examining the mind and methods of a serial fire setter.
John Orr's reputation in the local fire-fighting community was becoming
significant.

And his personal life seemed to be taking a turn for the better in 1983,
despite what he saw as his third wife's argumentative style. He reported,
"I typically stayed home evenings helping her daughters with homework,
preparing brown bag lunches for the next day, along with Ozzie-and-
Harriet-like family amusements."

Except that later in the year, Ozzie hauled ass yet another time. They
eventually were divorced, but remained friends.

He reported that during this period in his career he and his partner
found a lot of incendiary devices, some of them involving a cigarette, a
few matches, and a rubber band, which, in the case of brush fires, would
be weighed down with a screw and tossed from a moving car.

But while the arson duo still made plenty of arrests, "like a typical
married couple" we grew apart, he said. Typical for John Orr, that is, who
by then had dumped *three* wives, while for Dennis Wilson, family took
priority over his job.

Another blow to the partnering came when Wilson designed new
business cards with two overlapping badges as a logo, fire and police, and
there was no surprise which one was on top. John seethed.

As he recalled the inevitable rupture with his partner and all the slights that had preceded it, he made a claim that contradicted everything in his life since his rejection by the LAPD in 1971 for being "unsuitable." It was later said that his self-appraisal was breathtaking in its self-deception. He wrote:

Dennis never quite got it. I didn't want to be a cop, and even resented it when citizens and crooks said, "You're a cop, aren't you?" I was a fireman. The good guy. All I wanted from Dennis was a little credit once in a while. I just wanted acceptance.

Perhaps the unvarnished truth, and the very last word, so to speak, on John Orr's obsession with, and paranoia about, *real* cops can be gleaned from his relationship with one he'd dated periodically.

Many years after they'd broken up she had occasion to talk about the cop fixation that had gripped him. She implied that she'd been a kind of enabler, because after he'd begged, and cajoled, pleaded, and badgered her, she at last agreed to indulge him, and they met furtively in the basement of the fire station, where in full uniform—Sam Browne, gun, handcuffs, the works—she proved at last that he was more than suitable. John Orr got a real cop to give new meaning to "civil service," and risk her job and his, by getting down and whacking his weasel right there in the basement of the firehouse.

After the breakup of his third marriage, John moved in with a private investigator friend and part-time employer, Bill McLaughlin. Working for McLaughlin as a fire investigator helped his finances, what with a couple of kids and three ex-wives out there, but truth be told, he could never get enough of sleuthing, public or private. McLaughlin and his wife rented him a room in their hilltop home in Chevy Chase Canyon, in brush-fire country.

Some good things were happening to him. His article "Problems of the Firefighter Turned Arson Investigator" was published. It only paid $106, but now he could rightly call himself a professional writer.

Sometimes his sleuthing became a bit peculiar. He liked to have a drink after work with Bill McLaughlin to discuss his cases and to learn about PI methods, such as how to use electronic eavesdropping equipment. He thought that his fellow firefighters might be interested, so the next time a few of them got together for a brew, he brought up a scheme to install a bug in the office of the labor-negotiating team to see what they were going to offer the firefighters during contract talks. Saner voices prevailed and his offer was declined, since nobody wanted to get caught up in a firehouse version of Watergate. Still, he was undaunted and inordinately curious. He surreptitiously installed an electronic bug in the secretary's break room.

He said, "It worked just fine." No telling what juicy tidbits he picked up, even though if he'd been caught, his job would've been terminated on the spot, or he might have been jailed. It didn't seem to strike him as risky or outlandish.

John Orr had a take-home car, all the overtime pay he'd care to earn, and the best job in the city, but he felt it was time to study for promotion to fire captain. After all, he had the experience.

It appeared that the city of Glendale was having far more than its share of incendiary fires, but John said it may have been that it only *seemed* that way because he worked harder at defining them. He was building a reputation among arson investigators in neighboring jurisdictions, and it got enhanced when he received permission from the California Conference of Arson Investigators to host their five-day fire-fighting examinations.

He choreographed a live burn of a derelict building, a big one involving forty helpers, role players, and coordinators. Everyone thought it was spectacular. They got to watch a building fire from inception through all stages, and it was easy to see how people described fires in anthropomorphic terms. It *did* lick and dance and leap, after which it growled and roared and devoured *everything*, including the air that fed it.

A Love Machine was loosed upon the San Gabriel Valley. John Orr chronicled some of his adventures:

During my single years in the early-mid 1980s, I simultaneously dated Glendale and Pasadena lady friends. My love life was no secret. I couldn't leave my pager on all night without a charger if I slept somewhere other than my home base. I had to let Verdugo Dispatch know my overnight phone number. If I called after 10:00 P.M., the dispatcher, no matter who answered, would say, "Hi, John. Who is it tonight? Miss 242 or Miss 795?" For the Glendale or Pasadena prefixes.

Women weren't drinking so much anymore. A lot of them were doing the twelve-step tango and the carefree bachelor decided that the ones he was meeting in gin joints weren't cutting it. He began answering singles ads but didn't share this secret with anyone. During that year he answered eleven ads and dated ten women. Most of them were worth a second date or even a third, a pretty good average.

His first date, though, might've discouraged some singles. After answering her ad, he agreed to meet the woman at a Chinese restaurant for lunch, but just as he was in the middle of a formal introduction, he got paged to an accidental fire where a homeowner, who'd been cleaning the gas range with a flammable liquid, ignited gas fumes that burned her to death.

He explained his predicament, that he'd have to hurry to the fire scene to meet the coroner's people, and she said, "Cool! Can I go with you? I've never seen a burned body!"

The women he dated from the singles ads were of a higher caliber than those he met in the bars, he said.

And then in the autumn of 1984, on October 10, he attended the most monumental fire of his career, the disastrous blaze in South Pasadena at Ole's Home Center. The morning after that fire, when they were sifting through the rubble for clues, the South Pasadena fire chief, who'd heard about the photos John Orr had snapped the night before, asked to see them. So John put down his shovel, headed for a one-hour photo mart, and returned just before noon.

He couldn't believe what was happening then, what with the L.A. County sheriffs clearing out debris on a D-9 Caterpillar tractor instead of crawling the scene on hands and knees. Even the cadaver dogs they'd brought in couldn't find a scent in all that mess.

John quit the scene in disgust. "I decided I had better things to do than lean on a shovel until some cop snapped his fingers," he reported. "The condescending cop attitude toward fire department investigators was never more pronounced than at that scene."

By 5:00 P.M., Sergeant Palmer of the L.A. County Sheriff's Department attended a press conference and the fire was declared accidental.

John later contacted the coroner's office and was stunned to learn that no law-enforcement officer was even present during the autopsies. He talked with a pathologist and learned that the bodies had very high concentrations of carbon monoxide. He later wrote, "They were dead before the fire trucks ever left the station. I considered quietly pursuing the case, but my partner warned me off."

In 1985, they celebrated the fifth anniversary of the arson unit, but John knew that yet another "marriage" was doomed. The following year his partnership with Dennis Wilson ended for good when John confidentially told the boss that things weren't going so well with him and his partner, and that for "the good of the unit Wilson had to go." This time John didn't have to run from a relationship. His partner was sent back to the police department with a face-saving attaboy from all concerned.

He'd gotten rid of one partner, but took on another, continuing to commit serial marriage. Wanda owned her own home, drove a nice low-mileage car, had no kids and no man in her life, only a dog and two cats for company. In November, in a civil ceremony in her home presided over by a Glendale judge, who, ironically, was a retired LAPD cop, Wanda became wife number four.

There was a thing about "arsonists-in-training," as he called them. In the beginning, when they were setting small fires, it was usually done to build self-esteem. He saw it in a young woman, a former "police explorer" who had worked at the police station preparing for a career in law enforcement. There occurred a series of small grass fires near her father's posh home, and she'd called to report all of them, even fighting one fire with a garden hose.

John decided to interview that young woman after he learned from a friend at the Glendale Police Department that she had been terminated from the police explorer program because she was suspected of theft, specifically the theft of a police badge.

He went to the police to confer about the fires and the suspected badge theft, but, as usual, "they smirked" and didn't seem to give a shit. So he went to her home alone and spoke with the young woman about the fires she'd reported, and about her termination from the police department explorer program, and about her depression now that the police department had found her *unsuitable*.

It didn't take long at all for the lonely girl to confess through flowing tears that she was bored and terribly lonely, and that she had trouble getting along with others, and that she was never truly appreciated by authority figures, especially her usually absent father.

She denied stealing the police badge, but he figured it was stashed somewhere. He told her gently that he would have to book her for arson, but that he'd allow her to surrender herself to avoid the humiliation of having to face all those asshole cops she'd known from her police explorer stint.

As he put it, "Firefighters *care* for people. There aren't many cops who would even consider the feelings of someone they'd arrested."

Someone like the lonely young woman, for instance, who felt abandoned by the frequently absent father with whom she shared the home, a young woman who was easily bored, rebellious, resentful of authority, and so in need of attention and approval that she'd set fires in order to report them. And so desperate for power and control that she might run the risk of stealing a badge from the police station where she worked—a world-class cop wanna-be. But instead of seeing herself as an "eccentric," the young woman called herself a "nonconformist."

John Orr later reported that he'd tried to give her a break by okaying a release on her own recognizance, and recommending a probationary disposition of her case, explaining about her daddy issues and low self-esteem. He never said whether or not she'd reminded him of anyone.

The police department employee who had put him on to that case, informing him of the badge theft that aroused his suspicion about fire setting, was Karen Krause, the sister-in-law of Carolyn Krause, who had perished in the Ole's Home Center holocaust.

4

INTUITION

The California Conference of Arson Investigators hosted a three-day seminar in Fresno starting on January 13, 1987. John Orr decided to go and delegated his new junior partner to remain in Glendale and mind the store.

It can seem a very long drive to Central California from Los Angeles, north through the San Joaquin Valley, past endless truck crops and grazing land. There are mountains, the Sierra Madres to the west, the Tehachapis to the east, and then one passes through Bakersfield, once a destination for the Okie migration of the Great Depression, still a vital agricultural zone where folks can tune their radios to *real* country stars such as George Strait and even the old Bakersfield homeboy Buck Owens, rather than crossover cowboys.

After Bakersfield, there's not much until you arrive in the town of Tulare, and if you weren't already aware of it, you'll have an idea how crucial the farms and ranches of California are, not only to the state but to the country. Then, somewhere around the fourth hour of driving, you'll arrive in the city of Fresno, site of the arson seminar, but if you drive like John Orr, you'll get there much faster. He could drive with even more gusto now that he was wearing glasses full-time to correct the nearsightedness that had started to affect his shooting scores.

There were 242 conferees—arson investigators, prosecutors, insurance investigators, cops, and firefighters—arriving that Tuesday from all over the state. The weather was foggy, cold, and miserable that year, and most of the seminar participants stayed in and around the hotel, networking and boozing it up in the restaurant and bar. Of course, some of the more restless ventured out looking for action, such as there was. Fresno was a growing city of 350,000, but it had managed to retain much of its rural ethic. The conferees from the big cities said there was nothing to do there except watch grapes turn into Fresno raisins.

That conference might have come and gone and passed from memory except for the stunning events that took place starting on the first evening, when the city was swarming with men and women whose lives were dedicated to fire prevention and suppression.

At 8:30 P.M., about an hour after some of the registers had been closed at Payless Drug Store on North Blackstone Avenue, an employee spotted smoke rising up from a display of sleeping bags that had been tightly packed in a cabinet. He saw the bags suddenly burst into flame, setting off the overhead sprinklers. Helped by the sprinklers' deluge of water, the store manager contained the fire with a handheld fire extinguisher. There was a lot of water damage, but nobody had been seen in the area at the time the fire was spotted, so it was difficult to say what had caused it. The store manager was issued a citation because his fire alarms were not in good working order.

A witness reported seeing a deaf-mute, or perhaps a firebug posing as a deaf-mute, in the vicinity of the fire's point of origin shortly before it ignited. Nobody thought too much about that fire at Payless Drug Store until an occurrence on Thursday evening that got everybody thinking.

It happened once again on Blackstone Avenue, this time at Hancock Fabrics, right across the street from Payless Drug Store. The first and best witness was a shopper who had been examining some fabric at the cutting table in the center of the store when she glanced up and saw smoke in the northwest corner of the building. The smoke was gray, but instantly turned inky black, and then the smoke cloud erupted in a ball of flame. And she watched slack-jawed as the fireball divided into fingers of fire that "danced" up the walls and along the ceiling. It all happened so unbelievably fast.

Then, pandemonium. An announcement of *"Fire!"* sounded on the intercom, and customers and clerks were running to the exits. The woman who had first spotted the smoke had a rudimentary understanding of heat, fuel, and air, and she told the others outside the building that they should close the doors to starve the blaze until the firefighters arrived. And she tried, but the fire would have none of it. With all of her weight pressing against the exit doors, the voracious blaze flexed and roared and in a blast of terrible power hurled her back toward the parking lot. She ran to her car and got out of there.

The fire department did not dare enter the building to fight the out-of-control inferno, but confined suppression activities to the outer walls. The conflagration was amazingly hot and intense. They learned why the next day, after they could get inside, discovering that the point of origin was in a storage bin, in Styrofoam beanbag pellets used for stuffing pillows. Everyone was relieved that customers and employees had escaped without injury.

Hancock Fabrics was just about completely destroyed, but a diligent sifting through the debris rewarded searchers with an incendiary delay device consisting of one partially burned cigarette with a tan filter tip and three paper matches fastened to the cigarette by a rubber band.

A witness at the Hancock Fabrics fire described a nonchalant customer who had been loitering in the area of the fire prior to its outbreak. He was a white male, about sixty years old, standing six feet six inches, weighing 250 pounds, with a snow-white beard, wearing a blue sea captain's hat and a bright yellow rain slicker.

The fire captain taking the report said, "So do you think he was trying to look inconspicuous?"

And as if enough arson hadn't struck Fresno, later at House of Fabrics, another retail outlet just a block away from Hancock Fabrics and Payless Drug Store, an employee discovered, in a bin stacked with foam pillows, yet another incendiary device consisting of a cigarette, matches, and a rubber band. It had scorched the wall in an inverted V pattern, but had not ignited into a full-blown fire.

Some said it looked as if somebody had been trying to burn down the city during a conference of the most prominent arson sleuths in the state.

What *was* the arsonist trying to do? Was a statement being made to the investigators, or what? Neither the media nor the fire department could figure out what in hell was going on.

At about 10:45 on the last morning of the arson seminar, one hour south in the town of Tulare—where people said the town's only claim to fame was that it was located midway between Fresno and Bakersfield, which were midway between San Francisco and L.A.—there was a fire. At Surplus City, a fire like the one at Payless Drug Store broke out in a display of sleeping bags.

And forty-five minutes later, at the Family Bargain Center in Tulare, the unthinkable happened: *another* fire broke out. A customer in the rear of the retail outlet saw smoke, and the store manager ran to a wooden display bin that was stacked with foam pillows. The manager jerked the pillows out of the bin and extinguished the flames. At the bottom of the bin, beneath the pillows, he found a partially burned cigarette with a tan filter, two burned matches, one rubber band, and some pieces of yellow notebook paper.

By the time a fire captain arrived, the store manager had a description for him of a white male with collar-length black hair, five feet ten inches tall, weighing 170 pounds, wearing a blue jacket and designer jeans. He looked as though he hadn't shaved in a day or two, and his age was described as "mid-twenties."

The store manager recalled that when this man had entered the store about fifteen minutes before the fire broke out, he'd been carrying a yellow piece of paper with lines on it, just like the remnants of paper the manager had found under the pillows.

As in Fresno, Tulare had never experienced two fires on the same day in retail establishments during business hours, and with the recovery of the delay device, it became obvious that the Tulare fires were incendiary in nature.

It later seemed as though this arsonist had just decided to take a lunch break before resuming his activities. At 2:00 P.M., an hour south of Tulare, in the city of Bakersfield, an employee of CraftMart, a retail store open for business, spotted a column of smoke and incipient flames emitting from a bin in the center of the store where there were materials on display for making dry floral arrangements. The store manager put out the fire with a dry powder extinguisher while the engine company was en route.

The fire captain called for a fire investigator, and Captain Marvin G. Casey of the Bakersfield Fire Department arrived in short order. Marvin Casey had nearly twenty years of fire experience, including training in cause and origin analysis, and he'd investigated hundreds of fires. The former Texan had thinning gray hair, a blue-eyed Panhandle squint, and a face creased from years in the dust and wind of the San Joaquin Valley. He'd have looked right at home in boots, a Stetson, and Wrangler jeans.

Casey headed straight for the gondolas that held the display material, and found the heaviest burn there among the dried flowers. Then his gaze moved over the gondola bin and up about four feet. He looked inside and there, under the dry yellow powder from the fire extinguisher, he found an incendiary device composed of a cigarette with a tan filter tip, and three matches, two made of paper, one of wood, and a scorched sheet of yellow lined notebook paper.

Captain Casey asked the captain of the engine company to guard the aisle, and he went to his vehicle to get some evidence cans and envelopes. When he returned to the point of origin he used a Swiss Army knife with a tweezer attachment to lift each item and drop it into a separate envelope.

The notebook paper looked as though it had come from a standard legal pad, but Casey wanted to ascertain whether it could have been in the bin before the incendiary device ignited, or if it was part of the delay device brought into the store by the fire setter. He asked the store manager to bring him every yellow pad or loose sheet of paper in the store, but there was no yellow notepad in CraftMart that matched the piece of burned paper in his hand.

It was destined to be a busy day for investigator Marvin Casey. At 2:00 P.M. that same afternoon, at Hancock Fabrics, Bakersfield branch, sales clerk Laverne Andress was waiting on a customer who had just returned twelve yards of flawed drapery fabric. The sales clerk was very solicitous, and very concerned because the customer was so pregnant that delivery might commence at any moment right there on the cutting table.

While the two women were checking for fabric flaws and cutting the sixty-inch material, the sales clerk smelled cigarette smoke. Neither customers nor employees were permitted to smoke in a fabric store, so the clerk excused herself and went looking for the smoker.

It was then that she saw a man browsing among the shelves and racks of fabrics. She later described him as a white male, wearing a cowboy shirt and boots, five foot seven to five foot nine, with medium-brown receding hair graying at the temples, weighing 170 to 175 pounds with a "large tummy." She guessed his age at thirty to thirty-five years. She looked at his hands, but they were empty. She could find no one smoking in the store, so she went back to her pregnant customer.

At 2:30 P.M., in the rear of the store, the sales clerk heard a hissing sound. Something was hissing in the vicinity of the bin that contained rolled foam-rubber batting. Then a very small blue flame appeared, and then a wave of fire rolled out of the bin and climbed up the wall. Just that fast.

The automatic sprinklers went off and drenched that part of the store, holding the fire in check and flooding the store with two inches of water. The fire department arrived and completed the fire suppression, again calling Marvin Casey.

When Casey arrived, he discussed the fire with the captain of the engine company and described the fire at CraftMart just two miles away. Casey said that it was unique to have two such fires within an hour in retail stores open for business. Such a thing had never happened in Bakersfield.

By the next day, Captain Casey had received a phone call and met with some investigators from Fresno, learning not only about the Fresno fires but about the fires in Tulare. They were all eerily similar. All had been set in displays of volatile material, such as foam rubber and Styrofoam, by someone who must have understood the speed, power, and ferocity of a fire fed by this fuel.

The remnants of the delay devices were the same right down to the number of matches and yellow notebook paper, but the suspect descriptions were varied. They had a deaf-mute, a tubby cowboy, a gigantic ancient mariner in a rain slicker. Nothing really matched when it came to suspect descriptions, but the M.O., type of establishments attacked, and merchandise that was set alight were all just about identical.

And all the fires took place very close to Highway 99, as though the fire setter had been in Fresno on Tuesday through Thursday night, then had driven forty-eight miles down the road to Tulare on Friday morning for two fires, then, maybe after a lunch break, resumed his busy schedule sixty-four miles farther south in Bakersfield, where he'd struck twice between the hours of 1:45 and 2:45 P.M.

And then he seemed to vanish from the San Joaquin Valley.

With all of this arson activity in three separate cities, the locals needed the resources of the Department of the Treasury's Bureau of Alcohol, Tobacco and Firearms. When Captain Casey returned to his office, he had his evidence packaged and sent to the laboratory operated by ATF in Walnut Creek, California, where it ultimately ended up in the hands of Special Agent Clive Barnum, a onetime NYPD cop, now an ATF agent with more than thirty years of experience as a fingerprint specialist.

Barnum was a descendant of Phineas T. Barnum, the legendary circus impresario, and was a well-known character in his own right. He tried processing the cigarette butt with a ninhydrin solution, and it brought out some ridge fragments of a fingerprint, but nothing identifiable. However, the ninhydrin processing of the partially burned yellow notebook paper produced a purple image that was eminently readable. When Barnum started charting points of identification on the fingerprint photo, he stopped counting at thirteen. The FBI was willing to go to trial with seven points of identification, and Barnum could see twice that many. This fingerprint would easily make a positive identification if they came up with a suspect. It was submitted to the state and national fingerprint databases, but drew a negative response. The owner of the print, whoever it was, had no criminal record.

Still, Marvin Casey had the fingerprint of someone who had set, or attempted to set, seven fires while moving south from Fresno to Tulare to Bakersfield, and such an arson series had never been seen in Central California before. Casey made a wry comment that maybe the fire setter was someone who just didn't like arson investigators, and the more he thought about it the more plausible it seemed. He started getting some strange but exciting ideas.

Casey made a call and got the conference roster of 242 names. He determined from their places of employment who would have driven home south from the conference, passing through each city where there had been a fire. Then he learned how many of those had traveled to the conference *alone,* because serial arsonists were solitary creatures. There were fifty-five.

And though he could have guessed at the response he'd get, he had to turn to the feds for help on something multijurisdictional like this. He phoned the ATF office in Fresno and spoke with Special Agent Chuck Galyan, with whom he had worked on other arson fires.

Galyan was far more than skeptical, and later said, "Fifty-five names of respected arson investigators? I wasn't at all comfortable with this. I knew some of them. They were neat guys with lots of integrity. I certainly didn't think that Marv Casey's *intuition* was worth a wholesale inquiry into travel records and so forth."

Using the baseball imagery that the Mighty Casey's name invoked, Galyan said, "I thought Marv Casey was out in left field somewhere."

Everybody else with whom Casey spoke also implied that he should get over it. Maybe if there were just a *few* names. Maybe then he could go a little further with his notions. But Captain Marvin Casey could not get over the eerie feeling.

He thought it was at least plausible that the fire setter had been somehow associated with the conference, maybe in some civilian capacity, even though the arsonist understood which materials were very combustible and how to place a delay device. Or maybe the arsonist was an outsider who truly *did* hate arson investigators. Maybe someone was mocking them, playing all of those arson sleuths for saps and suckers.

Well, he had that someone's fingerprint successfully analyzed by Clive Barnum, whose ancestor P. T. Barnum said, "There's a sucker born every minute."

It remained to be seen who would be the sucker.

It had been nice working alone, but with John Orr's blessing, they had chosen another partner for him. At least this time the new cop would be the junior man. His name was Doug Staubs, an eight-year veteran of the Glendale Police Department. John thought it might work out. Staubs stood six foot three, weighed 220 pounds, and was ten years younger, so he could do any running and wrestling that needed to be done. He was as country as sweet potato pie, and was crazy about bowling alleys. Staubs called everyone "Buddy."

But it was the shortest of all his "marriages." By October, Doug Staubs was history. John insinuated that Staubs was worn out from working an off-duty job. Moreover, he said that Staubs had too much of the "typical cop persona." Staubs was thanked and bounced back to the police department with a diplomatic memo that said, "Returned to ranks due to manpower shortage."

In 1988, John was assigned a third partner, his hunting pal, Don Yeager. But John had plenty of doubts about what he described as Yeager's abrasive personality, calling him "Don Rickles without humor." At least Yeager was a firefighter instead of another Glendale police officer, but this made "a little resentment simmer at the cop shop," John said, especially since rumors had circulated that John had dumped the cop in order to make room for a firefighter.

John insisted that the working cops knew all about Staubs's off-duty commitments but had never revealed it to their superiors. "Apparently, the unthinkable had happened," John said; "a secret was being kept at the police department."

This was an allusion to what everyone who'd ever worked with cops knew to be true: they were the most gossip-obsessed blabbermouths on earth. If you wanted a rumor to circulate among every law-enforcement agency and media outlet in the county by Thursday, tell one cop your "secret" on Monday. If you wanted it on the same-day news shows, tell *two* cops. They'd compete to disclose it.

John published another piece for *American Fire Journal* entitled "Profiles in Arson—The Serial Firesetter." Between his writing and his organizing training sessions for other agencies, there weren't too many fire investigators in Southern California who hadn't heard of John Leonard Orr.

There was another important arson conference to be held, this time in the town of Pacific Grove, near Monterey. It was called the Symposium

IV Arson Conference, a four-day affair scheduled to begin on March 5, 1989. As before, Glendale's senior arson investigator opted to go, and Don Yeager remained in Glendale.

The drive, though not much farther in miles than the trip to Fresno, was slower and more scenic: north through Santa Barbara with those ocean vistas, on to Santa Maria and the Sierra Madres, past the Los Padres National Forest and rolling hills dotted with California oak, into San Luis Obispo, and north on Highway 101 through the Coast Ranges and Salinas. It was John Steinbeck country all the way west to Monterey and the conference site, in the town of Pacific Grove, population fifteen thousand.

This was an ideal place for a conference, with spectacular scenery all along the Monterey Peninsula. Every golf enthusiast in the world had seen some of it on TV from Pebble Beach, and who wouldn't like to visit Carmel, where Dirty Harry himself, Clint Eastwood, was mayor? And just a short drive away, perhaps the most staggering vistas of all were at Big Sur. Of course, many of the conferees would arrive early and stay late for this one, taking advantage of the weekend before the sessions actually began.

On Friday, March 3, 1989, at 5:49 P.M., two and a half hours south in the lovely coastal town of Morro Bay, business was brisk at Cornet Variety Store when a clerk heard a woman yelling "*Fire!*"

The clerk grabbed a fire extinguisher, ran toward the screaming voice at the southwest corner of the store, and saw an incipient fire licking out from a pile of foam pillows in an aisle display. The blaze was extinguished quickly.

At 1:25 P.M., on Saturday afternoon, the day before the conference was to officially begin, and while people were still arriving, a second fire broke out, just nineteen miles away in the town of Salinas at the Woolworth's store, in the bedding stock where foam pillows were stored. The building was heavily charged with smoke and heat and experienced severe damage, but no one was injured. The fire was thought to be incendiary in nature.

The conference was a success, ending on the eighth of March. Most of the conferees checked out of their rooms that day.

The next morning, two hours south of the conference site, just off Highway 101 in the town of Atascadero, there began a startling spree. At 9:30 A.M., an employee at Pacific Home Improvement noticed a scorched roll of foam padding on one of the shelves. He pulled the padding from the box and found a cigarette with three matches attached by a rubber band, all of it wrapped in yellow notebook paper.

Almost two hours later, at the Atascadero branch of Cornet Variety Store, a fire erupted in the back of the building in the shelves that contained plastic bags full of shredded foam rubber. The sprinkler system activated and confined the fire until the arrival of an engine company.

Suspicious customers included a sandy-haired couple in their twenties and an incredibly anal customer in his forties who insisted on paying for his merchandise even as the store was filling with smoke and flame and everybody else was hauling ass.

At 12:09 P.M., at Coast to Coast Hardware, a fire erupted in rolls of plastic sheeting and foam products, but was extinguished by employees using dry chemicals. There were no suspects worth reporting. All three fires had erupted on El Camino, near Highway 101, as though the fire setter had just been trucking along, going, "Eeney, meeny, miney . . ."

"Moe" occurred that evening at 7:55 P.M., twenty minutes south of Atascadero in the city of San Luis Obispo, at The Party Exchange and Et Cetera, a retail outlet selling gifts and decorations. The store manager, who was new on the job, was alerted by a customer to a column of smoke and flame behind the staircase. While ushering customers out and scrambling for a fire extinguisher, she was overcome by smoke and had to be helped to safety. The building was totally destroyed. Fire investigators believed that the blaze had been set in combustible packing material.

And then, after six fires in Morro Bay, Salinas, Atascadero, and San Luis Obispo, all in retail stores open for business, the spree ended. The weather station reported that it was cool, calm, and cloudy once again.

Captain Marvin Casey of the Bakersfield Fire Department was forty-five years old and had nearly twenty-two years on the job on the day he heard about the fires on the Central Coast that had broken out before, during, and after the Pacific Grove arson symposium. He was energized and adrenaline charged. It had happened again!

Casey once more quietly obtained a roster of symposium participants, but this time he could pare down a suspect list to only those from Southern California who had attended *both* the Fresno seminar two years before and this one. Instead of fifty-five names, like last time, there were now only ten.

Marv Casey reported that his superiors scoffed. "I couldn't get anyone to believe me," he said, "because they didn't *want* to believe me."

The people on the list were respected arson investigators. One of them, John Leonard Orr from the Glendale Fire Department, Casey knew rather well. Two years earlier he had taken a class from John Orr in Glendale in order to get his state certification. Prior to the training session, Casey had heard about John Orr and was excited to meet him. He had hoped to mix and network at the Holiday Inn in Burbank where they gathered after class. Casey had found a group of fellow students in that bar, but John Orr was schmoozing a blonde that evening. Marv Casey figured correctly that he wasn't going to get any networking with his instructor that night.

While Casey had never been able to stir up enthusiasm for his idea, at least the Bakersfield fire marshal had given him permission to indulge himself in his spare time. So he once again phoned ATF Special Agent Chuck Galyan in Fresno, who agreed to submit the photo negative of Casey's latent fingerprint, along with the ten names Casey had culled from the rosters of both conferences, to the Department of Justice Regional Criminalistics Laboratory in Fresno.

After the fingerprint cards of the ten arson investigators were retrieved from the state database of people who hold public-safety jobs, they were analyzed by a veteran Department of Justice fingerprint expert. His report, dated April 3, was sent to Galyan. It said that the usable impression appearing on the submitted photograph was compared with the inked fingerprints of the ten men in question. The results were negative. No match.

Casey thought that everyone could just have a good laugh at the hick from Bakersfield, a "city" they thought of as a sprawl of industrial parks, truck stops, and 7-Eleven stores, with a Kmart or two sprinkled in. They could chortle. This not-so-mighty Casey had finally struck out.

———————

A month after returning from the arson symposium in Pacific Grove, the results of the exam for fire captain were announced by letter to contenders. John Orr's score on the exam was 98 percent. He had placed number one, and was appointed a fire captain on May 1. His pay jumped an extra six hundred dollars per month. With his daughter Carrie Lyn turning eighteen in June, her child support would end, so he'd realize a monthly boost of a thousand bucks. He immediately went out and bought a white Chevy Blazer.

Captain Orr wrote three "Profiles in Arson" for *American Fire Journal* that year, and toyed with the idea of trying a novel. But on his days off it was too tempting to just join his wife Wanda in the backyard hot tub, with their Siamese cat and their dog, Cody, lazing nearby. Life was good.

There were several brush fires in and around Chevy Chase Canyon that year, and the newly appointed captain complained that his partner, Don Yeager, wasn't pulling his weight, and that Yeager resented the distinct supervisor-subordinate relationship now that John had been promoted. He said that none of his three partners had been dedicated to the arson unit, and he discussed his dissatisfaction with the fire marshal, Battalion Chief Chris Gray, explaining how difficult it was to be a supervisor with someone he considered a good friend. Captain Orr began wondering if, like wife number four, a firefighter partner number four might be the answer.

In early 1990, John Orr began to have more of a yen to try a novel. He took a writing class, picked up a few tips, and in the spring began writing *Points of Origin*.

5

POOL OF FIRE

There was another Fresno arson symposium in June 1990, but this time John Orr decided that his junior partner should go and he should stay behind tending to duties in Glendale.

The temperature neared ninety degrees by 7:00 A.M. on Wednesday, June 27. By noon it was topping one hundred degrees. Santa Ana winds were blowing into the Los Angeles basin from the desert, and with humidity down to 10 percent, that spelled trouble. Every year there had been brush fires in the foothills of Glendale during the hot dry summers, when the hills were parched and brown. The arson unit had been called upon to investigate all of them, but never had much luck in locating or arresting likely fire setters. This year was hotter and dryer than usual, and the Santa Anas were blowing thirty-five miles per hour. This was the season to fear. This was the time of fire.

At 3:15 P.M. that day, with the temperature in Glendale at 110 degrees, it felt like someone was firing a hair dryer in your mouth every time you took a breath. The Santa Anas were swirling through Chevy Chase Canyon and all along North Verdugo Road, where the local news media had covered brush fires every year, fires that John Orr had told them were probably set by the same person.

And then a call came in. There was a brush fire sweeping up the hillside by North Verdugo. At 3:24 P.M. the first alarm was dispatched. One of the firefighters with Engine Company 226, the second to arrive, was rookie James Frawley. His truck raced along Verdugo Road on the wrong side while cars scrambled out of the way of an onslaught of emergency vehicles blowing air horns and sirens. Just as Truck 26 was turning the corner to the reported fire location on Sweetbriar, the young firefighter saw a man standing at the base of the hill where the fire had reportedly been set, "sifting through things." He recognized the man to be Captain Orr of the arson unit, and Frawley figured that he must have come with the very first engine. He thought no more about it and they set about helping Engine 25 deal with the several homes that were already threatened.

Engine 29 had arrived at the fire scene with orders to set up structural protection from the leapfrogging flames that were being swept by the Santa Anas across the 134 Freeway. Captain Greg Jones, a contemporary of John Orr, saw him standing by his white Blazer on Swarthmore Drive. He wondered how his colleague could have driven to that uphill location near the area of origin without Jones seeing him arrive. Then John approached Captain Jones and asked if he needed help.

Jones told the arson investigator to grab a line and take it to the adjacent house, where a fire was very close to the structure but had not yet reached it other than burning the wooden fence in the backyard. Jones then went next door and began working on a house whose roof was on fire.

A few minutes later, when he returned to the street, Jones saw that John had removed a salvage cover from the engine and was dragging the tarp into the house that Jones was hosing down. Captain Jones was puzzled. Protecting the contents was a low priority when the attic was still involved in fire and the whole damn area was threatened. But John Orr simply covered a living-room couch with the tarp, walked out of the house, and drove away, with embers falling into every room. And he had *not* hosed down the house next door.

Jones later said that he'd seemed "agitated and not in control of what he was doing."

There were outbreaks everywhere in College Hills. The land was smothered by smoke and the skies were full of low-flying aircraft: helicopters belonging to the police and fire services, others from networks and local affiliates, and even fixed-wing observers, all of them having to veer and climb and dive to avoid one another in the blinding smoke storm.

The College Hills fire was described by Los Angeles newscasters in terms both hyperbolic and sensational. One claimed that the devastation resembled a Vietnam carpet bombing. But John may have looked with a more aesthetic eye. As he later described the scene:

> The winds had again subsided as the water-dropping helicopters dove at the hottest flanks of the fire, unleashing over 350 gallons of water each time they swooped down. . . . The big Hueys looked like dragonflies in slow motion, skittering over a pool of fire.

Engine companies arrived from every jurisdiction in the San Gabriel Valley and from the rest of the Los Angeles basin, as a blizzard of ash and soot, whipped and propelled by the Santa Anas, covered the ground for miles around with charred debris. Eventually, engines, trucks, and police units blocked every street and were parked helter-skelter like so many bumper cars at a theme park. And it seemed that every street was crisscrossed with hose lines manned by firefighters in yellow or red helmets.

The cops were manning barricades, and in many ways were the most frustrated and helpless, as houses all around them were burning to the ground and residents of College Hills were racing home through red lights and stop signs, ignoring all speed limits, frantic to rescue irreplaceable belongings, precious pets, and *children.*

Susan Raggio worked all the way across Los Angeles in Century City. She was the mother of six, including thirteen-year-old twin daughters and fifteen-month-old triplets. She had employed a nanny who left her the previous weekend, and her twins had to stay home that Wednesday to mind the three babies. Sometime after 3:00 P.M., Mrs. Raggio received a call from Jennifer, one of her twins, who said that she was frightened because there was a fire somewhere nearby and the entire sky was orange.

Susan Raggio phoned her husband at his job and he said he'd leave work and go home. And she phoned the Glendale Fire Department, but was told not to worry because the fire was on the other side of the freeway from her home. She then called her daughter to reassure her.

But Jennifer could see that vivid, violent sky, could smell the smoke in the air, could see the ash swirling, and she said to her mother, "We're really *afraid*."

Her mother replied, "Get the babies all together and listen for the firemen if they come. I'll be there as soon as I can."

She hung up and hit the freeway, but on any weekday afternoon in Los Angeles the traffic at 3:30 P.M. is horrendous. Couple this with the continual radio updates about a growing brush fire in the Glendale area and the traffic was worse. Then one of the helicopter newscasters announced that they could see flames around the Foxkirk area, and that was *her* street!

By the time Susan Raggio reached Glendale the streets were closed off, so she took back roads and detours, and drove up Chevy Chase right through a barrier where she explained to the fireman, "My children are up there!" Then she saw houses burning all along the ridge.

There were fire department engines and trucks on her street pumping water through a dozen lines, and she just drove over those charged lines and parked, and ran to the house that stood in front of hers. A fireman was hosing down the neighbor's house and she couldn't see *her* house at all through the wall of black smoke, but she sensed that her house was *gone*.

She asked the fireman if he had seen two little girls and three babies, and the harried firefighter looked at her desperate face, left his hose line, made a call on his radio, but then shook his head.

The fireman said, "You can't go back there where your house *was*. You *can't* go back there. Just stay where it's safe and look around for them."

He returned to his duties, and Susan Raggio did not know if her children had perished in their home.

Now the road behind her was blocked by more trucks, and she didn't know what to do or where to look so she just started walking up the hillside, just walking, perhaps for an hour but she couldn't say for sure. She walked until her skirt caught on fire.

After she beat out the flame, she continued along the streets in all that chaos, past those other properties that firefighters were trying to save. By then, seventy-four emergency vehicles and three hundred firefighters were doing battle, but the fire kept skipping over the San Rafael hills, taking houses at random, sparing some. And there in the street she saw her babies' stroller!

Susan Raggio plunged forward more frantically toward the unburned homes, until she was overcome by smoke and fainted. When she was revived, she found herself lying on the front lawn of one of those intact homes, and she walked inside that house while firemen were on the roof soaking it with hoses. She phoned her husband's office and his secretary told her that she had received a call from one of the girls. They'd been evacuated by neighbors and taken to the home of relatives, and other than the twins suffering third-degree burns on their feet when they had to flee barefoot with the triplets in their arms, they were *safe*.

The house and everything in it was lost. But the children were *safe*.

Late that afternoon, while in his West Covina office, Moses Gomez of the California State Fire Marshal's Office heard a report of a major fire in Glendale. He called, offered assistance, and was asked to respond to a command post that had been set up in the 1100 block on North Verdugo Road. Due to rush-hour traffic he didn't arrive until 6:00 P.M., and he identified himself at the police barricade and was waved through. Before getting to the command post, Gomez saw a white Chevrolet Blazer parked on the street. He recognized John Orr standing behind the Blazer removing his coveralls.

Moses Gomez waved to John, offered his help, and was invited to join him.

"My partner's out of town," John explained to Gomez.

Gomez saw a nearby area that was marked by crime-scene tape, and John pointed and said, "That's the area of origin."

But Gomez was not invited to leave the sidewalk and enter that burned-out brushland for a closer look. Since he would not impose on another investigator's crime scene, Gomez asked, "Did you find anything in there?"

"I found a delay device," John told him.

A few minutes later, when they were in the Blazer touring the fire that was still raging all over the foothills, John produced an evidence vial with a disposable lighter inside, and said that the extinguishing cap was jammed open by a clip attachment which allowed the butane to flow. That was the incendiary device used to start the fire, he told Gomez.

As they toured, Gomez offered the resources of the state for the fire investigation. He told John that the next day he could have personnel on the scene to assist, and hopefully to get a lead on the person who'd set the incendiary device.

When they arrived at the mobile command post, John was asked by Battalion Chief Gray to give some kind of statement to the press. The arson investigator told Gray that he didn't have much to report, but when eager reporters spotted him and surged forward sticking a boom mike in his face, John not only gave a statement, but told them *everything* that he'd told Gomez about the point of origin, the butane lighter with the cap clipped open, *all* of it. Things that arson investigators *never* reveal, things that only the arsonist would know about and therefore must be kept secret.

They began to drive some more, where the fires were still sweeping up the hills, burning anything in the way. As an investigator, Gomez kept wondering, Why aren't we interviewing potential witnesses? Why aren't we doing something? What are we doing up here?

Thirty-five minutes later they were back at the command post where Glendale detective Robert Masucci told them he'd been assigned to assist the arson unit in interviewing some possible witnesses who lived in the apartment building across from the fire's area of origin.

They knocked at the door of a woman who'd reported something of great interest. She said that prior to observing the fire, she'd seen a man standing across the street where the brush begins, and that he was about five feet ten inches tall, had dark hair and a mustache, and wore khaki pants. He'd been standing with his back to her. The man drove a white or tan car, she said. The cop wrote down what she'd told them and they left.

John hadn't opened his mouth during the interview. In fact, he'd spent the interview time in her bathroom, standing in the spot where the woman had stood when she looked out the window and saw a man hunched over in the brush right where the College Hills fire had ostensibly originated. It was at the mouth of a ravine, where the wind would take that fire up, creating a chimney effect.

At 11:00 P.M. Gomez thought they were finally going to *do* something when John drove him to a residential street and said they should surveil for a while, and wait for a suspect who he thought might be worth checking. So they sat. And they sat. When Gomez asked questions about the suspect's car, John was vague and distracted and said he'd know it if he saw it again. After wasting another thirty minutes, they left.

John thanked Moses Gomez and said he would call. The next day he did not call, so Gomez called him. But John told Gomez he had "everything under control" and that he'd send the fire marshal a copy of his report. But he never did. Gomez was the second person to say that the behavior of the Glendale arson investigator seemed very peculiar.

That evening in Fresno, at the California Conference of Arson Investigators, John Orr's partner, Don Yeager, and the other conferees had finished their training classes and had arrived at their hotel just in time for a wet-T-shirt contest that was about to begin.

But a Pasadena arson investigator walked up to Yeager and said, "Hey, do you know what's going on down in your city?"

Don Yeager turned on the TV and called Glendale Dispatch for an update. He decided there was no point leaving at that moment, but first thing in the morning he checked out of the conference and hit the highway south. By then he knew that this wasn't just a major fire; this was the largest fire in the city's history.

Twenty minutes after he arrived at the command post, John showed up and said, "What're *you* doing here?"

"I thought you'd need help," Yeager said.

But John said, "No, I have it under control."

Under control? What did *that* mean? Yeager asked, "Have you had time to do any canvassing?"

John answered, "I've turned that over to the police department."

Yeager had been his partner for almost three years and he'd known John since he'd joined the fire service, but he couldn't figure this out. Canvassing should be kept in-house, done by the arson unit, not turned over to the cops.

Yeager took it upon himself to do a little canvassing on his own, but he didn't find *anybody* who claimed to have already been canvassed by cops. The police weren't doing any canvassing for witnesses!

The next day John told Yeager that he'd found a possible delay device consisting of a modified butane lighter, and he talked in a general way about a possible area of origin at a hillside where lots of trash had been littered around.

There was a giant pin board in the office of the arson unit that Don Yeager called a war board, and he began pinning things to the board, and working on leads, and witnesses, and useless tips that were flooding in. But he seemed to be working alone. He didn't feel that his partner was doing much of anything in regard to that calamitous fire other than writing a lengthy report on fire damage, listing reasons that the fire had spread so rapidly. But there was no cause-and-origin report, nothing specific about an arson investigation. He felt he was constantly having to *push* the fire captain into any investigative work on the College Hills fire.

John kept explaining that his damage report was keeping him tied up, but finally Yeager had had enough. He said, "I'm going up to Chief Gray and I'm going to demand to have my partner back, because you're having to spend all your time doing things other than investigating the College Hills fire, and it's frustrating."

John said he agreed completely, and as far as Yeager complaining to the boss, John said, "I wish you *would*."

Yeager went to see the fire marshal, Chief Gray, and made some heated demands about his partner being so overburdened with niggling details that they had no time to properly investigate the most disastrous fire the city had ever experienced.

Gray finally had to chill him out by saying, "Hey, wait a minute. You're getting kinda borderline here! If you've got a problem with John Orr you're gonna have to address it with John Orr."

But Yeager tried to explain that John Orr wasn't the problem. They were not able to work on the College Hills fire because of being loaded down with all the other jobs that Chief Gray was giving to John.

The puzzled fire marshal said, "You don't know what you're talking about." Then he informed Yeager that John had been assigned to work *only* on the College Hills fire, and didn't have to work on *anything* else. And that he had carte blanche on overtime or anything he needed!

And Yeager had to slink back to his partner in confusion. After he told John what Chief Gray had said, his partner swore and disputed what Gray had told Yeager, and Yeager ended up befuddled by all of it. He didn't know *what* to believe.

———

There never was a cause-and-origin report written on the College Hills fire. There was never a "D.R. number" requested from the police department to delineate a crime investigation that commanding officers could monitor. It was all treated rather informally, this terrible event. There was the fire-incident report, John Orr's lengthy summary of damage, and general opinions on how and why the fire had spread so disastrously. It was almost as though the fire had just happened—an act of God, perhaps.

Captain Orr had a whole lot of autonomy. There was little or no arson-unit oversight from his superiors. As far as arson investigation and proper reporting was concerned, the College Hills catastrophe just seemed to slip through the cracks.

The news media wallowed in disaster coverage for a few weeks, interviewing homeless property owners from College Hills who had lost pets, heirlooms, treasured memorabilia, photos of loved ones both living and dead. When it was all over, Glendale, California, had suffered its worst disaster. Sixty-six homes were damaged or destroyed, but miraculously, nobody had been killed or seriously injured, and that muted some of the criticism of the fire department that follows in such cases.

For the Glendale Fire Department, one good thing had come out of it. The budget cuts they'd been facing were called off. The argument could be made that the fire department needed an even *bigger* budget. The fire setter, if there was one, had made their argument for them.

Heat from the College Hills fire ended up cooking the goose of arson investigator Don Yeager. After he'd gotten vocal with Chief Gray about the arson unit being overloaded with trivial duties, John Orr pointed out to Gray that he could now see for himself how hotheaded Yeager was. John said that Yeager irritated everybody with his abrasive personality, and he worried that his armed partner might someday snap and "go postal." He suggested to Gray that it was time for Yeager to be transferred back to the firehouse, but Gray said, "Let's keep him until December. Then he'll have his three years on the arson unit and we can call it a normal rotation."

John later wrote: "I had no choice but to accept the chief's decision. I would have to endure Don for another five months."

By August, the College Hills telephone tips had petered out and the Glendale arson unit began getting back to normal, but in the first week of September John again went to the fire marshal, and the topic of their meeting was once again Don Yeager.

John reported to their boss that Yeager had angered the detectives with whom the arson unit had been working on a minor case, and that the Glendale Police Department now refused to work with Yeager on any future cases, so they must take extreme measures. Yeager had to leave *now*.

Chief Gray finally concurred, and Yeager was called into the chief's office and informed that "department needs" necessitated his immediate return to the firehouse. He got an attaboy and a pat on the back, and the selection process for a new arson investigator was begun. So ended John Orr's third professional partnership.

In October, the Arson/Explosives Unit of the Glendale Fire Department received a transfer from the ranks. Joe Lopez, a ten-year firefighter, was assigned to Captain Orr as his junior partner. Lopez was a fitness buff who worked out at the YMCA several times a week, and John said of him, "If I end up in any foot pursuits I can just let Joe off his leash." The canine analogy must have seemed apt because he also said that his new partner had "the pliability and devotion of a six-month-old puppy."

In November, Glendale conducted its fourth annual Fire Investigation 2B Class. It lasted a week and involved thirty students and sixty staffers. John Orr, at this stage of his career, was one of only six arson investigators in the entire state of California who had the honor of administering the session for certification as level I or II California arson investigators. There would be a five-day final examination for students, all of whom had also completed three one-week pretesting sessions.

It went well, but John never conducted one of these without recalling that a few years earlier, a police chief from Northern California who had sent one of his cops to the training course wrote a glowing tribute about Captain Orr, but in his letter mistakenly referred to him as *Detective* Orr.

That accolade resulted in John being ordered into the office of a police department captain who presented the attaboy along with an admonition not to represent himself as a detective or any kind of cop, because he was a fire department employee. The police captain sent a memo to the fire chief saying that Captain Orr should be counseled about implying that he was a *real* police officer. John Orr would never forget it.

It was in such a training session that John had instructed and accredited the arson investigator from Bakersfield, Marvin G. Casey.

In December 1990 it was hard to imagine how John Orr's life could get any better. He thought that both his fourth wife and fourth investigative partner were keepers. Wanda had a good job at Warner Brothers Studios in Burbank, and John believed he had the best job in his city. He wore civilian clothes, never had a roll call to attend, worked four days a week, and had a take-home car and as much overtime pay as he cared to earn whenever he needed more than his annual pay of sixty-five thousand dollars. And after taking a writing class, his novel was progressing nicely.

He said that he was proud to have earned "the respect of my peers in the fire service." But that would never be enough, not for John Orr. He also reported: "Even more valuable to me was a degree of respect shown to me by most Glendale police officers and detectives, as well as from many of those at outside agencies."

There it was, and it would *never* go away. He couldn't get past it. More valuable than anything in his life was what he seldom got: respect from *them*—the *real* cops who had long ago rejected him.

Beginning in December 1990 and continuing through March 1991, the Los Angeles area was blitzed by an arson series of a kind never seen before. Nineteen arsons or arson attempts were made in retail stores from one end of the Los Angeles basin to the other. These brazen and frightening attacks would eventually focus the attention of many arson sleuths in the L.A. area.

The first occurred on December 10 at People's Department Store on Figueroa Street in Los Angeles, not far from the Eagle Rock residence of

Captain John Orr. The Glendale arson investigator's partner, Joe Lopez, was having lunch with his wife that afternoon, and John reported that it was his day to go home and check on one of the "children," a setter/Labrador mix named Cody, who had belonged to his wife Wanda before their marriage. The old dog was dying, and John said he needed to visit him at midday to take him outside or clean up after him if Cody hadn't been able to control his bowels or bladder.

Just after 1:00 P.M. that afternoon, People's Department Store, catering to a clientele interested in bargains, was busy with shoppers, mostly Hispanic women, many with small children. In the fabric department, at the northwest end of the store, mothers shopped while kids wandered through the toy department. Along the west wall was a curtain display, and one of the shoppers, who had been searching in vain for her children, suddenly saw flames rising four feet from the floor. The curtains were on fire. Another shopper spotted those flames just a moment later, when fire from the burning curtains was already lapping at the ceiling. And *her* children were also missing.

Employees Ana Ramirez and Maria Chavez began rounding up children and adults and rushing them toward the exits. There were no injuries and the children were all safe, but the entire building was ablaze. The roof collapsed and fed the fire even more.

Captain Orr later reported that he'd spotted a "header," a column of dark smoke, about three miles south, drifting over Highland Park when he was arriving home to care for Cody.

He said that after dealing with the dog he noticed that the header was bigger and knew that it must be from a major structure fire. He carried an eight-millimeter video camera in case of just such events, so he jumped in his car, flicked on his red light, and raced toward the header.

He reported that when he arrived, the building was engulfed and firefighters were busy suppressing, so he shot some video of the spectacular event.

On Thursday of that week, John had some private business that required him to leave his partner behind. He said that he needed to pick up the daughter of a friend at a La Cañada day-care center, and then drive the child home to Burbank, where her mother lived and worked. The "friend" was a petite brunette named Chris, and it appeared that Ozzie and Harriet might once again be needing lawyers.

Two miles from Chris's apartment was Mort's Surplus, a sporting-goods outlet on Victory Boulevard where John sometimes shopped. At 3:41 P.M. a fire broke out in a stack of cardboard boxes, quickly sweeping up and spreading along the Celotex ceiling until the entire structure was threatened. The first engine from the Burbank Fire Department reported that the building was charged with very hot smoke. Within minutes, more engine companies arrived and the super-hot smoke billowed out of the building and enveloped it.

John reported that it was after dropping off the child that he heard the crackle of activity on his radio frequencies. Then, he said, he saw brownish smoke rising in the sky and he thought it would be something to videotape for his training films, so he sped to the fire scene. During the fire suppression, he stood across the street from the building videotaping the efforts of the firefighters, wondering, he said, if the high-voltage lines overhead would melt and drop onto the sidewalk.

John was surprised when his partner, Joe Lopez, who knew he was in Burbank on private business, showed up at the three-alarm blaze and found him videotaping. John said of Lopez, "He was taking this joined-at-the-hip stuff rather seriously." The senior arson investigator had never been *anybody's* Siamese twin. This Siegfried-and-Roy stuff had to stop.

Captain Steve Patterson, an arson investigator from the Burbank Fire Department, arrived at Mort's Surplus while the fire was still burning, when the roof was sagging and it was unsafe to enter. Captain Patterson could not find any remnant of a delay device, but wrote in his report that he believed one could have been used because no one was seen in the area of origin just prior to the fire.

The next afternoon at 1:00 P.M., on Laurel Canyon Boulevard in North Hollywood, Constance Schipper, manager of the paint and plumbing department of Builder's Emporium, was stunned to see fire billowing up from a shopping cart filled with throw pillows. She ran to the cart and began pulling out the flaming pillows; the fire was extinguished by other employees. There on the floor among the pillows were a cigarette butt, two matches, and a rubber band.

Hollywood was next. On Monday, December 17, at 1:43 P.M., J. J. Newberry's, on Hollywood Boulevard, sustained moderate fire damage and heavy smoke damage after a fire broke out in display racks packed with blankets and comforters. Arson investigators listed the fire as being "suspicious in nature."

On the biggest shopping day of the year, December 26, Sherman Oaks in the San Fernando Valley was struck by an incendiary blitzkrieg so brazen that retail establishments soon started hiring security guards for fire watch.

The first was at 11:43 A.M. on Ventura Boulevard, at a dry-goods outlet, Bed Bath & Beyond, in a rack of plastic-wrapped throw pillows. The overhead sprinklers were triggered and the fire was contained very quickly. But just four blocks away at Pier 1 Imports, also on Ventura Boulevard, and at Strouds Linen Warehouse, fires broke out almost simultaneously at 12:07 P.M.

The fire at Pier 1 Imports came shooting out from under the mezzanine, and the ten customers in the store started yelling and running for the exits. The fire burned through the roof and ventilated itself. At Strouds Linen Warehouse, the cashier working at the rear of the store spotted smoke and flames bursting from a display of comforters. The heat got so violent that the metal beams holding up the roof became distorted and pulled away from the wall, causing the roof to cave in, which fed more fuel to the blaze.

A team of arson investigators from the L.A. Fire Department interviewed thirteen people before hearing of a suspect of any kind, but then they encountered a pair of security officers from the Thrifty Drug Store a few doors away from Strouds. The guards described a medium-size white male, thirty-five to thirty-nine years old, with slick black hair, wearing a purple shirt, black pants, and a black jacket. He was said to have had "soot" on him when spotted just prior to the fire at Strouds.

The description of the sooty suspect was broadcast on the LAPD frequency to all units in the vicinity. The arson team then interviewed the owner of a nearby newsstand, and again the description of the man in black popped up. This time he was described as a "fast-walking mumbler."

Later that day they contacted still another employee of Thrifty Drug Store, who said that just before the fire, the same man in black had walked into Thrifty's and made an announcement to one and all. He'd shouted, "There's a guy out there that was looking in Strouds' window! The guy was so ugly that he caught the window on fire!"

The next day, at 9:00 A.M., the arson team got a call they'd been wanting. A witness had spotted the man in black. He was in a restaurant men's room on Ventura Boulevard near the fire scene. The investigators immediately called LAPD asking that a police unit get to the location and detain the guy.

Thirty minutes later the arson team arrived at the restaurant, where a pair of LAPD officers were holding the man in black. The arson team instantly noted a strong odor of smoke coming from his clothing, and while the cops watched the suspect, the arson guys went into the restaurant men's room where they detected a stronger smell of smoke. In the toilet bowl they saw charred toilet paper. And there was a puzzling discovery. On the floor and in the sink were short pieces of hair. The hairs were all over the place, as if the man in black had been shedding. It was *weird*, they said.

"I was pulling my gray hairs out," he informed them. "Don't *you* pull your gray hairs out? And I went into Thrifty's yesterday to sample the aftershave and deodorant."

When they asked why his clothes smelled of smoke, he said, "Because I was burning newspapers in that old abandoned hotel down on Ventura."

That stopped them. Burning newspapers? For what?

"To keep warm," he said. "There's no heat in an abandoned hotel, you know. And there's no lights. No room service either."

And because lots of fires are set by fruit loops, the man in black was booked at North Hollywood Division Jail on a charge of 451 (c) of the penal code, "arson of an uninhabited structure."

For a time he was truly thought to be a spree fire setter, and he did not return to his abandoned hotel where there was absolutely no room service.

Before the year ended, the fire setter had demonstrated that retail establishments open for business were not safe on weekends either. He struck twice within an hour on Sunday, December 30.

The first attack occurred at National Store on North Broadway, not far from Dodger Stadium, a store that catered to many residents of nearby Chinatown. The mezzanine sustained heavy fire and smoke damage from burning pillows and polyfoam.

Forty-nine minutes later, a few miles away on Sunset Boulevard, at Crystal Promotions, a fire erupted in the rear of the store in a display of plastic decorative products. Once again, the LAFD arrived fast enough to save the structure.

When Desert Storm was launched, in January 1991, the workload increased for the Glendale Arson/Explosives Unit because of terrorist paranoia. Any abandoned briefcase, shopping bag, or unwanted postal package could prompt a call to the investigators. Other than that, it was a fairly uneventful month—except for the arson team almost blowing themselves up.

They had decided to burn off a pound of homemade fireworks at their training center, and assumed that the flash powder would burn, as usual, with a bright, smoky flash. It didn't. The blast was heard two miles away at fire department headquarters and knocked off part of the roof of the blast room. Captain Orr decided that his impulsive personality was not suited for the methodical defusing and disarming of explosives.

Meanwhile, his first attempt at fiction writing was moving forward. On weekend mornings he began writing at 8:00 A.M. and would some-times produce twelve pages a day. He chose the title *Points of Origin* because of its obvious importance in arson terminology, but also because he felt that it had significance for the two main characters, Aaron Stiles, a firefighter turned serial arsonist, and Phil Langtree, an arson investigator who is committed to hunting down the fire setter. He said that he'd orig-inally wanted to present the two characters as similar men from similar backgrounds who had gone diverse ways only because of "psychological triggers" in Aaron's life, but that the character of Phil Langtree was so strong and tenacious, he took the story away from the author and turned the novel into a manhunt/thriller. The moment of moral divergence was originally to have been their "points of origin."

Within a year, readers of that novel wished that those "triggers" had been explored by the novelist for what they may have revealed.

On March 3, once again on a Sunday, the southern districts of Los Angeles came under attack. The first fire, at 1:32 P.M., occurred at Thrifty Drug Store in the Wilmington area. There were more than one hundred customers milling around, and people charged the exits. Employees saw a fire column three feet in diameter boil out from between two stacks of pillows and then instantly mushroom across the ceiling.

Arson investigators were still arriving at the raging inferno when they received word that another Thrifty Drug Store, in nearby San Pedro, had been attacked at 2:09 P.M. The sprinkler heads above the fire had activated and extinguished a blaze that had begun in a stack of pillows.

Two weeks after fires in the south, arsons occurred back up in North Hollywood. There were two on Tuesday, March 19. The first broke out at the Goodwill store on Laurel Canyon Boulevard, where employees spotted mattresses burning but got them outside before much damage was done.

Twenty-one minutes later, at the House of Fabrics on Victory Boulevard, employees and customers managed to extinguish a small blaze in a display of foam-rubber pads and other synthetic products used in the construction of pillows.

Another Pier 1 Imports store, this one on Hollywood Boulevard, was the next target, on Friday of the same week. The fire erupted at 1:02 P.M. in pine shelving stacked with pillows.

John Orr no longer used his Chevrolet Blazer as an on-duty car. He sold it after being given a white five-year-old Ford Crown Victoria on which the police department had logged 110,000 miles. It was a take-home car, and gas and maintenance were provided, but John spent five hundred dollars of his own money to add a few custom touches, such as a siren speaker, which, he said, put out the decibel level of "a low-flying F-16."

Joe Lopez asked John if he could take off on a weekday to join a bunch of firefighters on a day trip to Big Bear Lake for some skiing. His senior partner granted the request, and on the very day that Joe Lopez left town, the most terrifying arson series yet struck Los Angeles County in the communities of Lawndale, Redondo Beach, and Inglewood: five fires occurred within a two-and-a-half-hour period on March 27, 1991.

At 11:40 on that Wednesday morning, business was relatively light at D&M Yardage on Hawthorne Boulevard in Lawndale. Employee Linda Zito saw a man, whom she later described as a white male of medium size with brown hair, roaming around the store. She approached and asked if she could help him and he asked if they carried camouflage material. When she said that they did not, he smiled and kept browsing. He left, and twenty minutes later the fire came: a column of flame appeared only eighteen inches from the floor. But in an instant it was spiraling up, all the way up to the ceiling, and she realized that the foam-backed display draperies were on fire.

Engine Company 21 had no chance. A cascade of flame blasted out of the doors and windows and heaved up, devouring the roof. The entire building was destroyed.

Less than two miles away, at 12:10 P.M., a customer at Stats Floral Supply was walking past a display of Styrofoam products and spotted a piece of yellow lined paper that was smoldering. She picked the paper out of the display and ran to the front of the store where an employee dumped a cup of water on the paper. Inside of the note paper was a cigarette butt, and three paper matches attached by a rubber band, just like the one recovered in Bakersfield by Captain Marvin Casey more than three years earlier.

Half a mile from Stats Floral Supply, and twenty minutes after that arson attempt, a fire erupted at Thrifty Drug Store on Aviation Boulevard in a display of foam patio cushions. The automatic sprinklers discharged and several employees kept the flames in check until the first engine company arrived and suppressed it.

At 1:28 P.M. in nearby Inglewood, at the J. J. Newberry store, a fire broke out in a pillow display. It was extinguished by employees, with only light smoke damage done to the premises.

And finally, on that afternoon of fire, again in the city of Inglewood, at the Pic N Save store, a customer began yelling, and employees extinguished a fire in a box full of stacked pillows.

The arsonist had had a very busy day, but had only succeeded in setting the one spectacular blaze that gutted D&M Yardage, leaving just the four walls, putting several employees out of work, and closing down the business for two years.

6

THE FINGERPRINT

Special Agent Michael Matassa of the Bureau of Alcohol, Tobacco and Firearms received a vibrating page that Wednesday afternoon. He had the audible page turned off because he was sitting in trial in Los Angeles Superior Court, assisting the district attorney's office with an arson fraud that involved over a hundred witnesses. Matassa was the acting resident agent in charge until the boss of the Los Angeles office returned from sick leave.

Deputy District Attorney Michael Cabral was prosecuting the owner of a furniture store on a charge of torching his own property for insurance, thus triggering the assistance of ATF with what otherwise would have been an L.A. Fire Department investigation. Mike Matassa liked working with Cabral and other deputy DA's on arson cases, because the U.S. Attorney's Office was notoriously hard to persuade when it came to filing criminal cases, and arson was among the most difficult of crimes to prove. State prosecutors were more apt to file the case and try to *make* it work without obsessing over a remote possibility of an acquittal.

When Mike Matassa left the courtroom to answer the page, he was asked to call the Los Angeles Sheriff's Department, who wanted ATF to assist with a commercial-structure fire in the L.A. suburb of Lawndale. He was told that the damage to D&M Yardage was obviously over one million dollars and could involve arson fraud, either scenario justifying ATF involvement. Matassa hung up and asked his office to send someone to Lawndale for a courtesy call.

It has always been remarkable that American law enforcement does as decent a job as it does, in spite of the Balkanization of the profession. The U.S. fear of a national police force has resulted in thousands of autonomous police agencies staffed by people who jealously guard their turf, their sources, and every scrap of information both vital and trivial. Many times the networking that takes place is appallingly fragmented and informal.

The vast-government-conspiracy theories floated in hundreds of books and films have never failed to produce howls of laughter when mentioned at law-enforcement gatherings, especially in the aftermath of JFK, when the vast government conspiracy included the FBI, CIA, and all the other three-letter agencies staffed by bureaucrats who are mostly loathed and distrusted by street cops. Those with an alliterative flair call them grandstanding government geeks in penny loafers, or bumbling back-stabbing bureaucrats who wouldn't conspire to peek inside a girl-friend's underwear without the approval of a U.S. attorney and a search warrant.

But what really brings down the station house is when, in order to make the JFK conspiracy work, all the revisionists had to include the Dallas Police Department. And *that* does it every time. Cops get to knee slapping and falling out of their chairs over the thought of it. Because everyone who's ever worn a badge knows that the moment a cop gets a *real* secret, the drums start beating and the asphalt jungle wireless starts humming, and the first leggy news chick with tits out to here will be blabbing the *secret* on the news at ten even before the cop wives get to tell it to the gang at the office and the girls at the gym.

All of this helps to explain why Matassa's arson team, when they arrived in Lawndale on the afternoon of March 27, hadn't yet connected the D&M Yardage arson to anything that had recently preceded it in other parts of the Los Angeles basin. Information was negligible, because everyone paid attention to his own little patch of turf and not the other guy's.

———

One of the arson investigators, Glen Lucero of the Los Angeles Fire Department, took a look at what was left of D&M Yardage and reported, "There's nothing left but four walls and a trash heap."

Lucero was forty-two years old and had been with the LAFD since 1973. Before that he'd served with the U.S. Air Force in Vietnam as a firefighter, and also in Air Rescue, where their job was to save downed pilots and to be prepared to get into hooded silver fire-fighting outfits, ready to suppress aircraft fires. He was a solidly built, good-humored Mexican-American who had been sent to the LAPD detective school and the LAPD homicide school in order to learn crime investigation.

His partner that afternoon was ATF Special Agent Ken Croke, an Irish-American from Boston who had relatives in the auld sod and considerable pride that a Dublin athletic stadium was called Croke Field. He'd played offensive guard in college, still pumped iron, and was very large. Everyone called the rookie agent "a musclebound party animal."

ATF and LAFD had a "memorandum of understanding," meaning that ATF assisted the city of L.A. with large commercial building fires, especially if it might entail arson for profit or arson by organized crime. ATF also responded to other state and local agencies if they had a church fire or an abortion-clinic fire, and they assisted at multiple-jurisdictional fires when an ATF umbrella was needed. Glen Lucero found it useful to have a fed with him, even one as inexperienced as Ken Croke. It impressed civilians, and even some of the cops from the smaller police departments. "The federal mystique," Lucero called it.

It was while they were there peering at the trash heap that used to be a thriving retail store that they heard about the attempted arson in nearby Redondo Beach at Stats Floral Supply, where an incendiary device had been discovered. Then they heard about Thrifty Drug Store, also in Redondo Beach, and after looking at the time of alarms called into dispatch, they thought they just might have a serial arsonist at work here.

Glen Lucero started recalling similar fires back in December, in pillows and bedding, up in the San Fernando Valley on Ventura Boulevard. The investigators on those fires hadn't given much thought to a time-delay device, but kept asking witnesses, "Who'd you see at the *time* of the fire?" Which had made everybody chase a lot of wild geese. But now, recalling a sheet of yellow lined paper and a cigarette and matches and rubber band, things started to jell, and Lucero began thinking about a pyro. Not some spree fire setter, but a *real* pyro with an uncontrollable need to set fires.

"The kind of guy," he said, "who starts out as a kid pulling wings off insects and setting cats' tails on fire, and then just branches out."

Michael Matassa had been with ATF for eight years, and before that he had served three years with the U.S. Marshal's Office in Los Angeles. Raised in Old Forge, Pennsylvania, he was the son of an Italian-American shoemaker. His maternal grandparents were from the Ukraine and Poland, so he was not an atypical Pennsylvania ethnic mix, and he grew up poor like everyone else he knew.

After graduating from Penn State in 1975 with a degree in criminal justice, Matassa had tried for five years to get a cop job. Like John Orr, he wanted to join the LAPD in that era before Rodney King and O. J. Simpson, back when the LAPD was the premier police agency in America. But when he'd inquired he was told that it would probably be a waste of plane fare; there were 10,000 applicants for only 150 job openings.

While working as an insurance adjuster in Williamsport, he tried for the Pennsylvania State Police. His brother Tony was a decorated state trooper who had been wounded by gunfire, and his cousin was a state police homicide investigator, and his next-door neighbor was a state police captain. Matassa took the state police exam twice, scored ninety-four out of a possible one hundred, but failed twice. A score of seventy passed for the right ethnic minorities, but nobody marched with signs for Italians, Poles, or Ukrainians. He then tried for the U.S. Marshal's Office and made it.

Matassa was sent to the Federal Law Enforcement Training Center, called "Flet-C," in Glynco, Georgia, where all feds except the FBI attend their training academies. He married an Irish firecracker, Linda Thomas, and they both quit their jobs, trading a twenty-six-thousand-dollar joint income for ten thousand dollars annually. Throwing everything into their Suburban, including a little mutt and a tabby cat, they drove across country to California, where they learned to live on hot dogs, hamburgers, and Chef Boyardee.

His training officer back in those U.S. marshal days had been the case agent on the hunt for fugitive Christopher Boyce, of *The Falcon and the Snowman* fame. While Boyce was in prison he'd seen a Clint Eastwood movie, made a papier mâché dummy, and escaped from prison through a manhole cover and drainage ditch. Matassa had to do a little surveillance on some of Boyce's mercenary friends, following them around the streets while they watched for reflections in store windows. Matassa called them a bunch of militia fruitcakes. Boyce got caught and went back to prison for life.

Mike Matassa liked the fugitive hunts best. It was a blast, he said, kicking down doors. All the hook-'em-and-book-'em street-cop stuff, he loved it. But he hated serving subpoenas, and court duty absolutely sucked, so he switched over to ATF, and was sent back to the ATF academy at Flet-C for another eight weeks. He returned again to L.A. as an ATF special agent.

Matassa had done well at ATF and was the acting supervisor when he received the page on March 27, 1991. He was thirty-seven years old then, with sandy hair, expressive dark eyes, and a long face that could look melancholy when he was not. If the lighting was right one could see a jagged scar over his right eye, between the lid and the brow. People who knew how he got it loved to make him explain to those who didn't. Did it happen in a violent arrest? From a knife maybe? Or a broken bottle?

Until he finally had to admit that yes, it *was* a broken bottle. He had fallen out of his crib, bottle and all, and the old-style glass baby bottle had broken in his face. And every time he'd be forced to explain, somebody would say, "And how old were you, Mike? Fifteen?"

After that vibrating page concerning the major fire in Lawndale, Michael Matassa would soon have occasion to remember another major fire at a commercial building over seven years earlier. As a rookie ATF agent he'd been called to the fire location because of the magnitude of the blaze and the multiple fatalities. Matassa had driven the bomb truck, a mobile crime lab. But before they could even assess the situation and decide whether or not to notify their National Response Team, they'd been given word that the fire at Ole's Home Center in South Pasadena had been called an accident by the Los Angeles County Sheriff's Department.

That horrific disaster had almost faded from memory, but within a matter of months, it would come back to him.

Prior to the five-fire spree on Wednesday, March 27, there had been something known as the Los Angeles Arson Task Force, an ostentatious military term for two L.A. Fire Department arson investigators assigned one block away from LAFD headquarters on Los Angeles Street. The job of the LAFD investigators was to coordinate with ATF on major city fires, particularly if they involved fraud or organized crime. In addition to Glen Lucero, the other LAFD employee was Mike Camello, a big guy with chiseled good looks and hair so coiffed it'd stay in place till Christ came back. He had worked as an extra on a movie, and he was rumored to be a member of SAG, so everyone called him "Hollywood Mike." The firemen found some of the feds to be a bit tight-jawed compared to the loosey-goosey gang in the firehouse, so they just kept "rolling turds" at them, as Lucero put it, and took the ATF guys to happy hour after work, and pretty soon all the feds acted pretty much like firemen and stopped worrying about getting the secret handshake wrong, or whatever the hell it was that feds worried about.

Another ATF special agent had joined Lucero and Ken Croke on the new investigation: April Carroll was an attractive blonde with good analytical skills, but she'd never worked an arson case. She'd joined ATF right out of college, where she'd played field hockey. She was more ambitious than a junior senator, and would run, not walk, wherever she went. The fortyish arson sleuths like Glen Lucero could barely keep up with her, and Mike Matassa, still the acting supervisor, said that Lucero should bring a skateboard to work when teamed with April. Matassa called Lucero, Croke, and Carroll the Three Amigos.

The day after the fire spree, Lucero and Croke went to the Redondo Beach Police Department to see the incendiary device found at Stats Floral, and they began examining reports of similar fires in recent months. Glen Lucero proved that John Orr wasn't the only arson sleuth in the L.A. area with a literary flair. He coined a moniker for the *new* task force now concentrating on a certain type of fire, in a certain type of commercial establishment, ignited in a certain type of combustible merchandise, possibly using the same delay device. They called themselves the Pillow Pyro Task Force.

On Friday, March 29, there was a meeting of the Fire Investigators Regional Strike Team, known by the acronym FIRST, in West Covina. It was an organization of smaller foothill cities—Pasadena, South Pasadena, Burbank, Monrovia, and Glendale—cities that did not have a staff of arson investigators but had formed FIRST in order to exchange information and help one another. The meetings were often attended by large agencies such as LAFD, L.A. County Fire Department, or LASD.

LAFD investigator Tom Campuzano had drawn up a list of seventeen fires that had occurred in recent months, all of which and more were being investigated by the Pillow Pyro gang. The fires had all taken place midday in retail establishments open for business, and the flyer described the signature device: a cigarette, three matches, a rubber band, and notebook paper.

Campuzano addressed the FIRST meeting that day and expressed the task force's opinion about the delay device being unusual in that such devices usually consisted of a cigarette and a book of matches. The arsonist had obviously included a piece of notebook paper in order to supply enough heat and flame to get the foam products melting and the flowing liquid ignited. The FIRST members were given a brief description of each fire, and Campuzano passed out a flyer to each member, but no one offered any information.

After the meeting, as Tom Campuzano was leaving, he was stopped in the parking lot by Scott Baker, an investigator from the state Fire Marshal's Office in the Central Valley.

Baker said, "Campy, I didn't want to say anything in there, but we had an arson series like yours back in 1987, and another one on the Central Coast in '89."

"And why didn't you want to mention it in there?" Campuzano asked.

Baker replied, "Because Marv Casey of the Bakersfield Fire Department had a theory that a firefighter might be involved, and Casey has a good fingerprint from one of the fires."

After Baker told him the story about Casey's hunch, Campuzano thanked him for the information and returned to his office.

When Mike Matassa was informed about the tip and who relayed it, he was impressed. He appreciated arson sleuths who came from a cop background, and Scott Baker was one of them. Matassa had attended a training session with Baker, who was, he said, "the arson and gun guy up there in the boonies. He carries about five guns including a hideout piece, and a Ninja knife, and whatever else he can tote and still walk without clanking."

Matassa liked that kind of arson cop, and thought his tip should be followed up.

One of those present at that FIRST meeting was the organization's treasurer, who was also one of the FIRST founders. He was the prime mover behind the very successful FIRST training sessions that brought fire investigators from all over the Southern California region, and he had listened while Campuzano talked about the Pillow Pyro.

After Campuzano had finished that afternoon, the treasurer of FIRST continued with business, discussing reimbursements to various members for postage, giving a report of finances, and arranging the monthly raffle.

The treasurer could barely tolerate Tom Campuzano of the Los Angeles Fire Department, and he later wrote: "LAFD's 'elite' prima donna investigators had always irritated me, and consistently bore a condescending attitude towards smaller agencies, so I avoided them except when required to mingle."

The treasurer of FIRST did not add that the Los Angeles Fire Department had washed him out of their fire academy, the third significant rejection of his life. First his mother's, who'd left him and whom he didn't see for nearly three years. Then came the LAPD, when they'd found him psychologically unsuitable. And finally, the LAFD, who'd accepted him, only to later find him physically unsuitable. The third rejection was cumulatively the most difficult, and had for a time left him "paralyzed" by grief and depression and outrage.

When the LAFD investigator had gone, and the treasurer of FIRST had the floor again, he put on an interesting fifteen-minute slide show detailing an arson arrest he and his partner had made of a young Glendale police explorer who had parental rejection issues, a fascination with authority symbols, and a compulsive need for attention, power, and control.

On Monday, April Fool's Day, the Pillow Pyro Task Force convened a group of about twenty investigators, mostly from ATF and LAFD, but also from other local agencies, to talk about the recent series of retail-store fires. The list they had compiled since the previous Wednesday had now grown to twenty-nine.

They met at task-force "headquarters," which was just a windowless room in the center of the Federal Building, across from Parker Center, the main headquarters of the LAPD. Both buildings were prime examples of the Gdansk school of design visited upon Los Angeles from the 1950s through two decades, a blight of concrete boxes the color of bacon grease, that had to pay homage to "art" by planting an ugly mosaic or sculpture vaguely resembling human beings smack dab in front, in order to assure all who entered that *this* bureaucracy cared about humanity. They all favored nuthouse-green interiors that graffiti artists sometimes improved with spray cans.

Everyone listened to what the task force had to say about the Pillow Pyro's series of assaults, and then they went back to their own investigative worlds. The Three Amigos sat in their headquarters with Mike Matassa and decided that the next move was for Glen Lucero, Ken Croke, and April Carroll to leave L.A. and head up country where folks don't look like Iggy Pop. They were going where everybody looked like Johnny Cash. The Pillow Pyro Task Force was sent to Bakersfield to meet Captain Marvin G. Casey.

Meanwhile, Special Agent Howard Sanders of ATF had the job of personally delivering another flyer to all local arson sleuths, spreading the word about the Pillow Pyro, and soliciting leads. One of the stops made by Sanders was at the Glendale Fire Department to see Captain John Orr and his partner, Joe Lopez.

Sanders talked briefly with the Glendale arson team about the incendiary delay device and the M.O. of the Pillow Pyro, and he gave them the new flyer. Sanders reported that the Glendale arson team had nothing to offer about the delay device or anything else, and he left after a few minutes. But John later said he'd informed Sanders that Glendale had brushfire experience with a cigarette-and-match delay device that had been weighed down by a coin and tossed from a moving car, and he told Sanders that his suspect could have graduated to retail stores.

John wrote about this encounter with the ATF agent by drawing a comparison to the old Andy Griffith TV show: "Sanders seemed more like a computer programmer than a cop, and had little interest in my Mayberry experiences, treating me like I was only a step above Barney Fife."

The only good thing John Orr had to say about ATF came later: "Though none of these special agents had any firefighting knowledge, and extremely limited fire scene experience, they did have the foresight to add an experienced LAFD arson investigator to their ranks to assist with the Pillow Pyro Task Force."

It was an attaboy for Glen Lucero, who never got a chance to hear of it at the time. He might have been pleased, coming as it did from a fellow firefighter.

Marvin Casey remembers the Three Amigos when they arrived at his office in Bakersfield as being like "kids in a candy store" when he regaled them with his strange theory that an arson investigator from L.A. had set the series of fires in the Central Valley in 1987 and on the Central Coast in 1989. Maybe that's the way *he* read their reaction, but it's not how the Three Amigos remembered it.

Glen Lucero said, "Marv Casey never stopped expounding on his idea, and we thought it was interesting, but he'd already worked it to death and there was no match with those ten L.A. area investigators who'd attended those two conferences during those years. So we were polite listeners, but definitely *not* excited."

After lunch, when the Three Amigos headed back to Los Angeles, they had no reason to believe they'd ever see Marvin Casey again. But they were wrong.

When Glen Lucero, Ken Croke, and April Carroll had returned from Bakersfield with the fingerprint photo, it didn't provoke any excitement or even much interest. After all, it had been run through the automated systems at the state and national levels in 1987 and in 1989. The owner of the print had no criminal record. And as for the Casey theory, the ten arson investigators who had attended those conferences had been *specifically* cleared by a Department of Justice fingerprint specialist, so really, the fingerprint was of limited use unless the Pillow Pyro had been arrested for something since 1989.

And that was the reason that Mike Matassa said, "So, let's run it through again. Maybe he got busted in the last couple of years for stealing pillows or whatever else he does to get himself off."

Glen Lucero took the photo and negative of Marvin Casey's fingerprint evidence to the L.A. County Sheriff's Department laboratory, where it was again reworked by fingerprint specialists. First, the latent print was enlarged photographically. Then tracing paper was placed over the enlarged photo, and the ridge structure was traced by hand, after which the tracing was reduced back down to its normal fingerprint size. Then it was put on a scanner that is linked to the fingerprint computer input terminal. It was a computer that scanned the print and gave a numerical score indicating how well the computer "liked" the print as a match to something already existing in the computer files.

The difference between this scanning system and the one that had initially scanned Marvin Casey's evidence was that the database in the Los Angeles Hall of Justice computer contained, in addition to criminal fingerprint cards, the fingerprints of all county law-enforcement officers and of anyone who had ever applied for a law-enforcement job—such as an applicant who had tried to join the Los Angeles Police Department twenty years earlier. And the computer "liked" that old LAPD applicant very much indeed. That 1971 fingerprint card was right across the street from the task force—at LAPD headquarters in Parker Center, where they could just stroll over and pick it up.

On April 17, 1991, Ron George, of the sheriff's laboratory, called the Pillow Pyro Task Force, spoke to an ATF agent, and said, "You oughtta tell your arson investigators to keep their mitts off the evidence. It was touched by John Orr. Left ring finger."

The agent thanked him, hung up, and informed Glen Lucero and April Carroll, who ran over to the sheriff's lab and had a meeting with a fingerprint specialist. They thought there had to be an explanation for this.

Mike Matassa, who was upstairs in the boss's office, got a frantic call later that afternoon from Glen Lucero, who said, "You better get down here right *now*!"

When Matassa asked what happened, Glen Lucero said, "I'll tell you when you get here!"

7

BIRD DOG

Never was the difference between fireman and cop displayed more clearly than it was following the astounding revelation of April 17. Glen Lucero, who knew John Orr and lived near his neighborhood, felt depressed. John was a personable guy with a big smile and a little laugh who'd invited the Luceros to a Christmas party at his home. Glen's wife, Martha, was shy around strangers, so they hadn't gone, but Lucero had appreciated the invitation.

John Orr produced interesting seminars with good speakers, was a respected member of the fire-fighting brotherhood and a fellow arson investigator, a man ostensibly dedicated to catching the people who set fires. Glen Lucero said that he couldn't see any way to come out a winner on this one.

Every member of that fraternity who needed to hear about John Orr—and it would include Lucero's superiors at the L.A. Fire Department—expressed similar sentiments. It was shocking and sickening. None of them wanted to believe it. Some of them refused to believe it. The task force was urged to go very slowly. There just *might* be a legitimate reason why Captain John Orr's left ring fingerprint had ended up on that scrap of paper.

Far-fetched scenarios were quietly floated. Maybe he'd been driving through Bakersfield at the time of the fire and stopped to assist the fire-fighters. Maybe Casey had just failed to mention that. Or maybe he'd stopped in Bakersfield for lunch and left his legal pad on a table at Burger King, and the real pyro happened to pick it up. And they all wondered why the DOJ fingerprint specialist hadn't been able to match the latent print with John Orr's fingerprint card back in 1989. How did *that* screw-up happen?

That's the way it was viewed by investigators and their superiors who came from a fire-fighting background. Those who came from the cop ranks, well, they saw it differently. They were so excited they were drool-ing. But for the sake of their firefighter cousins, they had to look pious, and they had to cluck and mouth sanctimonious things like, "This is a somber moment. This is one of ours. This is a family member gone bad. A hush and a pall has settled over the task force." And so forth.

When really they were thinking: This is awesome! This is a career case! This is so high profile I might end up on *60 Minutes*! Maybe even *Ger-aldo*! This is fucking fan-*tas*-tic!

Nobody working in emergency services can ever hope for stock options, or performance bonuses, or incentive pay, or golden parachutes, as in many other walks of life. And most other citizens don't have to end up in one of those How-the-fuck-did-I-get-in-this? situations where their violent death or even their murder is a real possibility. But there is a payoff that the firefighter does get from the public which the cop does not: love. John Orr himself said it many times: everybody loves a fireman.

So perhaps the arson sleuths from the fire-fighting ranks could never hope to fathom the cop investigators who don't have a payoff, cops who were keeping repressed with the greatest effort a burning question: When they make the movie, I wonder who they'll get to play *me*?

Mike Matassa was itching to return to the ranks and get involved now that things had taken this dizzying twist. "I wanted to go back to being a street hump real bad" is how he put it.

Glen Lucero sensed how thrilled the cops were, but he couldn't share it. "It was exciting," he said, "but there was this dark cloud over it. I kept thinking, why couldn't it have involved a *volunteer* fireman?"

There was now much to do before they could think about making an arrest, and this is where a federal investigation differs starkly from a state case. The U.S. Attorney's Office had come on board and U.S. attorneys want *more*. In a case destined to be as high profile as this one, they wanted still more. There was a *lot* of work to do before John Orr could be arrested.

The Three Amigos were ordered to make a fast second trip to Bakersfield to see Marvin Casey.

It was a lovely spring day in Glendale and John Orr was up to his old tricks: police work. He and Joe Lopez were cruising in the arson car, even though that big Crown Vic didn't exactly look undercover cool. In fact, it carried more antennas than a Radio Shack catalog. They were out of their city, cruising in nearby La Crescenta, but telling John Orr to stay in his bailiwick was like telling a salmon to just hang out downstream.

Suddenly, they spotted a guy leaving a drugstore with an employee chasing him. The young store clerk yelled "Stop!" But the guy jumped in a beat-up Toyota, pulled out, and aimed the car toward the kid, who had to jump out of the way.

"That," John said to his partner, "is assault with a deadly weapon."

Because of the prior overzealous conduct of the senior arson investigator, the fire chief of Glendale had rewritten a "Code Three Response Policy" that stated:

> The arson investigators will not engage in police-type pursuits
> of arson suspects. If an investigator needs to chase a suspect, contact
> with police dispatchers will be made on the radio and responding
> uniformed police will effect the stop.

The guy in the Toyota had given them the first opportunity to test the new policy. It specifically referred to arson suspects, John noted, and he grinned at his partner, and said, "This dude isn't an *arson* suspect."

It didn't start out as a pursuit. They just tailed the guy discreetly, and called in their location, and requested police units to assist. And they fudged a bit by saying they were following on city streets rather fast at fifty miles per hour, when actually they were doing seventy. But John was not about to back off because of a dumb-ass no-pursuit policy now that he had started broadcasting their location on the air. What, and let some cop taunt him because he wimped out? No way!

Finally, he had to hit the red lights and siren while flying across a busy intersection, and he made a few hair-raising sliding turns and U-ees, and when they managed to box in the Toyota, they jumped out with 9mm handguns, dragged the guy from the car, and put him down in a felony prone-out until the black-and-whites arrived.

So, Captain Orr was still nailing shoplifters and doing what he loved: *police* work. And Joe Lopez was learning fast what their boss already knew: asking John Orr just to chill out and cut the cop capers was like asking Islamic Jihad just to kick back and milk goats.

Captain Marvin Casey was justifiably suspicious when the Three Amigos arrived back at his office in Bakersfield.

"Two visits from the feds in one month?" he said. "To a country boy in Bakersfield?"

They told him that his latent print was "promising." That they might have a few suspects in mind, but nothing definite.

When he asked them what he could do to help, April Carroll said, "We want to establish the chain of evidence."

So Marvin Casey had to gather evidence techs and everyone who had anything whatsoever to do with the collecting, storing, photographing, packaging, or delivering of the incendiary device that he'd taken into custody on January 16, 1987. And by the end of the day, the Three Amigos were satisfied by what had been said, and what had *not* been said: that no outsider could have touched that evidence in any way. They now could proceed without fear of embarrassment from learning otherwise.

But of course, they never mentioned John Orr. It would always be, "And did anybody *else* come by that day?" As April Carroll put it, "We played Columbo."

But though Marvin Casey might have been a country boy, he was far from buying the Columbo act. He kept trying to pry some information out of them because he knew something was up.

"But feds are feds," he later said, rhetorically. "They want, but they never give. They just squirrel away all their information."

Perhaps that day his brother firefighter, Glen Lucero, might have felt

Casey's frustration. He later said that fire investigators were used to sharing vital information, not keeping secrets. Lucero might have empathized
with Marvin Casey, who'd had the intuition and the brains and the nerve
to work on the arson series of 1987 and 1989 when everyone else, even
his ATF helpers, were rolling their eyes. When they were even chortling
behind his back because he was only a fireman with a half-baked idea.
But he had been *right* all along.

This was the result of his work, his intuition, so shouldn't it have been
his to know, then and there? Among themselves the task force said that
they would have arrived at the same result without Casey's theory, that all
he did really was to collect and preserve the fingerprint evidence. But
they could never refute that only a colossal error by a fingerprint examiner at the Department of Justice had kept John Orr on the streets for the
past two years. If John Orr proved to be their arsonist, Marvin Casey had
solved the case back then. *Solved* it. And that could never be fairly denied.

But feds were feds and they were not about to play you-show-me-
yours-and-I'll-show-you-mine. The Three Amigos left Casey utterly in
the dark as to the true nature of their visit, and went back to Los Angeles.
And Marvin Casey was not to learn of his vindication for months to come.

Now that the task force believed they had the identity of the Pillow Pyro,
the M.O. reports they were collecting were turning into a paper ava-
lanche. It was time to inform John Orr's superiors at the Glendale Fire
Department. They needed his telephone log, and anything else they could
secretly gather as they began cementing a case that a jackhammer
couldn't chip.

Within days their list of need-to-knows had grown alarmingly. There
were at least two dozen in the know, and not just ATF and LAFD superiors at the highest level. Word had leaked to *everyone* in the ATF Los
Angeles office, and had been whispered around LAFD headquarters, not
to mention the L.A. County Sheriff's Department. That was most wor-
risome of all, because everyone knew what happens when street cops get
a "secret" of this magnitude. Mike Matassa predicted that by June there
would probably be enough government employees with knowledge that
John Orr of the Glendale Fire Department was the Pillow Pyro to form
a militia large enough to overthrow Castro.

A secret meeting was held at the U.S. Attorney's Office with Battalion Chief Christopher Gray, John Orr's immediate superior. Predictably, the disclosure hit him like a stun gun, but he quickly moved from denial to acceptance. They informed Gray that they might be working for a long time before making an arrest, and they described the magnitude of the fire reports they were revisiting. Without alerting John Orr, they had to get a recent mug shot for a photo spread to show witnesses, and they told the chief they'd have to subpoena telephone records from the Orr home and would need call-out sheets as well as phone records from the Glendale Fire Department.

When they were all finished, and the thunderstruck battalion chief could get his thoughts in order, he informed them that Captain Orr was not only a writer of articles for trade publications, but that he had written a novel about fire fighting. Chief Gray said that John had given him the first couple of chapters to read, but all Gray could remember about the story was that it was full of filthy dialogue. Chief Gray, a devout Christian, was decidedly unimpressed with his arson sleuth's literary style but thought they should know about the novel.

Nobody at the meeting could think of how John Orr's fiction efforts could assist the task force, but they thanked the chief and swore him to secrecy about their investigation, and that was about it. They promised to keep him apprised of any developments, and warned that even with this devastating news, he must not betray his feelings. It must remain business as usual back at his fire department.

Before leaving, Chief Gray did verify a piece of news they'd already heard. John Orr was scheduled to go to San Luis Obispo at the end of the month, to the California Specialized Training Institute, where he was taking a course on peace-officer safety. The session was to begin on April 29 and end May 3.

The task force shot some sidelong glances, because this was more than they could have wished. He might just try for another fire series after leaving the conference, just as he'd done twice before.

On April 23, John received a phone call from Mike Matassa of ATF, whom he knew from having his assistance on a couple of Glendale cases. Moreover, Matassa had attended a training session on firearms identification hosted by the Glendale Arson/Explosives Unit, so they were well acquainted.

In that phone call, Matassa first asked if he could send two of his ATF agents to a Fire Investigation 2A class that Glendale was hosting. John told him about the new laser technology on postfire flammable-liquid burn patterns that they'd be demonstrating, and that he could squeeze in the two ATF agents as a favor. Then Matassa switched the subject to the Pillow Pyro case and said he sure hoped that one of the local arson investigators might come up with something, and if John happened to remember anything, to please call.

Then Matassa said, "The guy's good, John. Real good. We got nothing on him, just that delay device from the Redondo Beach fire that Campy told you guys about."

And John said, "No, I've never encountered anything quite like this."

"Be sure to call if you think of anything," Matassa said to him. "Anything at all."

"Sure will," John said.

But before he could hang up, Mike Matassa added, "By the way, you going up to San Luis Obispo for the CSTI seminar?"

"Yeah, I'm going," John replied.

"Taking your wife?" Mike Matassa asked. "I was thinking about taking mine."

"Maybe," John said. "Haven't worked it out yet."

"Our boss won't let us take our G-rides," Matassa said. "How about you? Allowed to take your company car or do you have to take your own?"

"I can take the city car but I'm not sure yet."

Mike Matassa said, "Well, be sure to call if you come up with something for us on our guy."

When Matassa hung up, he looked around and said, "Nothing. He told me nothing. I still don't know which car he's taking."

They were planning an elaborate surveillance to follow John Orr on his trip to and from the San Luis Obispo conference. ATF had brought in undercover agents from their gun groups and dope groups, guys with long hair and beards, people that John Orr could not possibly have come in contact with during his arson investigations.

Six surveillance cars and a fixed-wing aircraft were ready, but the task force had a dilemma. What they needed was a court order allowing them to attach an electronic tracking device, or "bird dog," to Captain Orr's car for the times when it would be impossible to maintain visual surveillance, even by aircraft. And to get the court order they needed a specific description of the vehicle on which the device would be attached. And since they didn't know if he'd take the city car or his own, they had to wait and see.

John Orr was scheduled to drive away from his Eagle Rock home on Sunday morning, April 28, 1991. The "eyeball" surveillance car at the point position relayed by radio that John would be taking his city vehicle, the big Crown Vic, when at 10:30 A.M. he walked out of his wife Wanda's little house in Eagle Rock and loaded travel bags into the trunk.

The fun began almost at once. By the time John got on the freeway he simply *buried* the speedometer needle off the dial. The eyeball car had to back off or be burned.

The fixed-wing aircraft, waiting at the Burbank airport and ready to taxi, was informed that the Ford was approaching the city, but John roared past Burbank before they got off the runway. They said he blew by Disney Studios so fast his draft sucked the shorts off Mickey Mouse.

The surveillance cars simply couldn't do any of their fancy loops, passbys, and handoffs from one eyeball to another. All they could do was a straight line, balls-out road race all the way to San Luis Obispo.

And while all this daredevil motoring was going on, Ken Croke was rushing to a magistrate after just filling in the last lines of his affidavit with the description and license number of the car John was driving. The federal judge signed the order at her home, and then Ken Croke was back on the road with the impossible task of trying to catch the rocketing caravan of G-sleds "surveilling" Captain John Orr.

As one ATF agent said in utter frustration, "That Crown Vic's topping a hundred! I gotta do a buck-ten to even have a chance!"

They had no chance for a customary surveillance. Meanwhile, they had a problem in their aircraft. One of the new ATF agents, a guy from New York assigned as a spotter, got airsick right out of the airport. The pilot had to return, put the plane down on the tarmac, and let the kid run into the hangar to barf. When the young agent came back he was green around the gills, but game. And off they went, the pilot thinking maybe they should've had a Learjet to keep up with *this* guy.

The amazing thing is, his driving didn't seem to attract any California Highway Patrol units. Everybody who knew John Orr always said how ordinary he looked, the kind of guy nobody ever notices. The kind that blends into whatever background there is and just disappears. The surveillance guys started thinking that maybe he had some way of doing the same thing in his car. Maybe this dude could make himself invisible!

He checked into the Embassy Suites in San Luis Obispo early that afternoon, and the surveillance units were placed strategically to monitor his movements. During regular workdays, "the arson nerds"—Mike Matassa and the Three Amigos—had to dress like police detectives in business attire they bought cheap in L.A.'s garment district. But the undercover guys were definitely California casual, in tees, tanks, and Levi's 501s.

Until he blew out his knee, Ken Croke had been a college football player, and he was still a side of beef, going about 255 pounds. He and Hollywood Mike Camello often played flag football in the Hollywood League with other piano movers from LAPD, LAFD, and ATF, and Croke swore that their version of flag football was tougher than what he'd played in college. To pass the time he played catch football, and the long-hairs tossed Frisbees while scoping out coed joggers from the Cal Poly campus, dreaming of kinky sex and Jell-O fights in frat houses while using government film to shoot pictures of the sweaty chicks.

They were detailed to work twelve hours on and twelve off. Glen Lucero and April Carroll had the night shift, from 7:00 P.M. to 7:00 A.M., and the first evening was utterly boring, broken up by pizza runs. But after the observers put their quarry to bed, certain that he was tucked in for the night, two of the ATF tac-team guys went to work.

The "bird dog" looked like a black cigar box, and at 2:30 A.M. the mobile tracking device was strapped to the chassis of John's car with the antenna hanging just enough to clear the rear bumper but still be unobtrusive. In a surveillance van was the bird dog's monitor, resembling a radar screen with lines around it. A direction finder would cause beeps as the target's car got closer. Beeping at the center of the monitor meant that van and target were bumper to bumper, so the bird dog still required a human eyeball to work in conjunction with it. They wanted him no closer than a hundred yards from the direction finder.

Sunday was even more boring than Saturday. It was exhausting to just sit, and it was stifling in the surveillance van, where the unlucky ones inside had to start stripping off clothing. The luckier task-force members were in the hotel room directly across the hall from John Orr.

On Monday, April 29, John attended the training session, but after it was over he got in his car and took a drive to the Thrifty Drug Store on Madonna Road. And the pucker factor was very much in evidence in the cars bearing the Three Amigos, who were only too aware of the Thrifty Drug Stores fires in Wilmington, San Pedro, and Redondo Beach.

Following him into the store at 6:25 P.M. was ATF's José Canseco look-alike, Sal Noriega, who saw his man at the checkout. John Orr put something in his shirt pocket and the checker offered him a receipt but it was waved away. Noriega saw the checker drop the receipt under the counter, followed John outside, and saw him open and close the trunk of his car, then get in and drive off.

After they surveilled John back to the Embassy Suites, Noriega and his partner sped to the drugstore, identified themselves to the checker, and asked if he remembered the customer.

The young checker recalled an "older" man wearing glasses, a red plaid shirt, and blue jeans, and remembered that he'd bought two boxes of Marlboro Light cigarettes. When Noriega told the checker that he'd seen him drop something under the counter, the checker produced the trash basket. On top was a dated receipt for two box packs of Marlboro Lights, purchased at 6:27 P.M.

The purchase produced quite a flurry of excitement among the task-force members, especially the Three Amigos, who knew that John Orr did not smoke.

On May 1, the acting group supervisor, Mike Matassa, showed up in San Luis Obispo, pretty well convinced that before this exercise was over they would catch their man in the act of trying to burn down a retail store, probably on his return trip to Los Angeles. Matassa wanted to be there when they popped the Pillow Pyro.

Nothing happened during the next day of training. John went to

CSTI, then back to the Embassy Suites; so on the second evening, Mike Matassa took Ken Croke to a Pismo Beach steak house. Ken Croke, a GS-5, "as low as you can get," as he put it, was making sixteen thousand dollars a year, and could just about qualify for food stamps given the cost of living in L.A. The twenty-five-year-old agent figured the price of this meal would send him to a loan shark.

In the restaurant they spotted John Madden, the colorful football announcer and former Oakland Raiders coach. Croke was wide, but Madden was wider. Croke consumed a twenty-two-ounce baseball cut, and then the ATF agents watched in awe as Madden devoured *two* baseball cuts, enough cholesterol to put the whole task force in the cardiac ward. One of the waitresses did her thing by standing on a chair and filling water glasses from five feet up without spilling a drop. It was the only excitement they'd experienced during the entire surveillance.

Still, they believed something would happen on the way home. That's what they were all waiting for.

When John Orr left his room on the morning of May 3, the task force knew two things from their spies: he had never taken a smoke break at the conference, and there were no cigarette butts left in his room. So he hadn't bought those Marlboros because he'd suddenly taken up the habit. The agents were strung so tight they were humming.

When their quarry took a break from the convention site at 1:30 P.M. that afternoon, Mike Matassa was the eyeball in the aircraft, but he couldn't see anything.

He'd say to the ground people, "Gimme a landmark."

They'd say "McDonald's" or "Burger King."

He'd say, "Don't see it. Gimme another."

They'd say, "A water tank" or "The bus station."

He'd say, "Don't see it."

Just as Matassa was getting used to the aircraft it banked suddenly and Mike Matassa completely lost the eyeball, but the ground teams picked up for him and followed their target to the vicinity of a car wash.

John Orr drove into a parking lot next to an auto dealership, and for some reason he stopped. He got out and walked around to the rear of his car.

Glen Lucero reported, "I saw him do a double take!"

And Ben Franklin was right: for want of a nail the shoe was lost; for want of a shoe the horse was lost; for want of some baling wire, a surveillance was lost.

The antenna had dropped and was hanging down low, in plain view. When John squatted to take a closer look, all hell broke loose.

The guys from the dope and gun groups started jabbering on the radios all at once. Things like "Surveillance is blown!" And "Let's pop him now!" And "Let's do a felony stop!"

But April Carroll yelled, "Hold your positions! Hold your positions!"

And while the whole scene went from Technicolor to bad dream black-and-white, John peeled out, tires smoking, and drove straight to the San Luis Obispo Police Department, where he jumped out of his car and ran inside the station, leaving everyone in the task force absolutely stunned and baffled.

April Carroll and Ken Croke waited outside the police station, and because neither of them were known by John, they got ready to sprint inside the second something happened.

And it did. John came running out, jumped in his car, and sped away with most of the task force not knowing *what* in the hell was going on.

April Carroll got on the radio and said, "Hang back! We'll go in the P.D. and see what happened!"

And as they exited the car, Ken Croke, in all the excitement, closed the door and locked Glen Lucero's keys inside with the engine running.

Croke and Carroll badged the stunned desk officer and spoke with a police lieutenant, hastily explaining what was going down. They were told the astonishing story that when John Orr had run inside he'd identified himself and informed the cops that he might have a *bomb* strapped under his car! But instead of calling for a bomb-disposal squad, or doing something reasonable, Captain Orr had simply asked for directions to their Explosives Ordinance Disposal range.

The police lieutenant had complied, but asked if it wouldn't make just a wee bit more sense to call for a bomb technician rather than drive the car further, thus running the risk of hitting a chuck hole or running over a chipmunk or something, triggering a device which might blow him clear into the next fucking county? But John Orr had said no, he was *kind* of a bomb expert himself, and he'd be fine since he'd already driven it *this* far.

The EOD range was two miles out of town, and if he'd driven like a NASCAR racer before, now he drove like the Dukes of Hazzard. Mike Matassa eyeballed him kicking up a dust storm as he bounced along that dirt road to the range, not at all like a man who thought there was an explosive device attached to his car. And pretty soon he skidded to a stop in front of a uniformed cop who was himself the size of a bomb truck.

While all this was happening, ATF fingers were being pointed at the tactical-operations officer, and the longhairs were yelling, "Have you ever heard of duct tape?" And the T.O. guy. was yelling, "I put it on *right!*" And others were hollering that they'd been tanked by a guy who couldn't put a decal on a license plate, and Mike Matassa was yelling, "We ain't leaving here without that twenty-five-hundred-dollar bird dog!"

During the short time that it took John Orr to get to the bomb technician, April Carroll, the police lieutenant at the station, and Mike Matassa up in the sky had cooked up a story which they relayed by phone to the bomb sergeant.

The sergeant crawled under John Orr's car, removed the device, and told him, Look! It's just a harmless, obsolete, inert, helpless old bogus bomb that couldn't hurt a ladybug. Or words to that effect. The cop then told Captain Orr that he'd keep the thing and check it out further with the training institute, and put a stop to their childish shenanigans.

But if he'd really bought the story, as the sergeant thought he had, one might wonder why John Orr took a camera from his car and shot some pictures of the device. Close-up pictures.

That afternoon, John returned to his hotel, attended the rest of the training sessions, and awaited his wife, Wanda, who arrived by train that evening. They checked out of the Embassy Suites two days after the conference ended, having used the extra time to tour and relax. They arrived back at their home in Eagle Rock at 3:30 P.M. on May 5, followed all the way by the surveillance caravan of losers.

———

Two days later, the bomb sergeant from the San Luis Obispo Police Department received a phone call from Captain Orr asking if he'd had a chance to examine the bogus bomb, and the sergeant said sure he had, and just as he thought, it was an empty box, the CSTI gang's idea of a sick joke. John thanked him and hung up, after which, the bomb sergeant immediately called the task force saying he was pretty certain that John Orr had bought the story.

The Pillow Pyro Task Force generally agreed. They believed they could continue with their investigation, and Mike Matassa didn't disagree. But when he got pensive, that jagged scar over his right eyelid grew more prominent, and in one of those moments, he said: "That arrogant prick. He's *on to* us!"

Still, they behaved as though he wasn't. Ken Croke tried surveilling him from his house, and it was disastrous. John would be driving along a Glendale avenue, nice as you please, and suddenly he'd slide across three lanes of traffic, jerk a hard left turn into a wrong-way alley, pull out onto another street, and repeat the exercise!

Or, he'd be moseying along a residential street in his city car, just out for a drive, and he'd turn onto another street, but suddenly he'd spin a U-ee and stop at the end of a cul-de-sac. Any G-sled turning onto that street would be burned. But Croke already had enough experience with John not to be burned, and the only way to assure that was to abandon any further attempts to tail him.

Still, from all they were learning, he had *always* driven like that. So they couldn't say for sure if he was looking for a surveillance or just liked to play cops-and-robbers head games with himself when he got bored. John Leonard Orr was not easy to fathom or predict—unless one paid attention to the profilers at the FBI academy who'd written about the violent serial offender's compelling need for *excitement*.

They had some heart-to-hearts, the Three Amigos did, while back at task-force headquarters. They still had the two choices: either pop him now and settle for the one sure count of arson in Marv Casey's Bakersfield fire, as well as trying to link in the others from the Central Coast and Central Valley; or wait and do it right by seeking out witnesses from every store he'd torched or attempted to torch and showing them a "six-pak" photo spread, building a monumental case brick by brick.

If they waited and did all that, and if he truly *had* bought the bomb-hoax story, he might feel safe enough to begin a *new* arson series some-where in the Los Angeles basin. But if the Pillow Pyro struck again and maybe killed someone in a fire, where would that leave the government as far as liability was concerned? And where would that leave *them* as far as their careers were concerned?

The U.S. Attorney's Office, ATF supervisors, and others mulled it over, and it was decided to let the fish run with the hook. A reason that they could afford to take the risk was that since Tom Campuzano of the L.A. Fire Department had first walked into that FIRST meeting on March 29 with the Pillow Pyro flyer, there had not been a single arson attempt at a retail store in all of Los Angeles County. Their conclusion was that knowledge of the existence of the task force had been enough to keep the matches out of John Orr's hands, and would continue to do so for the foreseeable future.

But Mike Matassa's doubts, which he kept squirreled away from everyone, suddenly jumped out of his pocket and landed on the desk in front of him, like a series of tiny, brightly burning fires. And he won-dered: Is John Orr really too scared to strike again? Or does it just en-hance the thrill?

By June there were only Two Amigos. April Carroll had been transferred prior to being promoted. Mike Matassa was told he'd soon be relieved of his supervisory duties and allowed to be a street hump once again. Glen Lucero was checking fire reports every day, but there was absolutely no activity that could be linked to the Pillow Pyro.

They still needed a recent mug shot of him in order to create a good photo spread to show employees from the retail-store fire series. His Department of Motor Vehicles photo didn't look like him, and they were trying to think of a way to get it done.

Then they had an idea. They asked the LAFD arson unit to put out a bogus request to the FIRST organization for publicity photos. Vanity car-ried the day, and they sent a photographer to a FIRST meeting and got a good shot of John Orr without his glasses for a six-pak. The photo spread

was shown five to ten times a day to potential witnesses at every one of
those arson fires in the Los Angeles basin, and beyond to the Central
Coast and Central Valley of California.

This time they didn't ask who'd been seen in the store at the time of
the fires, as the original investigators had done. This time it was: "Is one of
these men a customer?" And "Have you ever seen any of these men? And
not necessarily on the day of the fire, but anytime?"

They scored their first hit when they interviewed former employees
from People's Department Store, the first arson that had been committed
in the L.A. series. People's employee Ana Ramirez looked at the photo
spread and said, "Yeah, that guy there, number five. He's a customer. He
wore a khaki shirt like a service person. I saw him a couple times a few
weeks before the fire. He was coming back from where you pay your bills
in the store."

She was a middle-aged woman and she was *certain*. Mike Matassa said
she'd be a great witness. They were off and running.

Evelyn Gutierrez, a former employee of the gutted D&M Yardage
store in Lawndale, was shown the photo spread and told them that number five was the person she'd seen in the drapery section of the store fifteen minutes before the fire broke out.

And while all this drudge work was paying off, Mike Matassa conducted a little experiment. He made a Pillow Pyro incendiary device.
And it worked.

The task force believed that all of the call-outs and log sheets and telephone records to be secretly supplied by Battalion Chief Gray of the
Glendale FD would point to one inescapable conclusion: John Orr was
always out of the office on pager, always unaccounted for and alone on
the dates and times of every single arson. They believed that there would
never be any recorded telephone traffic on any of the records at the time
of the fires that could later be used to alibi him.

A problem occurred when a witness picked out one of the other faces
from the photo lineup. The mug shot she picked happened to look like
the composite they'd originally drawn with her help. They questioned
her repeatedly until they finally realized that the guy she'd originally
described for the composite sketch never could have started the fire. She

admitted she'd only seen him at the store *after* the incendiary device was discovered.

When the frustrated task-force interviewer asked, "Well then, why in the world did you choose *him* for the composite sketch back then?"

They'd only asked her if she'd *remembered* anybody, she replied. And yes, she had. She'd remembered him, she said, because he was cute, and had a nice ass.

8

POINTS OF ORIGIN

I n June 1991, John Orr and his wife, Wanda, drove to Orange
County to attend his daughter Lori's high-school graduation. Also
that month he wrote a cover letter to a New York literary agent
who'd been referred by an author he'd met at a book signing in Beverly
Hills. After phoning the agent he was invited to send his manuscript,
Points of Origin.

By July, Mike Matassa was back at work as a co-lead investigator, or "case
agent" as ATF called it, with Glen Lucero as the other co-lead. And it was
during these dog days of summer that Lucero could see the stark difference between a complex government investigation and one done by the
locals. As Lucero put it, "The state prosecutor gets the dregs and tries to
make it work. A deputy D.A. says, 'We might convict him, let's give it a
try.' It's very different when you're dealing with a government case and
assistant U.S. attorneys."

Then another opportunity to catch him in the act presented itself.
That is, if they were right, and old habits die hard. If he'd regained the
nerve he had prior to March 29, before he'd heard of the task force. The
California Conference of Arson Investigators was holding its summer

session in Fresno from July 31 to August 2, and John Orr had signed up for it.

This time there would be no bird dog attached to his car, nor an airplane spotter, and once again John Orr took what Mike Matassa called his "plain white wrapper," the white Ford Crown Victoria. And once again, when he got behind the wheel and on the freeway, the speedometer needle vanished.

On the afternoon of July 30, the surveillance caravan surrendered by the time they reached the highway known as the Grapevine. John Orr was over the hill and rocketing toward the Central Valley before anybody's lunch had settled. The task force tried to stay in the game with Ken Croke acting as eyeball in the lead car. His G-sled was a black Lincoln Mark IV, but the Grapevine climb proved too much and it overheated. When steam came pouring out from under the hood, the G-ride pulled over, the door flew open, and Ken Croke jumped out yelling for a fireman.

When Mike Matassa found out what had happened to the eyeball he got a frantic radio message from the rookie Boston agent asking, "What'll I do, Mike? What'll I *do*?"

With John Orr out of sight, and for all they knew, somewhere just south of Seattle, and this surveillance turning to shit even faster than the last one, Mike Matassa said, in the accent of Ken Croke's hometown: "Just call Triple A, Ken. Put it on your *Veezer* card."

Glen Lucero, who was hanging back in another G-sled, could not be the eyeball because John Orr knew him, so he floored it and picked up Ken Croke. Though they topped out at one hundred miles per hour all the way, they would not catch up with the surveillance caravan until they all arrived in Fresno.

Matassa's boss, Larry Cornelison, had been assigned to attend the CCAI seminar in order to monitor the activities of their suspect, and he was already there when John Orr arrived at the Holiday Inn. He watched his man check in, make a stop at the bar, and go to his room.

The next day, Cornelison was also with John Orr for the morning session, and for lunch at the hotel with several other CCAI committee members. Those who *knew* were giving one another and John Orr quick nervous glances like patrons in a Pussycat theater, but at 2:30 P.M. Captain Orr left the seminar and did not return. Cornelison notified the surveillance teams by radio.

At 3:00 P.M. the ATF resident agent in charge, William Vizzard, who was participating in the surveillance, was parked in the vicinity of the Fresno Convention Center when he saw dark smoke rising. He drove to the location and saw that a trash container by the convention center was on fire. He put it out with a fire extinguisher from his car. In the trash receptacle were pieces of foam among cigarette butts and other debris.

The fire could have meant nothing at all, but Mike Matassa asked, "Is this guy fucking with our heads, or what?"

At 8:48 A.M. on August 2, Mike Matassa watched through binoculars as John Orr checked out of his hotel, loaded his bags into the trunk of his car, and closed the trunk. But before getting in for the drive home, he got down on the ground and looked under the car.

The trip home was uneventful and, of course, *fast.*

Task-force members found themselves wondering how their colleague John Orr was different from them. Mike Matassa was in some ways quite unlike John Orr. Matassa, four years younger, had ethnic roots with recent forebears and was a product of the Northeast. He wore his father's gold crucifix on a chain around his neck. John Orr was from western America, the white-bread variety among whom ethnicity is unknown or so far back nobody cares. And his family had no religious affiliation. Unlike Orr, Matassa was childless, but his marriage worked. John Orr's fourth marriage was in jeopardy; his affair with Chris had reached the point where he was listed on her daughter's emergency-call card at school. The child even called him Dad.

One thing that the two men had in common was that early in their adult lives their first career choice had been the Los Angeles Police Department, which had rejected John Orr and had seemed an impossible dream to young Mike Matassa. They had both settled for other investigative work, and both had done well.

Neither had ever gotten past a preference for street police work. Matassa liked to point out that ATF agents were more like the cops who policed the streets of L.A. than they were like the other feds so distrusted by street cops. And he said that ATF would do the down-and-dirty police work that needed to be done, and was proud that back when he was a new agent he'd assisted the LAPD in making a case that helped convict the Wah Ching gang members who'd shot two LAPD officers in a botched jewelry-store robbery.

And of course, John Orr's love of street police work was legendary in the city of Glendale, if distressful to his bosses. It set him apart from both his fellow firefighters and the street cops he tried to emulate while hungering for their respect. In the end, Matassa, and Glen Lucero as well, belonged to things larger than themselves, but John Orr had never quite belonged anywhere. Everything he did and everything he wrote indicated that. Whereas Lucero believed that his position as a fireman turned crime investigator gave him the best of both worlds, John Orr, with the identical background, saw himself as a "bastard child" belonging to neither world, appreciated by no one.

Meanwhile, Captain John Orr was getting very anxious about his novel. He sent his 104,000-word manuscript and a check for three hundred dollars to the Writer's Digest Criticism Service, hoping to learn how he could make it acceptable for publication.

About the time that John Orr was waiting for comments from hired critics, Mike Matassa and the task force had come up with a new wrinkle to catch him in the act of setting a fire, thus speeding up the maddeningly slow and methodical investigative moves required by the assistant U.S. attorneys. John Leonard Orr was about to become a law-enforcement footnote: the first crime suspect on whom a Teletrac device would be tested.

He couldn't have known of its existence. The L.A. Sheriff's Department had obtained the Teletrac from a Los Angeles dealer who'd been using it like the Lo-Jack device that locates stolen cars. Upon hearing about it, sheriff's arson investigators who'd done work on the Pillow Pyro case said, "Let's give it a *real* test on John Orr."

With the Teletrac they didn't need an eyeball at all. The device could relay information to a receiver screen that looked like a Thomas Brothers map grid. A little cursor traveled on the map and could feed back the tracker location every second or every hour, as they wished. They decided to set it up so that it relayed information every five seconds when they had a surveillance team on him, and every fifteen minutes when they did not.

The monitoring equipment included a printout that told them where it was within their selected time frames, and the assistant special agent in charge of the L.A. ATF office scanned the printouts. For their computer cursor, they chose a little rectangle with a single word inside it: "Fire."

Now they only had to wait for Captain Orr's city car to be taken to the garage for its regular service. The device would be installed behind the dashboard, hardwired into the electrical system to run off the battery. And this one had no antenna for him to see.

For the remainder of the hot smoggy summer, the task force was taking trips to the Central Valley and Central Coast to interview more witnesses for the assistant U.S. attorneys. On one of those trips by Mike Matassa and Ken Croke, they found themselves at a shit-kickin' bar in the boonies, looking for a former employee of a burned retail store. Both Matassa the Pennsylvania guy and Croke the Massachusetts guy learned just how far away the rural Central Valley of California is, culturally speaking. There wasn't a single copy of *The Hollywood Reporter* for miles around.

When they walked into the saloon in their arson-nerd business attire, the music literally stopped, or so they claimed. Somebody might've pulled the plug on Travis Tritt or Vince Gill or whoever the hell it was singing about bad love, bad booze, and hangovers. And the two feds found themselves part of a frozen tableau in a place where there were no waitresses named Crystal or Brittany. All the ones there were called Mavis and Flo, and there were no busboys named Chad. In fact, there were no busboys. And all the guys around there, and a few of the women, dipped snuff and drove trucks with NRA bumper stickers that said, "GUNS, GUTS AND GOD," with more firepower in those pickups and possibly on their persons than ATF had in its entire L.A. gun group.

So the feds were extra polite, and if they bought a brew they drank it straight out of the bottle, wiped the foam away with a coat sleeve, and became acutely aware that they had left the L.A. city limits.

More bricks and mortar were added in September when Constance Schipper, an employee from Builder's Emporium in North Hollywood, talked with Glen Lucero and chose photo number five as having been to the store at some time before the fire. Also in September, the official review of Captain Orr's personnel file from the Glendale Fire Department revealed that he'd been scheduled to work on the date of every fire that had occurred between December 10, 1990, and March 27, 1991. A week later the review was completed on Glendale call-out sheets, which showed that he was not at any fire scenes in the city of Glendale during the dates and times of Pillow Pyro fires. In short, he was still unaccounted for when every one of the arson fires had occurred, and he had always been alone. Joe Lopez was on a day off, or in training, or elsewhere, when the arsons had taken place.

Mike Matassa said, "Let's see him chalk it all up to coincidence. Let's see him produce an alibi witness for even *one* of them."

The U.S. Attorney's Office was talking about affidavits for search warrants as the time to arrest John Orr drew near. The lawyers wanted Mike Matassa, for the record, to specifically ask Marvin Casey of Bakersfield if Captain John Orr of the Glendale Fire Department ever could have touched the notebook paper that Casey had collected back in January of 1987. And that meant that Marvin Casey had to be let in on the secret.

Mike Matassa called Marv Casey and asked the question and was given the expected negative answer, and Matassa explained how he would like to have informed Casey sooner, and Casey asked to be allowed to take part in the arrest of John Orr. Understandably, he felt a proprietary interest in the case and wanted a piece of it. Mike Matassa told him that he'd be in touch when the time came.

And when he'd hung up, Marvin Casey at long last had his vindication. They had scoffed for years, even ATF agents. And now an ATF agent had phoned to say that Casey had been right all along. Marv Casey wondered if he'd ever be given proper credit for what he had done. He doubted it, feds being feds.

———

Around the first of October the task force was reminded of something that Battalion Chief Gray of the Glendale Fire Department had advised them of back in April: John Orr was writing a novel about fire fighting called *Points of Origin*. What piqued their interest for the first time was that Gray had found his secretary doing some typing for John. It was a cover letter that he was sending to publishers.

Gray took a look and discovered that in his letter John indicated that the novel was about a fireman who is also a serial arsonist. When Gray relayed this to the task force, it was decided that they should find a way to take a peek at his literary effort. They thought there just might be something in it after all.

They lost Ken Croke that month to an assignment back at the academy for two months of new-agent training. Mike Matassa told Croke they'd try not to pop John Orr until he returned.

On October 2, on a hot and dry Indian summer afternoon, another brush fire broke out in Glendale, in Chevy Chase Canyon, where so many had occurred in the past. This fire's point of origin was determined to be just off the street, in a gully that formed a perfect chimney to take the flames up the hill in the direction of a house perched nice and high with plenty of brush around it. The house was a sitting duck for an arsonist.

Deputy Rich Edwards of the L.A. Sheriff's Department arrived twenty-five to thirty minutes after the alarm was given, but by then the house on Kennington Road was completely engulfed. Edwards was one of the sheriff's arson investigators who'd learned back in August, when the Teletrac was installed, that John Orr was the one and only suspect of the Pillow Pyro Task Force. He looked for John at the fire scene but at first did not see him.

Five minutes later, John arrived in his city car, got out and accompanied Rich Edwards to the point of origin. The fire had begun beside Chevy Chase and had swooped up the hill in a classic V pattern. Both Rich Edwards and John Orr concurred that it was an arson fire. Nobody had been in the house at the time of the fire, but the dwelling had burned to the ground.

———

What do cops in L.A. do when they're up against a tough situation? They draw on Hollywood, except it usually comes in the form of movie memories. "Here's how Bruce Willis did it." Or, "Remember how Mel Gibson drove in that movie?"

Well, this time they went *directly* to Tinseltown. Producer-writer-director John Herzfeld was a friend of Hollywood Mike Camello of the task force. He was fascinated by arson and fire-related themes, and had met Camello when he'd made a fire-fighting film.

The task force thought that Herzfeld might feign some interest in John Orr's literary effort and get his hands on the manuscript on the pretext of movie possibilities. They invited John Herzfeld to the L.A. police academy for lunch, where they gave him a general overview, then took him to the U.S. Attorney's Office in downtown Los Angeles for a confidential meeting. They told him some of it, as much as they had to, and he seemed very curious.

And then an assistant U.S. attorney started talking about confidential grand jury information, and warned that a leak could be considered obstruction of justice. But it still looked as if Herzfeld was on board. Then the assistant U.S. attorney used a word that Mike Matassa wanted to grab out of the air and shove back in the lawyer's mouth. He said to Herzfeld, "You'll become an *informant*."

And there it was: The Informer! Victor McLaglen dying on a Dublin street, gunned down by the IRA. The informer was *always* gunned down, or had his throat cut, or worse. And was always despised as a rat. The producer thanked everybody and said adios, as Matassa knew he would. You don't use the word *informant* around *any* respectable witness, let alone a guy who's in a business where the snitch is always tits up in the last fucking reel!

They had to come up with another plan, and John Orr helped them do it. A week after the Hollywood debacle, John himself called the L.A. Fire Department to find out if they had a firefighter by the name of Aaron Stiles, or any firefighter named Stiles. He said that he was writing a novel and one of his characters was an L.A. city firefighter. He didn't want to be sued for using the name of a real fireman.

The task force couldn't believe his timing. They knew of a retired LAFD arson investigator, A. A. Jackubowski, who lived in Santa Maria and was himself a writer. And John Orr knew him too. The task force had Jackubowski call the Glendale arson captain and say that he'd heard that John was writing a novel and was glad to hear it, and wondered if there was anything he could do to help a fellow firefighter get published. And that maybe they could exchange and compare manuscripts.

Jackubowski told John he was in Hollywood for the day and could meet him in a restaurant, but for once John couldn't get out of Glendale. However, he was clearly excited, and he sent a copy of the manuscript by overnight mail to Jackubowski in Santa Maria. And the day after that, *Points of Origin* was being photocopied at task-force headquarters, about to be eagerly read by Mike Matassa, Glen Lucero, and a couple of assistant U.S. attorneys.

A memorable moment happened during the copying of the manuscript. The assistant special agent in charge of the ATF office was pulling out pages as they flew into the paper tray, and it got very interesting very quickly. Mike Matassa received a phone call from that ASAC, who said, "Believe it or not, John Orr is writing in detail about the *very* fires we're investigating!"

In a matter of minutes everyone was ganging up on the machine operator, grabbing at copies. In chapter 6 the author described how his villain set an arson fire at "Cal's," a hardware business in a "small community south of Pasadena." In the novel, five people died in that fire, one of them a little boy named Matthew.

The residential fire on Kennington Drive in Glendale was not brought to the attention of the Pillow Pyro Task Force, or if it was, nobody paid much attention to it. They were working on M.O. crimes, and the M.O. of their man had to do with fires at retail stores, not brush fires, even if they did take place in John Orr's bailiwick and destroyed houses.

By then the task force had enlisted the aid of behavioral analysts who did serial-arson profiles at the FBI Academy in Quantico, Virginia. It was surprising to learn that government profilers had studied only half a dozen *organized* serial arsonists who had been caught and incarcerated. All of the others they'd studied fell into the *disorganized* category, mostly young men who torched random targets of opportunity, unsophisticated loners with poor social skills. Often they were nocturnal walkers who would just set a fire by applying open flame to anything combustible.

The organized serial arsonists, the few they'd studied, went through a target-selection process. The task force was told that retail stores open for business would represent one of the most risk-filled, hence most fulfilling, of targets. The organized serial arsonist didn't just want to start a fire, he wanted to start *the* fire, his own fire, his way. He was a somewhat older offender with experience. He had unlimited mobility, and sometimes drove for miles selecting targets. It had to be the best fire possible to meet his needs. A fire set in foam material, the task force was told, would certainly provide that kind of bigger, faster, better fire.

The organized serial arsonist was generally employed and often vain about his appearance. He might project an image of authority, even cocksure competence in his other life, but his personal life was dismal. There were no monogamous relationships among those they'd studied.

The serial arsonist, like other violent serial offenders, was conscience-less, egocentric, manipulative, cunning, and indifferent to societal rules and restrictions, with a compulsive need for excitement. In short, his was the classic psychopathic personality, with a unique component: the fire.

Only the fire could temporarily satisfy the lust for power and control and possession. Only the flames could provide the irresistible thrill, the indescribable reward. The fire. The best fire. *His* fire.

Having been installed in John Orr's car during a "routine maintenance," the Teletrac was up and running and being monitored on Friday, November 22, 1991. The system sent out signals from some forty towers covering the Los Angeles basin and far beyond. The signal was coded and got picked up by the transmitter on the target vehicle. The system measured the time it took a signal to travel from the target vehicle to the towers, after which a telephone line sent all information to a master computer, and then out to the star center at the L.A. County Sheriff's Department.

At the star center the deputies could watch on screen as the target moved on a computer map, and could tell within one hundred feet where the target vehicle was located. There were some Teletrac printouts that afternoon that soon caught the attention of the task force.

It was about 3:30 P.M. when a Burbank fire inspector was driving his city car toward his office and spotted a plume, a column of smoke rising in the air. He drove toward it and heard on his radio a full alarm assignment being dispatched to Warner Brothers Studios.

By the time the fire inspector arrived through the studio gate there was already a Warner Brothers fire engine at the scene laying out lines, while other engines from the Burbank Fire Department were on the way. A large facade in the form of a house, barn, sawmill, and chicken coop, which had been used by *The Waltons* TV series, was engulfed, and a crowd of studio employees had gathered to watch.

After several minutes, the fire inspector was joined by Captain Steve Patterson, the lead arson investigator for the city of Burbank. As the two men began looking for possible causes of the blaze they examined electrical substation boxes and found no obvious short circuits. But the fire inspector thought it was probably an electrical fire.

Patterson found burn patterns on the floor of the chicken coop that resembled residue from flammable liquid, and he saw a tree next to the coop that was burned more on one side than the other, which puzzled him as to the direction of the fire. Steve Patterson, who had only eighteen months' experience as an investigator, felt he needed some assistance in solving this one. He used the studio phone to call a colleague, Captain John Orr, who had hosted an arson-investigation class in Glendale which Patterson had attended that very day. Patterson was five years older, but considered the more experienced John Orr his mentor.

John returned Patterson's call, and was told by his friend that he could use some help investigating a fire at Warner Brothers Studios. John said that, coincidentally, he happened to be just a short distance away having dinner with a friend, and he'd be there in a jiffy. He told Patterson he was at Oak and Hollywood Way and asked for directions.

Steve Patterson said, "Well, if you're at Oak and Hollywood Way, you just proceed south on Hollywood Way to Olive, and make a left turn and . . . I can't recall the first street you come to, but there you make a right turn and . . ."

John interrupted him and said, "You know, your directions are somewhat complicated. Would you mind going out and meeting me on Warner Boulevard?"

"Sure, John," Patterson said. "See you there."

John added, "Make sure you have a flashlight. If you see a car coming your way, flash the light at me so I'll know where you're standing."

Steve Patterson waited five minutes and looked at his watch. He looked again after ten minutes had passed. After fifteen minutes, he went to his car, got on the radio and contacted John, asking his colleague if he'd gotten lost. John told him not at all, that he was actually inside the studio at the Waltons set.

As Patterson drove back to the fire scene he was puzzled. John had said he didn't know how to get there and needed directions, yet he was inside at the fire scene. But Patterson didn't question his colleague about why he'd been left standing outside in the dark with a flashlight; he was too glad to have his help.

The two arson investigators pretty much reached agreement, as they assessed the cause and origin of the fire, that it was arson. Nothing was said to Patterson by John as to how he'd found his way in, or about having been in the vicinity earlier in the day.

At a later time, John reported that after giving his partner, Joe Lopez, that afternoon off, he had to go to the school of his lady friend's daughter for a parent-teacher meeting, and the school was only a mile from the fire. He'd seen a header of smoke and heard the fire call over his car radio, and since he was fifteen minutes early he'd decided to drive to the fire for "videotaping possibilities." But due to traffic and time constraints he'd returned to the school and the parent-teacher conference. He also added that because he'd seen the header of smoke earlier, he knew approximately where to go, and had arrived quickly at the fire scene after leaving word for Patterson with a gate guard.

He later denied that he'd agreed with Patterson's assessment of arson, but that he was tired and hungry and "placated Steve, instead of arguing with him." They both agreed to call for Blanche, the FIRST organization's arson dog, to come the next morning and sniff for traces of any flammable liquid.

But Steve Patterson never did learn from his colleague that evening that Wanda Orr worked at Warner Brothers, or that he'd been to Warner Brothers many times. And Patterson didn't hear that Jack Egger, the studio's director of security, said he'd seen John Orr badge his way through the pedestrian gate sometime before 4:00 P.M., when the fire was still raging, and that for a few minutes John had watched it burn.

When the task force learned about the Warner Brothers fire that burned down John Boy Walton's house, barn, sawmill, and chicken coop, and that John Orr had been there, somebody said, "So now *our* John Boy's a TV critic?"

But the task-force supervisors weren't laughing. This was the first suspicious blaze at which they could place him since the inception of the Pillow Pyro Task Force. And the Teletrac hadn't been very helpful. The printout showed him in the Warner Brothers parking lot at 6:18 P.M. when he came to assist Steve Patterson. It did not show him there prior to the fire's ignition at about 3:30 P.M., but only in the vicinity.

Had the Teletrac malfunctioned? Or did he have two cars? Did he drive his girlfriend's car there at 3:10 P.M., set a delay device, leave for a quick run to the girl's school one mile away, then return to be seen by the security director prior to 4:00 P.M.? If so, why two cars? Did he guess there was some sort of tracking device on his city car once again? Or had he gotten in and out between the raindrops, during the fifteen-minute window in Teletrac "hits"?

They had many questions, but one certain answer: he was dissembling. He pretended to Steve Patterson that he didn't know the way, and yet he had *been* there two hours earlier when the fire was burning, according to the director of security.

The day after the Warner Brothers fire, while certain members of the task force were just hearing about it and trying to get their hands on Captain Steve Patterson's report, Gary Seidel, a past captain of the LAFD's arson investigation section, was driving east on the Foothill Freeway in his red-and-white city car. He was getting ready to turn off on Ocean View Avenue when he saw a white car next to him, driven by John Orr. Seidel had his son and three other kids with him when he honked at John, who honked back.

Seidel happened to be one on the growing list of people who knew that John Orr was the suspect in the task-force investigation, so he watched John turning south. Fifteen minutes later, Seidel saw a column of smoke, and saw fire engines heading toward the Foothill Freeway. He asked his son to jot down some notes regarding the time and location of John Orr's sighting. It was 2:25 P.M.

A minute or two before Seidel asked his son to record the time, a dispatcher at the Verdugo Fire Communication Center had received a call regarding smoke in the area of San Augustine Drive. The call was dispatched to Engine 23, but after additional calls came in, the fire was upgraded to a full brush-fire response that called for additional engines and a battalion chief. With all brush fires, the Glendale arson team was automatically notified, and as the dispatcher was in the process of paging him, John acknowledged the San Augustine dispatch on his radio.

Then the dispatcher received another fire call, but this was at a different location, on Hilldale Avenue. The dispatcher redirected Engine 29 to the Hilldale fire and did not redirect any other units to Hilldale, but one unit rerouted himself, the arson investigator, John Orr, who did not inform the communication center.

A firefighter from Engine 31 in Pasadena, Denis Imler, responded to the first brush-fire call on San Augustine Drive, but he never made it there. His engine spotted the fire at a different location. It was on Figueroa Street, down slope from the house on San Augustine Drive that was threatened. The fire had burned from the edge of the road and was running up the hill, but Engine 31 managed to suppress it within three minutes.

During that three-minute interval the Glendale arson investigator arrived on the scene in his city car. Imler was surprised to see John Orr because the closest Glendale engine to this fire had been dispatched to the wrong location on San Augustine, so how did he find it?

On Truck 29 that afternoon was Engineer Glenn Brink. After Brink and the crew were rerouted to a second brush fire on Hilldale Avenue, the Glendale arson car was behind him, siren howling. The engineer was surprised that John Orr could be behind them already because he'd heard the arson investigator broadcasting on the radio, supposedly from San Augustine Drive.

Ronald Ablott, an arson investigator from the L.A. Sheriff's Department, was sent the next day and determined the area of origin for the Hillside fire to be off the road by twenty feet, near the base of a fallen tree. The area was obliterated by mud from the fire suppression, so he couldn't tell if it was a "hot set" or if the fire had been caused by a delay device, but he deemed it to be an arson fire set at or near the crotch of the tree. It seemed possible that one fire was diversionary to draw away the closest engine company, so the other fire could be allowed time to burn before engines would arrive.

———

The Warner Brothers fire report worried the assistant U.S. attorneys and the supervisors of the task force. John Orr had been at the scene. And now, a day later, he was all over the place at a pair of arson fires in Glendale. They couldn't continue to hope that he had lost his nerve upon hearing of the task force's existence. It was looking as though he may have regained it, perhaps not for retail stores, but how about movie studios? How about brush fires? Some of those on the task force and in the U.S. Attorney's Office were saying that another College Hills disaster could happen.

Mike Matassa phoned Ken Croke at the academy and told him he was sorry, but they couldn't hold off until Croke returned to L.A. This was the end. An arrest had to be effected within days. Events had tapped into one of mankind's two primal fears, of dark water and bright flame, ominously expressed in the spiritual:

The Lord gave Noah the rainbow sign.
No more water, the fire next time.

9

THE PRISONER

John Orr himself chronicled the events of December 4, 1991:

> At 7:10 A.M. I walked out of my house to find a cool clear day
> and a man crouched behind a neighbor's juniper bush. Odd sight.
> Even odder was the fact that he had a gun. My first thought was to
> reach for my own off-duty gun, a Walther PPK/S .380 strapped
> securely to my left ankle . . . I also had a Ruger .41 Magnum in
> my hand, but it was in a zippered case . . . An LAPD black-and-
> white pulled halfway into my driveway . . . I looked back at the
> juniper and saw I recognized the man. He was an LAFD arson
> investigator and a friend.
>
> "John . . . John! Don't move! Stay where you are!"
>
> The shouts came from behind a camper parked in front of my
> house . . . I recognized Larry Cornelison, head of the L.A. area
> ATF office, who was holding a gun as he jogged toward me. He
> repeated, "Don't move! You're under arrest!"
>
> "Wanda, step inside!" I heard myself say, as Cornelison ordered
> me to put my hands on top of the car.
>
> "John, you're under arrest!" he repeated.

"For what?"

"Arson, John."

Arson? I couldn't believe it! I was quickly handcuffed and led to a plain Ford parked on the street. I counted at least five undercover cars and saw people I'd worked alongside for twelve years. Rich Edwards and Walt Scheuerell of the LASD arson unit, Tom Campuzano and Glen Lucero of the LAFD arson unit, and Mike Matassa of ATF. There appeared to be more than ten investigators in front of my house.

Glancing over my shoulder I took a last look. Wanda was being shown paperwork at the front door where Domino joyously barked at all the attention he received. A piece of paperwork now in Wanda's hands was a search warrant. I was sure. I wasn't worried, however. I'd done nothing wrong. We didn't even cheat on our taxes.

John Orr's black canvas bag was taken away along with his guns. Inside the bag were a tape recorder and a wine opener, small binoculars, seven brown paper bags, a pack of unfiltered Camel cigarettes, two books of matches, a plastic baggy containing rubber bands, and a cigarette lighter. In his city car, behind the driver's seat and under the floor mat, was a steno pad of yellow lined paper. Camel unfiltered cigarettes were used in the delay devices found both in North Hollywood at Builder's Emporium and at Stats Floral Supply in Redondo Beach. And similar notebook paper had been found at a number of the fires.

The ride to the LAPD station was silent except when John Orr asked, "Are you guys gonna tell me what this is all about?"

Mike Matassa's boss, Larry Cornelison said, "We'll talk when we get to the police station, John."

John Orr also chronicled the moments subsequent to his arrest.

Larry Cornelison rode in the backseat of the Ford with me, as I was driven by Mike Matassa to the LAPD Northeast Division. There I was paraded past several uniformed officers while being taken to an interview room.

"How's it goin', John?"

I looked up to see Officer Will, the beat cop who worked the

day watch in my neighborhood . . . I shook my head as I passed
him, not knowing what to say. His query was neither contemptuous nor probing, just a greeting. I don't think he knew I was handcuffed . . . I was outraged and confused, and prepared to strike out
at anyone handy, particularly the ATF idiots.

Mike Matassa later said, "Serial arsonists are the hardest people to
interview. They're convinced that any real evidence has burned up in
their fires."

After the three men had been settled in the interview room, and John
Orr was Mirandized, the preliminaries did not last long. The prisoner was
informed that the case against him for serial arson was built on many
things, including a fingerprint.

John Orr asked, "How many points does your print have?"

Mike Matassa answered truthfully, "Thirteen."

And then their prisoner asked, "How many prints?" But they chose
not to answer.

"You guys are on a fishing expedition," John Orr said. "You're running a game on me. Find me a motive!"

The detectives at LAPD's Northeast Station had switched on the tap-
ing equipment when the ATF agents took their prisoner into the interview room. The tape recording of the conversation is not inconsistent
with John Orr's version:

> The interrogation was brief and inept. I was shown an affidavit
> supporting the search warrant . . . Matassa took the lead, obviously
> the case investigator. Cornelison didn't allow it for long though.
> Matassa faltered somewhat, expecting an immediate confession . . .
> A lack of response baffled Matassa, and Larry attempted to gain
> some headway by making a half-assed compliment about my repu-
> tation.
>
> He added, "When we developed you as a suspect, none of us
> believed it. We didn't want to believe it, but you did it all."
>
> His blatant declaration, not just an accusation, pissed me off
> enough to have decked him had I been uncuffed . . . I couldn't
> understand what he meant by "all."
>
> The affidavit mentioned three different retail store fires in the

greater Los Angeles area. I was aware of only one of the three. It had occurred at the People's Department Store in nearby Highland Park.

I looked at Cornelison and Matassa and said, "You're fucking crazy. This is fantasy! This has got to be a joke."

Overwhelmed by the situation and afraid to say anything, I limited my responses and let Cornelison rattle on. An old interrogation trick is to maintain silence and let the other person fill the void. I let Larry do his trash talk.

I said, "Larry, I haven't done a fucking thing. This is all bullshit!"

This was followed by a feeble good cop/bad cop routine straight out of *Police Academy III*.

Cornelison saw me ready to clam up and ask for a lawyer, and reverted to another textbook maneuver.

"All right, John," he said. "This is as hard on us as it is on you. Let's talk off the record for a minute."

Matassa chimed in, "John, you're the last person we wanted to arrest. We just need you to help us to understand why."

I saw Larry grimace at Matassa's intrusion that effectively diluted the original off-the-record offer. While watching Matassa, I missed Cornelison's eye or head jerk, but I expected it anyway. Matassa mumbled something to his superior and stepped out.

Cornelison looked back at me. "Off the record, John. Why?"

Tempted to jump into his face with a comeback, I felt pity for this middle-aged man who, by his lack of interview skills, confirmed my theory of ATF as Keystone Kops. I was disappointed as well as angry.

I said, "I don't want to talk to you anymore. I didn't do anything, so let's just get the procedure moving."

Cornelison stepped outside. While he was gone I scanned the affidavit and the support information attached. I found several pages and maps listing two or three series of fires that occurred in Central California. I then realized the scope of the ATF's investigation. I was aware of the 1987 Fresno series but never heard about the discovery of a fingerprint associated with one of the fires. The documents relating to the fingerprint indicated it was mine. I'd never been in Bakersfield in my life. Through it, yes, but never in it. The accusation seemed indefensible.

The interview lasted an hour. The last thing Cornelison said to the arrestee was, "After we get our case together will you talk to us?"

John Orr answered, "I won't close the door on it. But you could have come and talked to me instead of embarrassing me in front of my neighbors."

The prisoner was taken downtown to federal court, where he met with a federal defender who informed the prisoner that the U.S. Attorney's Office had recommended no bail. At 5:00 P.M. he was transported a short distance away to the Metropolitan Detention Center, where he was told he would remain until the preliminary hearing and bail review, both set for December 18.

John eventually ended up in an eight-by-eight-foot isolation cell with a stainless-steel toilet, a sink, and a table with a swing-out seat. There were three ragged novels there which he read in the next two days. He couldn't eat and only drank milk.

When he called Wanda she told him that the task force had searched the house, garage, and her mother's studio behind the garage. "They were gentlemen," she said, and they'd even played with Domino.

The Orrs' conversation was broken by long silences, and he finally asked her to contact a Glendale attorney, Jack Dirakjian.

Just about everyone who worked with the task force had an opinion on the interrogation of John Orr, which pretty much mirrored that of the arrestee: that it was inadequate. The task-force critics seemed to think that they should have tried addressing his allegiance to the fire-fighting service.

ATF serial-arson profilers had briefed the task force on suggested interrogation techniques and later also voiced dismay with the results of this interview. But all of these critics had been quick to diagnose John Leonard Orr as a classic sociopath, a term that criminologists as well as cops use synonymously with the more precise *psychopath*. To most criminologists a sociopath is produced by his environment, but a psychopath's emergence depends on a number of factors, including genetic predisposition, as well as biological or psychological factors. The term *psychopath* is more disturbing, less certain, and probably more accurate in most cases.

But if John Leonard Orr was a classic psychopath—that is, a man with a giant ego and a dwarfed superego; a conscienceless, manipulative, deceptive creature with shallow emotions who cannot truly give or receive love; an impulsive thrill seeker who is glib and grandiose, who cannot empathize or feel responsibility for his criminal behavior—then how could *any* interrogation have worked? He could never have felt the burden of guilt or empathy or brotherhood that they wished to extract from him in the interview room. A psychopath would not confess in such a situation unless faced with a cattle prod and branding iron. It seemed that the critics were faulting the interrogators for not playing upon the conscience of a man who, by their own definition, didn't have one.

The search of John Orr's office that day, in the presence of his shocked and dismayed partner, Joe Lopez, revealed more items of possible value to the task force, including videos and photographs of fires, and something that settled the long debate as to whether John had bought the story from the San Luis Obispo cop about the tracking device being a bogus bomb.

In the arson unit's office they found, clipped together in his desk, photos that he'd taken of the tracking device that day, the business card of ATF Agent Howard Sanders, who had delivered the Pillow Pyro flyer to his office, a Post-it note bearing ATF frequency numbers, and the ATF megahertz rating. Along with ATF's property ID number for the tracking device was the name of a Glendale electronics store where John had obviously collected the information he'd needed.

At the end of the day, an orange folder inside John Orr's canvas bag was found to contain other prints of the tracking device, so it had to have been a matter of great concern to him. The optimists had been wrong. He had known all along that he was the object of an ATF investigation, yet he'd never come forward to make an inquiry. And that would be *very* hard for him to explain from the witness stand.

The "gentlemen" searchers at the home of Wanda Orr had found two drafts of *Points of Origin*, one of them consisting only of the first three chapters, up to page 36. An item of no particular importance to the task force or the U.S. Attorney's Office, but nevertheless interesting, was found in his briefcase that day—a badge. It was a special sort of badge whose "fire department" banner could be popped off, and a banner saying "police" could be snapped onto the shield in its place. The task force believed he must have been posing as a Glendale police detective.

John Orr later wrote that he sometimes used a tactic of posing as a burglary detective so as not to alert arson suspects when he was questioning witnesses. His chronicles tell of the tactic, and the badge:

> It was used on those few occasions when I truly needed it. The last thing I ever wanted to be was a "real" cop. My loyalties were with the fire service; law enforcement was a sideline.

But many who knew him said that he was forever a cop wanna-be, and the badge was validation of their opinions.

The day after the arrest of John Orr was indeed a busy one for the entire task force as well as for Assistant U.S. Attorneys Stefan Stein and Walter Brown, who'd been consulting with the task force since early summer.

Of greater interest to the lawyers than anything found in the searches of John Orr's car, home, and office were copies of letters that he'd kept with the manuscript of his novel. One of the letters was designed for any potential publisher or agent in order to explain something about the story accompanying it. This one was sent on April 17, 1991, to the L. Harry Lee Literary Agency:

> "Common" criminals seem to have one characteristic they all
> share, the need to distance themselves from their crimes as quickly
> as possible, all criminals, that is, except the arsonist. The arsonists
> stay close by, and sometimes even participate in the discovery and
> eventual extinguishment of "their" fires. Bizarre? Indeed it is.
> With the criminal so close at hand why is it that the crime of

arson has the lowest arrest and conviction rate of all? The reason
is simple. The arsonist is weak and insecure, and usually perpe-
trates his crime in the dark, generally in seclusion. Sometimes he
uses time delays. Additionally, the evidence is almost always
destroyed, if not by the fire, then by the firefighters during extin-
guishment. Arsonists are not greed motivated like the "common"
criminal.

I have been a professional firefighter for over twenty years
with the last ten devoted to full-time arson investigation for a fire
department in the Los Angeles area. With the clearance of over
400 cases I have found that the true pyromaniac is responsible for
only five percent of all fires, but generally causes the most
destruction and sets the most dangerous types of fires.

My novel, *POINTS OF ORIGIN,* is a fact-based work that
follows the pattern of an actual arsonist who has been setting
serial fires in California over the past eight years. He has not been
identified or apprehended, and probably will not be in the near
future. As in the real case, the arsonist in my novel is a firefighter.

The second letter found in the search of the Orr residence was dated
July 28, 1991, was addressed to the Writer's Digest Criticism Service, and
had been sent with a check for three hundred dollars. Again there were
certain passages of great interest to the task force.

My completed manuscript (started in 5/90, finished in 4/91)
is my first attempt at fiction, after writing a series of articles for a
fire service magazine, *AMERICAN FIRE JOURNAL.* I am a
firefighter, an arson investigator, actually, with 21 years of fire
service. *POINTS* is the story of a serial arsonist and the investigator who tracks him in Southern California. Aaron, the arsonist, is
actually a firefighter, and Phil Langtree slowly develops the theory
that the suspect is somehow related to the fire department.

My arsonist is sexually/psychologically motivated, and
POINTS is somewhat fact-based. There is an arsonist plying his
trade in the west, and he sets the same types of fires portrayed in
my novel. The investigation is continuing . . .

There was a letter addressed to Natasha Kern Literary Agency, Inc., the postscript of which caught the attention of the task force:

> My novel is fiction, but is based on a real arsonist who has again hit the L.A. area earlier this year doing over $12 million in damage. The investigation now has federal assistance and could be linked to fires outside California. It is my feeling that the arsonist could be a firefighter, but I'm not directly linked to the investigation and can't confirm this fact.

The most interesting letter the task force found was one addressed to the Dominick Abel Literary Agency, dated June 3, 1991.

> My work is a fact-based novel of an ongoing investigation here on the west coast. A serial arsonist is setting fires throughout the west and is quite possibly a firefighter. The series has been going on for over five years and I was even considered a suspect at one point. In early May of this year, I found a radio tracking device attached to my car in San Luis Obispo while I attended a training conference. Ironically, my protagonist experiences the same situation. I had already written the chapter dealing with the protagonist being tailed *before* I found that I was being followed. By the way, I'm not the arsonist and the investigation out here continues. My work is fictional.

In that the Pillow Pyro Task Force hadn't even known about the series of fires in the Central Valley in 1987, and on the Central Coast in 1989, the letters to the agents and publishers were among the most damaging evidence they'd found. John Orr's novel was depicting some events he shouldn't have known about, and he'd indicated that they were arsons committed by a firefighter, when only a few people in Central California knew about Marvin Casey's theory.

As if anyone needed any more convincing, John Orr had not believed for one moment the bomb hoax story, and knew "he was even considered a suspect at one point" of a federal investigation. And yet he had never come forward to ask any questions, to comment or to deny, as his fictional arson investigator had logically done in *Points of Origin*. The assistant U.S. attorneys believed that the letters might ultimately prove more of a problem for the defendant to explain than the novel itself.

One of the people Mike Matassa had phoned first was Mike Cabral, the deputy district attorney whom he had been assisting in court back in March when the extraordinary fire series had struck Redondo Beach, Inglewood, and Lawndale. When the fingerprint match had come back on April 17, Matassa felt bad that he couldn't explain to Cabral what they were doing and why he had to partly abandon Cabral's case.

He'd said then to the prosecutor, "It's something I can't share, Mike. But when it happens, you'll know it. Sorry."

When he explained it all to Cabral on December 5, the prosecutor said, "I knew it was big, and I understand why you couldn't tell me about it. It's okay."

After prosecutor Mike Cabral hung up the phone that day he couldn't have known that in the years to come, this case was going to consume a larger portion of *his* life than Matassa's.

On December 6, John Orr received a visit from his Glendale lawyer acquaintance, Jack Dirakjian, who handled mostly civil cases and decided that John would be better served by his associate, Douglas McCann, who handled criminal matters. John wrote of that meeting:

> I hated McCann instantly, but it was obvious that Jack wanted Doug to represent me . . . I listened to the staccato presentation of McCann outlining defense strategy. Only thirty-two years old, he cut off his superior and me, choosing to take total control of our brief interview. He was arrogant, opinionated, sly, and a complete asshole . . . I retained him on the spot. I wanted a cutthroat to go after the feds who had exposed Wanda and me to this travesty.
>
> He required a ten-thousand-dollar retainer. Wanda made the arrangements, and early the next week, Doug announced that he'd moved up the bail-review hearing to December 10. This pleased me immensely and renewed my faith in the man despite both Wanda

and I initially wondering if he was the right choice. He was young enough to be our son. Later, I'd wish he'd been devoured at birth.

Actually, Douglas McCann was not young enough to be the prisoner's son; John was forty-two years old at the time. And one might question John's strategy of selecting a lawyer he hated, especially in this complex case involving multiple counts and multiple jurisdictions. Defender and defendant would need to work closely.

Wanda Orr had to use her home as collateral for her husband's fifty-thousand-dollar bail, which was set on December 10. Eight days later, the prisoner was released on bail subject to home detention with a transmitter anklet. Once home, Wanda prepared a cup of freshly brewed coffee laced with a shot of Kahlúa.

Close friends and family offered loans, and John's mother frequently dropped by to run errands and do Christmas shopping for them while they tried to get by on Wanda's salary. The accused and his wife forged an agreement that he alone would deal with their lawyer, Douglas McCann, and his defense investigators, insulating Wanda from the trauma as much as possible. She was a private person and tried not to talk about the case with friends. She ducked reporters as best she could during a time in which John's face or, rather, photos and videos of him in action as a fire-fighter were shown almost daily by the print and electronic media.

The task force spent part of the day following the arrest making further notifications to people who had worked closely with John. One of these was Jim Allen of the state Fire Marshal's Office, who was a personal friend of the Orrs as well as a respected arson investigator in his own right.

Mike Matassa made that particular courtesy call, and began it by saying, "Jim, I didn't want you to have to hear it cold on the news . . ."

When he had concluded, and Allen had recovered sufficiently to ask perfunctory questions, and Matassa was about to hang up, Allen said simply, "You ought to look at the Ole's fire."

When Matassa asked Jim Allen to clarify that, Allen said, "Ole's Home Center in South Pasadena. October 1984. Do you remember it?"

And Matassa said, "Yeah. I was there the day after, driving the bomb truck as a rookie agent. What about it?"

Jim Allen said, "John's been obsessed for years about that one. He was very angry that they called it an accident. He brings it up. *Often.*"

Matassa thanked Jim Allen and later said, "A light went on!"

He grabbed his copy of John Orr's novel and paged through it until he came to the chapter dealing with a fire at "Cal's Hardware Store." When Glen Lucero came in the office that day, Mike Matassa said, "You ain't gonna believe this!"

Neither Matassa nor any of the task-force members who had read the manuscript had matched Cal's Hardware with Ole's Home Center. Too many years had passed. But as Mike Matassa talked and read, Glen Lucero remembered. In the novel five people die, including a little boy. In real life, four people had died, including a little boy. In the book, the arson cops were too stupid to figure out that it was an arson, and they called it an accident. So the firefighter arsonist had to set another fire at another hardware store to expose their ignorance.

Glen Lucero had never shared Matassa's confidence that they had a rock-solid case, and being a member of the fire-fighting brotherhood, Lucero had mixed emotions about the arrest of one of their own. But as he sat and listened to Matassa, he began to change.

He later said, "It all became easier for me after I thought about the people who'd died in the Ole's fire. Then I thought, okay, let's really *get* him."

The two lead investigators of the Pillow Pyro Task Force, Mike Matassa and Glen Lucero, reread chapter 6 of *Points of Origin* that afternoon, but this time they read it with new eyes.

10

FIRE LOVER

The general public might think that by the time the suspect in a major investigation is arrested, the work of the investigators ends, but in reality, it gets more intense. In this instance, they had to ensure their case against a prominent arson investigator, a case based entirely on circumstantial evidence. Even with the best piece of circumstantial evidence, the fingerprint, the assistant U.S. attorneys could think of several scenarios whereby a clever defense lawyer might convince a jury that there could be an innocent reason why a piece of notebook paper touched by John Orr had been found on an incendiary device in Bakersfield.

Stefan D. Stein was an attractive and effective thirty-five-year-old government prosecutor who, prior to joining the Pillow Pyro Task Force, had been part of a team that had won an important guilty verdict against a DEA agent in a corruption case. Stein was assigned to the Public Corruptions Group, and a month after the major DEA case had concluded, the chief of the Major Crimes Section came to him and said, "I've got a phenomenal case for you. You think that *other* case was something . . ."

Stefan Stein, along with Assistant U.S. Attorney Walter Brown, another talented prosecutor even younger than Stein, worked out of the federal courthouse in downtown Los Angeles. Stein, a graduate of Hollywood High School, had previously been in private practice for seven years, near his boyhood home on the west side of Los Angeles. He'd done entertainment litigation, but lacked trial experience and had always heard great things about the U.S. Attorney's Office. He'd taken a big salary cut when he joined them, and he had to make a three-year commitment. Those three years were almost up when he became involved in the day-to-day monitoring of the John Orr investigation.

Like everyone else connected with the case, Stein knew how dicey it could be: an M.O. case, a circumstantial case. He'd had the fingerprint examined half a dozen times before he could relax about it, knowing that without the fingerprint they had no chance at all. More investigators were now assisting in the witness interviews; Mike Matassa mostly assisted Stein, and Glen Lucero primarily helped Walt Brown. There were lots of man-hours being expended.

As Stein and Brown began examining the evidence seized on December 4, their confidence grew. Like all the others in the task force, they said it took a while to digest the manuscript of *Points of Origin*. One of the fires set by John Orr's fictional arsonist, Aaron Stiles, happened in a fabric store during the summer seminar in Fresno, and mirrored the actual blaze.

And on page 239, Aaron Stiles sets a brush fire in a canyon, very much like Chevy Chase Canyon in Glendale, causing him to "stroke himself wildly."

There was a passage in the book describing a fire on Victory Boulevard, where the Pillow Pyro had actually struck on two occasions. This one was set by the novel's Aaron Stiles in a display of curtains, as had happened in at least one of the Pillow Pyro series.

This passage, like all of the book, had been written before the Pillow Pyro Task Force had been formed. The author seemed to have had knowledge about the L.A. fire series that they did *not* have.

The author of *Points of Origin* was very much aware of the proprietary feelings of the serial arsonist, as evidenced in a chapter describing Aaron Stiles setting a grass fire when the Santa Anas are blowing, admiring *his* fire, "wanting to be near *his* fire."

The task force thought that the fictional arsonist offered clues to the defendant's ability to compartmentalize and rationalize his activity, when Aaron Stiles attends a Fresno arson conference, "blocking out his history . . . divorcing himself from the fact that he was an arsonist."

There were dozens of calls made to the task force by firefighters and arson investigators who were having second thoughts about fires they'd suppressed or cases they'd worked with John Orr. As for the brush fires in the foothill areas, it seemed that the proliferation had occurred after John had gone to work in Glendale. They found fire reports from 1985 about an arsonist who'd set sixteen fires in Glendale homes, carports, and garages during an eight-month spree. At the time, John Orr had given interviews to the *Los Angeles Times* about his hunt for this serial arsonist, claiming that six incendiary devices had been found at Glendale brush fires during that hot summer.

Stories began to surface about some of those devices found by Captain Orr. Arson investigators from neighboring cities described incidents to the task force when they'd gathered at fire sites trying to find an area of origin when John Orr would drive up, gaze at the area, stroke his mustache, and like a water seeker with a divining rod, say, "I believe the point of origin is . . . there."

And lo! The Glendale arson investigator would go to where he'd pointed and find the remnant of an incendiary device under a rock. At the time they'd felt like *applauding*.

There were stories about afternoons in the foothills when they'd tried stakeouts to catch the elusive brush-fire arsonist. One afternoon, Lucero and others met at a Glendale fire station near Chevy Chase Canyon, where so many grass fires had occurred, and found John Orr with a map board that he'd marked off in quadrants.

The cluster of investigators were assigned to one-man cars for a patrol of these quadrants, and each man had a radio set to the same frequency. John was the rover; the others were assigned to fixed positions. Lucero wasn't out there any time at all before a fire occurred at a location he'd driven past a moment before. When the engine company arrived to suppress it, Lucero met with John and said, "I couldn't have missed the arsonist by a minute! He's a ghost!"

So it was better luck next time. But when Lucero drove from that grass fire to his fixed location, he found another grass fire burning from where he'd just been! At sunset they'd called off their stakeout and gone back to their respective fire departments. The phantom arsonist was never caught.

Glen Lucero said to the task force, "Now I know it was John toying with the big guys, the L.A. Fire Department arson investigators. The people who washed him out of their academy. It must have done a whole lot for his ego."

There was a passage from the novel, spoken by Phil Langtree, that was as prophetic as an omen, concerning the number of identification points needed in a good fingerprint. The man who had penned those lines could not have foretold how his own life story would teeter on the number of points in a latent fingerprint.

Assistant U.S. Attorneys Stein and Brown soon began listing similarities between the fictional serial arsonist, Aaron Stiles, and his creator, John Leonard Orr. They came up with nine:

1. The defendant and Aaron Stiles are both firefighters.
2. They're both nonsmokers.
3. They both use a delay device that gives them a ten-to-fifteen-minute escape opportunity.
4. In the original three-chapter manuscript found during the search, the delay device used by Aaron Stiles is a match attached to a cigarette, placed inside a paper bag, similar to the match, cigarette, and lined paper used by the defendant.

After reworking the manuscript, the completed version had changed the device to a bead of glue on a cigarette, which they interpreted as John Orr realizing that he was getting too close to writing a diary.

5. Aaron Stiles and the defendant start fires in retail stores in the L.A. area during business hours by placing a delay device in combustible materials.
6. Aaron Stiles also starts a fire in the drapery section of an L.A. fabric store, as did the defendant.
7. Aaron Stiles starts a fire in an L.A. retail store in a display of Styrofoam products, also the Pillow Pyro's M.O.
8. Aaron Stiles starts fires in hardware stores, specifically, "Cal's,"

which mirrors "Ole's Home Center" to the point of being macabre.

9. Aaron Stiles starts fires at various retail stores in close proximity to one another within a short time span on the same day, an M.O. for which the Pillow Pyro was notorious.

In addition to the nine points of similarity, the young prosecutors found other similarities in the book written before the task force had any knowledge of the Central Valley fire series.

1. Aaron Stiles starts fires in Fresno, Tulare, and Bakersfield, while driving to or from an arson investigators' conference at the Holiday Inn in Fresno.
2. Aaron Stiles starts fires in fabric stores in Fresno.
3. Aaron Stiles starts one of the Fresno fires in a display of pillows.

But with all that, it was still the correspondence to publishers and agents that Stefan Stein and Walt Brown believed would drop like a fire door and suck the air from the defense. First, in his cover letter to potential agents and publishers, John Orr described his novel as a "fact-based work that follows the pattern of an actual arsonist who has been setting serial fires in California over the past eight years."

Stein and Brown also noted that in his letter, John Orr had written that the real serial arsonist "has not been identified or apprehended." And, "As in the real case, the arsonist in my novel is a firefighter."

They absolutely cherished the letter to literary agent Dominick Abel, wherein John Orr wrote, "The series has been going on for over five years and I was even considered a suspect at one point. In early May of this year, I found a radio tracking device . . ."

This was a prosecutorial bonanza, and Walt Brown longed for the day when they had John Orr on cross-examination, making him explain to the jury why, if he had known that he was a target of the Pillow Pyro Task Force, he had never come forward to inquire or discuss his status as a suspect in a major criminal investigation.

"I can't *wait* to hear his explanation," Brown said.

To the rest of the task force, the evidence was so compelling that they had every confidence; to Stefan Stein there was not enough. Walt Brown was more easygoing, but Glen Lucero found Stein to be a nitpicking fretter. Lucero said, "Stefan can find a hundred ways to ask you for information, until you run out of answers. Then you gotta go out and dig some more. His mind's always working. He's high-strung, hyper, intense, and can drive you nuts."

And the task force learned that their prosecution approach based upon the book manuscript and the letters to publishers and agents might be countered by the suggestion that some years earlier, John had heard from a Fresno arson investigator, Tom Kuczynski, all about the arson series in the Central Valley—that Kuczynski had told him that an unknown arson investigator who'd attended the CCAI conferences was suspected. That rumor, if true, could be used by the defense to claim that John's plotline was based on information fed to him, not from personal experience.

So much had been called to their attention about Ole's Home Center that they'd begun examining everything about that "accidental fire," and in so doing they learned of another attempted arson at Ole's sister store in Pasadena two months after the calamity. In the second arson attempt an incendiary device had been found, consisting of a cigarette, three paper matches, and a rubber band. It was found in a stack of polyfoam that had not fully ignited. The fictional arsonist does the same thing after he doesn't receive "credit" for setting the disastrous fire at "Cal's Hardware Store."

Mike Matassa was absolutely convinced that they had enough evidence, but Stefan Stein would worry and say, "No, not enough. McCann's talking about an ironclad alibi."

And Matassa would say, "Stefan, Orr's guilty! He *can't* have an ironclad alibi!"

Matassa thought the prosecutor was more anal than Woody Allen, and because Stein's early career had been at the entertainment-law firm that also employed Howard Weitzman, lawyer for O. J. Simpson, Matassa called Stein "The Mole," as in defense mole.

Stefan Stein got something with which to bust Matassa's chops when they took a trip to the Central Valley and Central Coast to re-interview witnesses, including Marvin Casey. On the way to Atascadero they were stopped for speeding by a CHiP officer. In the front seat were Matassa and Lucero, in the back were Stefan Stein and Walt Brown.

When the CHiP approached the car, Matassa and Lucero showed their hands and Matassa said, "We're cops and we're packing."

The CHiP officer stuck his face in the car window and said, "Yeah? So *what*."

For months thereafter, whenever he was called "The Mole" by Matassa, Stein would throw up his hands, and cry out in falsetto: "We got guns! We got guns!" And then in the deepest bass he could manage, reply, "Yeah? So *what*, asshole!"

After reading *Points of Origin*, the Pillow Pyro Task Force decided that you couldn't find that many erections at the Playboy Mansion on New Year's Eve. It seemed that every time Aaron Stiles so much as thought about setting a fire he'd end up choking the ferret. And the erections didn't stop with the arsonist. The "good" firefighter, Phil Langtree, had his share of woodies as well, causing task-force banter about the author's description of what happens to Phil Langtree after fighting a blaze.

When Phil Langtree wakes up the next morning in the house he is sharing with his friends Bill and Judy, he staggers into the kitchen in his underwear and Bill embarrasses him by calling attention to the bulge in his shorts, saying that it must have been "a pretty good fire."

So all of the firefighters turned arson investigators, like Glen Lucero, got hit with the question: "Do you guys really get chubbies from dragging that big hose around?" And, "Do *all* you guys check each other's bulge in the firehouse to see if it was a pretty good fire?"

There were so many contemptuous references to cops in the novel—even more by the "good" fireman Phil Langtree than by the "bad" one Aaron Stiles—that it seemed both despise the police equally. And it surprised the task force, even the firefighter investigators like Glen Lucero, that many members of the arson-investigator community were suspicious of the allegations against John, and some were downright hostile. The publisher of the magazine for whom John had written eight articles opined, "If they arrest John Orr for writing a book, they'd arrest Conan Doyle for writing Sherlock Holmes."

Mike Matassa responded that Conan Doyle couldn't have written some of the scenes from *Points of Origin* unless he'd been there. When Matassa first learned about the arson attempt back in 1984 that had been made at Ole's Home Center's sister store, he verbalized for the others how he thought John Orr felt after the sheriffs called the Ole's calamity an accident:

"How *could* you call this an accident? It's my *work*! And you cops are too stupid to figure it out! Cops! I hate them! What do I gotta do, burn down *another* Ole's to convince you fucking idiots?"

John Orr's protagonist, Phil Langtree, has a romantic involvement with a woman named Chris, as did the author for months prior to his arrest. In the novel, the fictional Chris learns about serial arsonists from Langtree, who mixes the disorganized serial arsonists with the organized kind, but nevertheless makes interesting comments.

In one passage of dialogue, Phil Langtree says of the serial arsonist that the fire becomes a friend and sometimes a lover, "actually a sexual thing," to which Chris replies, "Bullshit."

Some members of the task force reacted like the fictional Chris does: Bullshit! The fire as lover? My lover, the fire? Pseudoliterary bullshit!

Others weren't so sure. The task-force interviews were already revealing that John Orr had often said to his present wife, and presumably the other wives and paramours: "My job is my life. My mistress."

Skeptics dismissed that as his rationale for philandering, but a few wondered if he could have meant it literally, as a reference to what they believed was his *real* job, the secret work that possessed him, allowing him to embrace the object of overwhelming desire.

My mistress. My lover. *The fire.*

II

CONSPIRACY

The legal reason used to justify the prosecution of John Leonard Orr in a United States district court rather than a California state court was that he was accused of torching buildings "used in interstate commerce and used in activities affecting interstate commerce." Of course, the fire at Ole's Home Center might have qualified for a prosecution by U.S. attorneys, but the government prosecutors slipped free of that because of the statute of limitations on federal arson, even when death results from it. With no statute of limitations on murder, the state could take its time and try to develop a case against John Orr for a capital crime.

Ole's was left to the Los Angeles County District Attorney's Office, along with all of the residential fires such as the disaster in College Hills, which would be almost as hard to prove as the arson at Ole's. But if the federal courts could convict him in the cases more easily proven, then any state prosecution to follow—including one that could charge four counts of murder in a fire that had been investigated and deemed accidental—might actually become feasible. It was for the federal prosecutors to decide in which U.S. judicial district he should be tried first for the retail-store arsons, and how many counts should be charged.

There were two reasons to let Stefan Stein and Walt Brown have at him initially in the Central District of Los Angeles: first, because Stein and Brown had been bird-dogging the case for nearly a year, and second, because the U.S. District Court for the Central District of California had the *clout*. If the case against John Orr could be won in Los Angeles, it would have judicial significance when it came time to charge and try him for arsons committed in Bakersfield, Fresno, and Tulare.

By April, Stein and Brown were raring to go. They'd been busy writing a twenty-seven-page opening statement for the jury, which was well crafted and very lucid given the complexity of the circumstantial case. And since prosecutors are uneasy when there's not a single reliable eyewitness who can point a finger and say "I saw him do it," the prosecutors tried to lay out a case in their opening that the jury could not fail to understand. The task force was proud of the prosecutors' work. There was just a matter of the few annoying motions *in limine* that John Orr's lawyer had filed with Edward Rafeedie, the district court judge in Los Angeles who would be presiding.

Stein, ever the worrier, sweated out one of the motions having to do with the fingerprint evidence that he'd had examined so many times he could have traced the ridge pattern himself. Then on April 6, a week before they were to go to trial, the judge ruled on what Stein and Brown thought was a frivolous motion.

Douglas McCann had asked that John Orr's novel and his letters to agents be excluded as hearsay. That made the prosecutors snicker. They thought that the manuscript and letters were amazingly probative of the arsonist's modus operandi. One only had to look at the list of similarities between the novel and the actual cases. They soon stopped snickering.

Judge Rafeedie was known as a jurist who wanted to move things along. Speed was important to him. His decision moved the case right out of his courtroom. The judge granted the defendant's request to exclude the manuscript and the letters, not because he agreed with the defense that it was hearsay, but because he believed the prejudicial effect of the manuscript was too great under general rules of evidence. That is, the M.O. of the fictional arsonist did not appear so unique as to justify a conclusion that John Orr had firsthand knowledge of the arsons charged against him.

As the judge put it: "Claimed similarities between the events in the manuscript and the actual events underlying the crimes charged in the

indictment . . . are not . . . sufficiently probative to substantially out-
weigh the tremendous prejudice to the defendant."

The government's arguments did not move him. The prosecutors
were stunned, but they pulled themselves together and asked for a stay of
proceedings pending an appeal to the Ninth Circuit of the U.S. Court of
Appeals. And it was granted by the judge.

That stay was a *major* victory for the prosecution. It meant that they
might not have to go to court without the book and the letters, but it
threw Stein and Brown into the appellate mode, drafting briefs instead of
preparing for trial. And it forced them to lateral the ball to their prosecutorial cousins up in Fresno in the Eastern District of California. Stefan
Stein and Walter Brown were benched until the Ninth Circuit Court of
Appeals could get into the game.

And while the prosecution of John Orr was being transferred to Fresno
with all the briefing that entailed, the task force had their own major dis-
traction—the Rodney King trial.

While Mike Matassa was out of town on an investigation, the LAPD
cops were acquitted of beating Rodney King, causing Matassa to say jok-
ingly to his partners, "Let's get back to town before the riot starts."

And it did. Within days, ATF was asked to do the cause and origin on
all of the riot's retail-store fires because, as Mike Matassa put it, store pro-
prietors were "burning down their own cribs." It was a perfect chance
to collect insurance for failing and failed businesses, and there were
enough store owners buying gas in five-gallon cans to jump-start OPEC
production.

Because of the danger on the street during the riots, the task force
was sent out in three-man cars. There were two ATF agents with one
L.A. Fire Department investigator. The agents carried MP5s or AR-15s,
and watched the investigator's back while he worked. It went on for
three days with everyone sweltering in their "BDUs," the standard
SWAT costume.

They might have looked imposing and they might have been well
armed, but so was the mob. The standard ATF repartee at that time
included the line, "Hey, we just did a cause and origin—at thirty-five
miles an hour. How about you?"

And as bad luck would have it, the Matassas had had the biggest vacation of their lives planned for Easter. They'd booked a trip to Italy, but Linda Matassa had to take it without Mike. And he couldn't even get a weekend off to visit his brand-new thirty-foot Catalina sailboat, which was growing barnacles in Dana Point harbor. He just worked and took care of Mikey, a black-and-white terrier pup they'd adopted at Christmas after it had been abandoned. On a couple of occasions he couldn't get home to the frightened pup until 4:00 A.M., and then he'd have to be right back on duty in L.A. by seven o'clock. Linda Matassa was more of an animal nut than Saint Francis of Assisi. If she'd known that the pup was alone and scared she'd have flown home and put a scar on her husband's *other* eyelid.

Glen Lucero loved Fresno's small-town atmosphere and hospitality. When they closed the shop for the day, the assistant U.S. attorneys would open the fridge and break out the beer.

Fresno wasn't exactly the boondocks, but the jury pool was drawn from eleven largely rural counties. One could drive for miles past citrus groves, cotton fields, and grazing cattle, so the guys from L.A. were hoping for a jury that looked like a monthly meeting of the Rotary Club, instead of people who were into "lifestyle experimentation" with spiders tattooed on their chins.

Forty-year-old Carl Faller, the chief of the office, and his thirty-four-year-old colleague, Pat Hanly, were aggressive and confident, more like state prosecutors. More like Mike Cabral or the other Los Angeles deputy DAs with whom Lucero usually worked.

An assistant U.S. attorney from L.A. had described Captain Marvin Casey of Bakersfield as "folksy," and "unsure of what he had." But Carl Faller saw him as shrewd, with full knowledge of what he had, right from the very beginning.

Carl Faller said of Marvin Casey, "When all is said and done, he's the ball game."

So they were back to the baseball metaphors, and the Mighty Casey was going to get another at bat.

Assistant U.S. Attorney Carl Faller liked to say that he lived by an axiom taught to him by an old cop when he was a young prosecutor:

"Don't screw up good police work." That alone endeared him to the task force, who believed that they had done some *very* good police work.

Matassa and Hanly hit it off at once. Matassa liked to address the young prosecutor as "Paddy, me boy" because of Hanly's Irish roots, which had been planted in the soil of Solvang, a famous Danish community near Santa Barbara. Hanly explained that Solvang had originally been settled by the Irish, but because the Irish are such a disorganized lot, the Danes took over and turned it into a tourist mecca to celebrate Danish pride.

When the prosecutors first met John Orr and his lawyer, Douglas McCann, in their office, Hanly made an observation about the defendant: "When we shook hands, his was fleshy, pasty; it was a small feminine hand. He just didn't strike me as a fireman."

Pat Hanly made it a point never to speak a word to the defendant either in the courtroom or out of it, and as to Douglas McCann's fast-talking nervous style, they said he talked like Daffy Duck.

Prosecution and defense were mutually contemptuous. John Orr said that Carl Faller was "a sneaky, backstabbing kind of prosecutor," and that Pat Hanly was "snide and slippery," always asking questions that he knew would result in an objection. The only lawyer in the case whom John hated more than the prosecutors was his own.

John did his share of interviews, including extensive sessions with his hometown newspaper, the *Glendale News-Press*, which also excerpted his novel, *Points of Origin*. He'd been featured on *Inside Edition,* but he accused them of "manipulating the interview." He was never happy with his television coverage, believing that TV journalists existed just to sandbag people for ratings.

The prosecutors had received a few offers from the defense that they'd rejected. The first was the offer to take a polygraph. The prosecutors believed that a polygraph would be useless. Their thinking was that a psychopath's underdeveloped superego, or conscience, made him unfit for the polygraph. An ego like a cruise missile, a superego like a BB, is how they looked at John Orr.

Then the defense had another idea: "How about a plephysmograph?" they asked.

And when the prosecutors said, "A what?" it was explained that a sensor could be attached to John Orr's frontispiece in order to measure blood flow, thus signifying an erection. It had been used with some success on child molesters in clinical settings.

The prosecutors said no, videos of burning buildings and brush fires and Campfire Girls roasting wienies probably wouldn't prove much. They said that even though the fictional arsonist was always waxing his carrot at fire scenes, having John Orr hang a wire on his wang wouldn't be admissible even if he did get a woody.

John Orr said well, he was game for just about any *other* test they could devise.

The press flocked to the courthouse for the first day of trial, Tuesday, July 21, 1992. Presiding was U.S. District Court Judge Oliver W. Wanger, a snowy-haired jurist known for his relaxed, laid-back courtroom and his booming voice.

The defendant, who'd been staying at a Fresno hotel under his lawyer's supervision, looked scholarly in a tweed jacket, a subdued necktie, glasses, and a gray-streaked beard.

The government lawyers had charged John Leonard Orr with five counts of arson: two in Fresno, one in Tulare, and two in Bakersfield. Judge Wanger began by explaining to the jury the difference between direct and circumstantial evidence. He used the example of a witness seeing a man take a gun from the trunk of a car, which was direct evidence, and a witness seeing a man standing by the open trunk and being found to have a gun. That was circumstantial evidence. The judge gave the obligatory admonishment about not reading any news articles or listening to any radio or TV reports about the case, and everyone thought, Fat chance. You couldn't walk without slipping on the drool left by slavering hordes of reporters.

Assistant U.S. Attorney Pat Hanly handled the opening argument, and after asking that witnesses be excluded from the courtroom, he described for the jury how John Leonard Orr, after attending an arson conference in Fresno, had set five fires in the Central Valley, then returned home and wrote a book about it.

He described the incendiary delay devices found in Tulare, Bakersfield, and Fresno at the retail establishments, and he used the term *signature device*. Of course, he talked about the fingerprint collected by Captain

Marvin Casey, and how it was eventually matched with the defendant's left ring fingerprint.

Hanly sketched the surveillance to San Luis Obispo when the tracking device was discovered by the defendant, as well as the defendant's failure to ever come forward to ask why he'd been targeted. Lastly, he discussed the letters that John Orr had written to agents and publishers discussing the arson series, including: "I was even considered a suspect at one point."

When Hanly's synopsis was concluded, Douglas McCann began his opening argument by discussing the arson conference, and pointing out that the defendant had received a "completion certificate" for attendance, implying that John Orr must have been there until the end of the last day, during the time in which fires were being set. He was concentrating on an alibi for the hours between 8:00 A.M. and noon on January 16, 1987.

McCann agreed with the government's thesis that one man had set all five fires, but not the man at counsel table. He disputed "consciousness of guilt," wherein the prosecutors maintained that because John Orr hadn't come forward after knowing he was a suspect, one could infer culpability. He summarized the evidence found in the black bag in the defendant's car, and implied that all the things in that bag were tools for an arson class that John Orr had been teaching, and that his partner, Joe Lopez, would verify it.

As to the most damaging piece of evidence, the fingerprint collected by Marvin Casey, McCann informed the jury that in 1989, a Department of Justice fingerprint expert had examined the defendant's fingerprint, but had found no match. And that two years later someone else supposedly found a match, and because of that two-year gap and stark difference in the analysis—and because Marvin Casey hadn't written a date on that piece of notebook paper—the jury could question whether it actually had come from the arson attempt or had been fabricated.

John Orr's attorney was more than hinting at task-force malfeasance by then, and he discussed John Orr's superior, Battalion Chief Christopher Gray, from whom the task force had heard details in October 1991 about the manuscript, according to the prosecution's version of events.

McCann then said, "Now the government, probably Mr. Matassa, will probably say, the first time he ever saw that manuscript was some time after the positive comparison. But we believe the evidence will show that the government had made contact with Mr. Gray prior to this positive comparison. And if it wasn't for the manuscript, there never would have been a positive comparison. That's what the evidence will show. That's why we are here today. At some point in time, the government decided, 'He's our suspect, let's follow him. Let's surveil him.' "

McCann concluded his opening with: "A big part of this case will be the manuscript in relationship to the fingerprint, and whether or not that yellow paper came from that particular fire."

It would be fair to say that the task force and prosecutors were very surprised. The defense case was almost completely based upon a government frame-up. An elaborate frame-up which would include Marvin Casey, unnamed fingerprint examiners at the L.A. County Sheriff's Department, the task-force investigators, and possibly the assistant U.S. attorneys, Stefan Stein and Walter Brown.

This would be a vast government conspiracy, even though, as Pat Hanly put it, "We're working for a government that can't conspire to get out of its own way. A government that can't get us our paychecks on time. A government that always leaks everything."

Hanly thought that Douglas McCann had picked a losing strategy. McCann had not only hurled down the gauntlet, he'd also thrown at them his sword, shield, and horse—the whole goddamn thing!

Hanly wondered how a former law enforcer could strike out at other law enforcers but *not* take the stand in his own defense. Now it seemed that John Orr *must* testify.

Prosecutor Carl Faller immediately wanted to meet head-on any defense assertion that the author of *Points of Origin* wrote about the fire series in the Central Valley only after learning about it from Fresno arson investigator Tom Kuczynski.

The important portion of Kuczynski's testimony began when Faller asked, "Now, after the fire took place in 1987, at some later time did you have an occasion to discuss this particular case with the defendant, John Orr?"

The witness said, "I asked him if he knew of any commercial buildings that were set on fire while they were open for business, and where a device was used. He said, basically, he hadn't heard of anything. And he told me about a hardware-store fire that he had a few years prior."

That testimony by the witness effectively countered any suggestion that "Ski," as he was called, had provided details to John Orr about the Central Valley fire series, including that an arson investigator from the Fresno conference was suspected, details that had wound up in John Orr's novel.

And if prosecutors Faller and Hanly were not very interested in the last few words in the witness's answer, another prosecutor certainly was: Michael J. Cabral from the Los Angeles District Attorney's Office, who had come to attend a part of the trial. The "hardware-store fire" that John Orr had gratuitously brought up to Kuczynski was the Ole's fire, which apparently had never been far from the defendant's consciousness.

Another witness that day testified that he'd worked at House of Fabrics, a few stores away from Hancock Fabrics, and that two weeks after the Hancock Fabrics fire he discovered the remains of an incendiary device in a pile of pillow stuffing. It was the first time the jury would hear from a witness about the cigarette, matches, and rubber band, which they would come to know as a "signature device."

The day's final witness had worked in Tulare at Family Bargain Center, and testified to a small fire and the finding of a delay device in a pile of pillows. The witness provided the jury another look at the cigarette, matches, and rubber band, but this time a piece of notebook paper had been found, partially intact.

Pat Hanly then gave this witness a chance to directly place the defendant at the crime scene when he asked, "Did you see anybody in the store who stuck in your mind, either before or after the fire?"

"Yeah," the witness answered, "there was a man that entered the store . . . basically looking down at a piece of paper in his hand."

"Could you describe the piece of paper for us?"

"It was a piece of yellow legal pad," the witness replied.

And then after some testimony about the yellow notepaper being blank, and the customer looking down at it, he recounted the description of the man that he'd given to investigators:

"He had dark hair, black hair, probably five-ten, medium build, mid-twenties, is what I put in the report."

And because the defendant was nearly thirty-eight years old at the time of the fire, Hanly asked, "Now, would you please tell us what mid-twenties means to you?"

The witness replied, "It's hard to judge somebody's age. I would say mid-twenties could be anywhere from twenty-four, twenty-five, up to maybe thirty-two, thirty-four."

As soon as the jurors were in place the next morning, the prosecution called its star witness, Marvin Casey, who began by testifying that he was a fire captain for the city of Bakersfield with twenty-five years of service. He listed his bona fides as an expert in fire cause-and-origin analysis, and arson investigation. Then they got down to it—the attempted arson at CraftMart on January 16, 1987.

Casey testified that there'd been a fire in a display rack and that he saw, in the dry powder from the store's fire extinguisher, the incendiary delay device: a cigarette, matches, rubber band, and scorched piece of yellow lined notebook paper. He described his careful collecting and packaging of the evidence.

Because of Douglas McCann's opening statement about the notebook paper not being dated, Hanly asked the witness: "On January sixteenth, did you initial the yellow lined paper and date it?"

"No," Casey answered.

"And why is that?"

"I didn't do it because I was afraid I'd mess up the evidence. I would never have initialed it, like I wouldn't have initialed the cigarette match device either. I wouldn't have put any mark on them."

Hanly asked if he'd initialed and dated anything, and the witness informed the jury of the protocol: he'd initialed and dated the evidence envelope, not the evidence inside it.

When he was asked if he'd taken photos at the store of the entire device, he said that he had not. When asked why, he responded, "Well, at the time I was dealing with just a fifty-dollar loss of some dry floral arrangements, and I didn't feel it necessary to take photographs. I had conducted what I considered to be a thorough investigation, so I felt like that was enough."

The irony was not lost on those familiar with the convoluted Pillow Pyro investigation. The seemingly insignificant arson attempt might become the key to unlock all of it—from the Ole's catastrophe through the astonishing arson series in retail stores through the College Hills fire where sixty-six homes were burned—all of it.

The first questions that Douglas McCann had for Marvin Casey concerned Casey's decision not to photograph the intact incendiary device when and where it was found at the fire scene, rather than back at the office.

McCann said, "So there's not one document anywhere that will tell us that this yellow piece of paper existed on January sixteenth, 1987. There's no document anywhere that will tell us that, is there?"

"No," Casey answered.

"And this report was made on the date of the fire?"

"Yes."

"You ever heard of the term 'chain of custody'?"

"Yes," Casey answered, with that blue-eyed Panhandle squint that said: You are pissing me off, boy!

There followed a series of short questions about missing links in the chain of custody, dealing with absent evidence envelopes and how some investigators had initialed the yellow notepaper, and the fact that it had only been signed by Casey in September 1991, when the government was putting together its case for the search warrant.

McCann said, "You didn't want to disturb anything on that yellow paper. That's why you didn't put a little pencil mark—'one-sixteen-eighty-seven'—is that what you are saying?"

"That's correct," Casey answered.

Then, after trying to indicate that the packaging, forwarding, unpackaging, and examining of the yellow notebook paper was sloppy if not suspicious, McCann said, "You have testified that you are an expert in cause and origin?"

"Yes," Casey answered.

"In fact, have you attended classes that John Orr instructed?"

"That's correct," Casey answered.

Questions continued coming fast, and not for the last time, the court reporter had to ask McCann to slow down his hyperkinetic delivery. The thrust of the questions was designed to persuade the jury that the piece of notebook paper in the courtroom was not the paper that Casey had found, especially because the paper had been torn into two pieces.

Nothing had been implied as yet about Casey being part of a conspiracy. At this juncture, the defense was hinting at careless collection and marking of evidence, and that Casey was there in court identifying a piece of paper that the government *told* him was the paper he'd collected in 1987, but that he really had no idea if it was or was not.

On the second day of the Fresno trial a *Los Angeles Times* news story was headlined: FIRE CAPTAIN CALLS ARSON TRIAL A CONSPIRACY.

> As his trial opened in U.S. District Court, Glendale Fire Capt. John Orr defiantly charged that the government's case linking him to five Central Valley arsons in January, 1987, is a conspiracy of lies to railroad an innocent man.
>
> "Have you seen the movie 'JFK'?" he asked The Times during a break in the opening arguments Tuesday. "They went down to the morgue and placed Oswald's hand on the butt of that rifle . . . The only difference is that my hand wasn't cold."

Well, that approach was guaranteed to draw a crowd in the court of public opinion, and it resulted in an inordinate amount of coverage in the print and electronic media. In 1992 the public's appetite for government conspiracy and police malfeasance already had been whetted, not just by the film *JFK*, but by the Rodney King beating and other high-profile cases.

John Orr didn't think that his thirty-two-year-old lawyer was old enough, smart enough, or even graceful enough. John Orr complained that his lawyer had tripped over his own briefcase three times while he was "flitting" around the courtroom. He thought McCann's machine-gun oratory was off-putting to the conservative folks of Fresno. And he deeply resented that his defense was costing him and Wanda forty thousand dollars.

But for all that, he had a lawyer with enormous intensity and belief in his client, and the fee was far less than many would have charged for such a difficult, time-consuming case. Douglas McCann had a good sense of humor, which his client was in no mood to appreciate, and his youthful high-wire style in the courtroom, with hair flying and eyes blazing—and the court reporter pleading for him to slow down—wasn't all bad, given what he was up against. The creation of reasonable doubt in the government's evidence was his only option. A phlegmatic approach when one is making an extravagant allegation against the U.S. government might not have carried the emotional appeal necessary. He needed, as it were, *fire* in his presentation.

Not the first to use the game of baseball in portraying his feelings about the crux of the case, McCann said, "Ordinarily, there's no defense against a fingerprint. It'll knock you right out of the box."

The defense was obliged to confront a former clerk from Hancock Fabrics in Bakersfield who had, in 1987, given a description that was very close to John Orr's at the time, and she related how she'd smelled cigarette smoke but that the suspect did not have a cigarette in his hand when she'd seen him. And she described how she'd picked John Orr out of a photo lineup. The defense did a good job with a good witness, and before she left the stand she admitted that she was only "seventy percent" certain that the defendant was the man she'd seen in the store.

The next witness called was Clive T. Barnum, the crusty fingerprint expert for ATF who'd been doing his job for thirty-five years. Barnum testified as to how he'd processed the piece of notebook paper that had been forwarded to his lab by Marvin Casey in 1987, and that the latent print that popped out of the ninhydrin solution was a very clear one that even a layman could read. The exchange between defense counsel and the grizzled lawman perked up the press a bit.

"Was it a pretty obvious make?" McCann asked Barnum, referring to the match.

"Well, I certainly think thirteen is a considerable number of points," Barnum answered, referring to the fingerprint points of comparison.

"If you were comparing an exemplar to a latent and there were seven points, you would make a note of it, correct?"

"Make a note of it how?"

"Would there be a number *less* than seven that you wouldn't draw a conclusion at?"

"There's no certain number you need for a positive identification of fingerprints," Barnum said.

"Even if there were only three points that matched?"

"I would have to see the print. I would have to examine it."

"Because it's more than just the points?"

"I know where you're going," Barnum said. "I know where you're going. I'd have to see the print."

"I don't think you're qualified as a psychic yet," McCann countered.

"Well, I know where you're going," Barnum repeated.

"Well, where am I going?" McCann challenged.

"You're going to start to count down."

"Actually, you *don't* know where I'm going. Where I'm going is, I'd like to know if you had five or six points of comparison, in *some* situations you'd draw a conclusion that there was a match, isn't that true?"

Not buying into hypotheticals, the crafty old fingerprint expert said, "I'd have to *see* the print."

When McCann asked how long a latent fingerprint could remain on a piece of paper, Barnum answered, "Forty years, under laser enhancement."

Carl Faller's next witness was Jerry Taylor, an explosives-enforcement officer for ATF who testified to M.O., crucial in linking this fire series as well as establishing a foundation for a future prosecution of the Los Angeles series. After lengthy testimony about incendiary delay devices, including how and where they were placed and in what sort of retail stores, Faller asked, "Now, based upon your training and experience, did you come to the conclusion as to whether the fires were started by the same individual?"

The witness replied, "Those fires were not only started by the same individual, but the same individual built the devices."

The last and most important witness of the day was Michael Matassa, and Doug McCann had to do his damage now if he had any chance of suggesting a government frame-up.

After being sworn, Mike Matassa informed the jury that he was the case agent in the matter at hand, and like almost every other law-enforcement witness, he said he'd been personally acquainted with the defendant for several years.

The first question from Pat Hanly seemed innocent enough, but it would prompt a lot of cross-examination. The prosecutor asked: "Now, could you please tell the ladies and gentlemen of the jury, when did Mr. Orr first become a suspect in this case?"

Mike Matassa answered, "April seventeenth, 1991."

"And why on that date?" Hanly asked.

"Because of a positive comparison by the Los Angeles Sheriff's Department between the known print of John Orr and a latent print that was recovered from the CraftMart device."

"Have you had an opportunity to review the manuscript *Points of Origin?*"

"Yes, I have."

"Now, how many different versions of the manuscript have you read?"

"Two."

"What is the difference?"

"Primarily, one version is shorter, and in that version the incendiary device consists of a match attached to a cigarette. In the second version, the incendiary device consists of a glob of glue attached to a cigarette."

"When did you become aware of the existence of the manuscript?"

"Late June or July of 1991."

"And how did that happen?"

"We became aware of that from Fire Marshal Chris Gray of the Glendale Fire Department."

The prosecutor then asked the witness to generally describe the story line, and Mike Matassa talked about Aaron Stiles, the arsonist, and how he travels to Fresno and sets fires in fabric stores, and also in Tulare and Bakersfield, always in foam products, using a delay device.

Then Hanly asked, "Is there any discussion in the book about what would happen if the arsonist knew that the information about the fires was being disseminated to law-enforcement agencies?"

The witness answered, "Yes, that he would then cease starting the fires."

"Is there any mention in the book about fires and their relationship to Fresno?"

"Yes, that they are always started close to the freeway."

Hanly then asked the witness to examine what Matassa called "the shorter version" of the manuscript, which was actually the first three chapters.

"When did you first become aware of this shorter version?" the prosecutor asked.

"December fourth, 1991," Matassa replied, indicating the day of arrest.

The witness described the material found at the time of the defendant's arrest, including the photos of the tracking device, paper bags, cigarettes, matches, rubber bands, and lighters. Then came questions about the interview of the prisoner at the police station.

"How would you characterize the defendant's attitude during the interview?" the prosecutor asked.

"It was a cat-and-mouse game. He was probing, trying to see how much information we had, how much evidence we had on him."

Of course, the defense objected to Matassa's conclusion, and the court sustained it. But Hanly wanted to stay with it and tried to lay a foundation that would permit Matassa to characterize the prisoner's responses.

Matassa told the jury that he'd conducted hundreds of interviews, and Hanly asked, "In fact, have you attended classes with the defendant on that subject?"

"Yes," the witness replied.

"And in those classes, did you go over how to interview witnesses?"

"Yes, we did."

Then, despite Douglas McCann's objection, the court permitted the witness to answer the next question: "How did the witness respond to your questioning?"

"By asking us questions along the lines of what type of evidence we had."

"And did he indicate whether he had actually found the tracking device?"

"Yes, he did. He said it made good grist for his book."

"During the interview, was the defendant asked anything about explaining his conduct?"

"Yes, we asked him if once he became convinced that we did have a case on him, would he then be willing to talk to us. And he said he would not close the door on that."

"Previous to that did the defendant say anything about lies?"

"Yes, he said he had interviewed hundreds of witnesses, and lying and guessing was part of the game. He implied that that's what he thought we were doing."

"That the evidence was all lies?"

"And guessing."

The prosecution then introduced the letters to literary agents and publishers, and had Matassa read them for the jury.

When the witness was given to the defense for cross-examination, Doug McCann had what he thought was a big surprise for the witness.

"One of the very first questions the government asked today was whether John Orr became a suspect on April seventeenth, 1991. Do you recall that question?"

"That's correct."

"Are you sure about that? Is that what you testified to here today?"

"April seventeenth is the day that the sheriff's department made the fingerprint comparison."

"He wasn't a suspect on April sixteenth, was he?"

"No."

Mike Matassa was obviously puzzled, not only by the question, but by the obvious relish with which it was asked.

McCann then dropped the hammer: "All right, are you aware that one week prior to April sixteenth, 1991, in Atascadero, California, Ken Croke had a photographic lineup with John Orr's photo in it? A week *before* this fingerprint result? You are not aware of that?"

The baffled witness replied, "That's not possible."

"Okay. It wouldn't be possible that he was a suspect a week before April seventeenth, 1991, because you said he wasn't a suspect until the fingerprint match, correct?"

"That's correct. I put the lineup together, and I did not have it done until July of 1991."

Then Douglas McCann didn't just drop the hammer, he fired both barrels. "Mr. Matassa, isn't it true that you had the manuscript *prior* to April seventeenth, 1991?"

"That is *not* true," the defendant said.

"Okay, and it's not possible that Ken Croke was showing this photograph of John Orr as a suspect in this case. That's not possible, is it?"

The witness looked from one prosecutor to another and said, "I don't understand how that could be."

"Now, you are under oath here today, right?"

"That's correct, sir."

"Did you make an affidavit in this case?"

"Yes."

"Did you lie in that affidavit?"

"No, I did not."

Hanly said, "Your Honor, I'm going to object on the ground that that is argumentative."

"I will withdraw that last question," McCann said. "I'm sorry." Then he came right back and asked, "Did you make false statements in that affidavit?"

"No," Matassa said.

"You've seen the photo lineup?"

"Yes, I had it prepared."

"Okay, when was the photograph of John Orr taken?"

"I would say in July of '91."

"Do you know where it was taken?"

"I believe it was at a FIRST meeting."

"Therefore, you are saying it's impossible that on April ninth and April eleventh Ken Croke was showing John Orr's photograph in Atascadero? That's an impossibility?"

"He was not a suspect at that time," Matassa repeated.

There were many questions about the interview with John Orr until Pat Hanly objected that the defense counsel was "rambling at the witness." After which McCann objected to the government's accusing him of rambling, and it was becoming clear that the lawyers wanted to spit on each other.

McCann's questions then tried to demonstrate to the jury that the government sometimes tells intentional lies. The witness admitted that the agents were instructed to lie to John Orr in order to obtain a copy of the manuscript through a retired arson investigator who also wrote books, and that they'd asked the San Luis Obispo police to lie about the tracking device.

The defense settled for those lies, called it a day, and the trial was recessed until the next morning.

12

ERRORS

O n the morning of the third day McCann got right at Mike Matassa: "Yesterday you told us it was an impossibility that Ken Croke would've been showing John Orr's photograph on April ninth, 1991, in Atascadero. Are you going to change your testimony since yesterday or is that still your testimony?"

"It was impossible for him to have been showing John Orr's photograph prior to April seventeenth, 1991," Matassa declared.

McCann then asked a couple of clever questions.

"You read these letters. These were letters to agents. Did you take them literally? For example, when John Orr says that there's an arsonist and he's a fireman. Did you take that literally that he knows there is an arsonist who's a fireman?"

"Yes, I believe he knew that there was one," Matassa answered.

"Did you also take literally the statement that he made, 'And by the way, I'm not the arsonist.' You didn't take that one literally, did you?"

"No, I did not."

"So you chose *which* portions you would take as true statements and which ones were false statements?"

"I chose that decision based upon the evidence that I'd uncovered during the investigation."

"Including the fact that in 1989 they'd compared his fingerprints and said it wasn't his print? Did you consider that?"

On redirect, Pat Hanly gave the witness a chance to read part of the transcription of the defendant's interrogation. Matassa read the words of John Orr:

"I want to know what's going on. I know how the game works."

The longest response involved a desire to know what the task force had by way of evidence: "I want to get ahold of your reports too. If I got to do this, I'm going to have to access all the reports. So if you are charging me with certain things, I have to start working on some kind of a defense for some of this stuff. I'm trying to control myself. I'm really, really pissed. I've never been in this position before. I won't close the door on anything, so I want to know as much as you got."

Matassa's superior, Larry Cornelison, asked, "Why? Why did you do this?" The defendant answered, "Larry, I can't talk about it. I just can't talk about it. I don't know where this is going."

When it was again his turn, McCann asked the witness: "When he says, 'I'm not closing the door on anything,' isn't it possible that what he meant was, 'Hey, look, tell me what you've got'? That he was trying to pursue what this was all about?"

"Exactly. To find out what we had on him," Matassa replied.

And after a lengthy sidebar about where the defense was heading, it became time for Doug McCann to prove that Mike Matassa was lying about *when* John Orr had become a suspect in the Pillow Pyro investigation. McCann approached the witness with reports of photo spreads and interviews.

"Mr. Matassa," McCann said, "have you ever seen this report which is initialed at the bottom by Ken Croke?"

"I would assume that somewhere along the line I must have seen it," Matassa said.

"And a final document signed by Ken Croke marked April ninth, 1991. You must have seen these documents, is that what you are saying?"

"I *must* have," Matassa repeated.

"I thought you said it was impossible that Ken Croke was in Atascadero before the positive fingerprint comparison? Now are you changing that?"

"No, I did not say that."

"What did you say?"

"I said it was impossible that he was showing a photo of John Orr. I did *not* say it was impossible for him to have been in Atascadero prior to April seventeenth."

"Don't they indicate that John Orr was in a photo spread prior to April sixteenth, 1991?"

"They are incorrect," Matassa said, simply.

"These federal government reports . . . let's be clear about this, the ones in front of you, prepared by Croke, are *incorrect*?"

"That's correct."

"All *four* of them? And they are all dated April ninth and April eleventh? They are all incorrect?"

"They have to be incorrect, because no photo lineup of John Orr existed prior to July of '91."

"So, by looking at those four reports, Special Agent Ken Croke was wrong four times?"

"Yes."

And there it was. The implication of frame-up was boiling down to a rookie ATF agent confusing the dates of two different photo spreads on reports he'd written months after the fact. The media onlookers were disappointed.

Television trials later in the decade would reveal to the general public that even the highest-profile cases are fraught with law-enforcement errors both large and small. Ken Croke was brought to Fresno to confess to his minor mistake. There was also the large error in the Pillow Pyro investigation committed by ATF agents who'd failed to properly secure the tracking device to John Orr's car. But the next witness was about to tell the jury about the gravest error of all.

Richard Kinney was a middle-aged, balding, bespectacled employee of the California Department of Justice who must have known very well what observers in the courtroom were thinking, those who believed that John Orr was guilty of all that had been charged and later would be charged in the courtrooms of Los Angeles. Kinney had to have known they were thinking that if he hadn't made his error, the Pillow Pyro fires would never have occurred, the College Hills fire would never have happened, and God only knew how many other fires. One had to admire the courage of the studious witness as he took the stand, preparing to fall on his sword.

After stating his qualifications as an expert with vast experience as a latent-print analyst and teacher of criminology, Richard Kinney told the jury that he'd testified as an expert in courtrooms on at least four hundred occasions.

When they got to it, Hanly asked, "What did you look at in 1989 when you made your report?"

Kinney held the photo of Marvin Casey's latent fingerprint evidence in his hands and said, "I looked at this particular photograph along with machine copies of inked fingerprints of individuals."

"Was one of those individuals the defendant, John Orr?"

"Yes," the witness replied.

"Did you come up with a conclusion in 1989 as to whether that latent print matched any of the subjects you compared?"

"I did."

"What was that conclusion?"

"I was unable to make a match against any subject. However, I felt the print was usable, meaning identifiable."

"Now, did there come a time after 1989 where you again compared a latent print to John Orr's known prints?"

"Yes."

"When did that occur?"

"That occurred on November seventh, 1991."

"And what was your conclusion?"

"At that time I was able to identify the impression with that of a subject named John Orr."

"And what finger did the analysis reveal that to be?"

"It would be the left ring finger."

"And can you explain why you reached that conclusion in '91 but not in '89?"

"Well," the witness began, "I had a second opportunity to look at the impression. I was also given better material with which to make my examination. And I also had information that the impression was, in fact, identified by other individuals. In fact, three other individuals."

The unfortunate witness was then handed over for cross-examination, and Doug McCann wasted no time: "Why would you *care* what another fingerprint expert found? You don't have enough faith in your own abilities?"

"When a fingerprint expert is confronted, he's got to prove the other expert wrong," the witness said.

"You testified here that what you looked at in 1989 was a usable and identifiable print. Correct?"

"That is correct."

"So it wasn't that poor, was it?"

"The latent print wasn't that poor."

"And in your report in '89, your conclusion was that it was a negative result?"

"Correct."

"Your conclusion is that you did not make a mistake in 1989, or you did?"

"I did."

"You did make a mistake in 1989?"

"Oh, yes," the beleaguered witness repeated.

"Is that the first time that's ever happened?"

"No."

"Happens all the time?"

"No."

"It's only happened *once* in twenty-two years?"

"To my knowledge it's happened two different times," the witness replied.

"How many prints have you looked at over all those years?"

"Millions," the witness answered, wearily.

Millions. The courtroom observers could only feel for the avuncular, bookish man on the witness stand. Could only imagine him at a table, maybe wearing an eyeshade—Bob Cratchit on Christmas Eve—day after day, staring at loops, whorls, and arches. And breaking those down to ending ridges, bifurcations, trifurcations, bridges, spurs, and the rest of it. For twenty-two years. Millions. He'd examined *millions* of fingerprints! And this had only been his second known mistake.

But this one was a pip.

On the fourth day the prosecution had no more witnesses, but before the defense witnesses could be called there was more bickering at the bench, and it was growing ever more hostile as the trial wore on. It quickly became personal when Doug McCann said, "Excuse me,Your Honor, the U.S. government is laughing as I'm speaking. I find that rather disrespectful."

When all of the lawyering was concluded at the bench, the defense called a customer of Hancock Fabrics who had been there on that cool winter evening when the terrifying fire struck. And for the first time, the jury would be given an idea of just how fast and violently a fire can build when given a fuel load of foam products.

Customer Mary Dummler described it vividly: "I saw a little puff of smoke in the back of the far corner. And it went from a kind of a wispy circular smoke suddenly to dark gray. You know, swirling puffy smoke. And then that exploded into flames!"

"Did you run out of the store then?" McCann asked.

"Not immediately. I said, 'There's a fire! That's a fire in the corner!' And it just started to jump. There were children in the store at the time. A mother with children, and the flames just went so quickly. And they literally jumped to the next row of fabric. And jumped! And within minutes the whole store was in flames and the lights had gone out and people were screaming and calling for help!"

There were a few chills up the back on that hot July afternoon in Fresno. It began to register in the minds of the courtroom throng just how it is possible for people to die a horrible death while shopping in a well-lighted, well-tended retail store. Where there is safety and security one minute, and the next . . . The astonishment was still in the faces of those witnesses who had been in the store. How could that terrible *thing* move that *fast*?

Defense witness Joe Lopez was six foot three, very fit, with salt-and-pepper sideburns: a recruiting-poster firefighter. He testified to having ten and a half years of fire-fighting experience, and more than a year as a full-time arson investigator and partner of John Orr.

The witness testified to the training sessions that he and his partner had conducted with incendiary devices made from a cigarette and matchbooks. And then came questions about the black bag that the task force had seized on the morning of John Orr's arrest.

"You had been inside the bag at some point?" McCann asked, trying to show that had there been anything sinister in that bag, the witness would have seen it.

"Yes, I had."

"How did that occur?"

"During two of the classes, I believe, we were having copies made at a copy center and John had forgotten his checkbook, which was located inside the bag in the trunk of his vehicle. He asked me if I wouldn't mind going out and getting the checkbook. That happened several times. And there was one other time that I can remember when we were at the police department and he needed some papers that were in there, so I volunteered to go out and get those for him."

"Now, what was your relationship to John Orr? Professionally?"

"We spent the majority of the workdays together, and we also spent a lot of off-duty time together preparing for the classes. And socializing at times."

"Was your office right next to his?"

"We had two desks in the same office facing each other."

"Was he your mentor, so to speak?"

"Well, he was training me, yes."

Then McCann got to the items that had been found in the bag. "Have you ever seen John Orr collect fire-scene evidence with brown paper bags?"

"Yes."

"Have you ever seen John Orr construct any incendiary devices that included yellow lined paper?"

"No, I have not."

"At some point in time, did you ever become aware that John Orr was writing anything?"

"Yes. At times he would have portions of his book on his desk, and I think I may have seen it and asked him about it."

When Pat Hanly took over, he bored into the credibility of the witness.

"So is it your testimony today that you have been inside Mr. Orr's black canvas bag, Mr. Lopez?"

"Yes."

"Do you recall testifying at a hearing on December tenth, 1991, in Los Angeles District Court?"

"Yes, I testified during that time period."

"Do you recall the following question being asked of you: 'Are you aware that Mr. Orr has a black canvas briefcase?' "

"Yes."

"Do you remember the following question: 'Have you ever looked inside that briefcase?' "

"Yes."

"And do you remember the following answer: 'No, I have not'?"

"Yes."

"Now would you like to change that testimony today?"

"No."

"You are aware, Mr. Lopez, are you not, that you are under oath today as well?"

"Yes. May I have an opportunity to explain my reason?"

"Go ahead."

"When I was asked at that time, I felt that the question was, had I ever gone into John's bag. The answer is no, I had never gone into John's bag *on my own*. After that I was trying to remember. I couldn't remember the specific times or the consequences if I ever had gone into the bag. And I recalled that there were several instances when it happened. At that time, I called up Stefan Stein from the U.S. Attorney's Office and told him yes, I *do* remember being in John's bag several times. And I also called up Douglas McCann and relayed the same information to him."

"But on December tenth, 1991, when you were asked point-blank under oath, 'Have you ever looked inside that briefcase?' you said, 'No, I have not.' Is that true?"

"That's true."

"But then after that was over, you had a sudden epiphany and realized, 'Oh, my gosh! I *have* looked in that bag before!' Even though you were asked twice and said 'No,' twice, under oath. Is that correct?"

"Yes."

"And do you think your testimony today is influenced in any way by your relationship with the defendant?"

"No, I don't."

"You *are* a close friend of his, is that correct?"

"I'm a friend of John's, yes."

"Have you ever undertaken any efforts whatsoever since his arrest to assist him in his defense?"

"No, I'm not part of John's defense team at all."

"No, but I mean have you done *anything,* provided funds or anything?"

"I provided funds to the John Orr family, to John Orr and his wife, for food, yes."

"Did he ever tell you that he considered himself a suspect at one point in the investigation?"

"Not that I can recall."

"Now, are you aware of any investigation regarding a firefighter who is also suspected of being a serial arsonist?"

"No."

"You would take steps, would you not, to investigate this firefighter/serial arsonist?"

"Yes, I would."

"If you found yourself to be in a situation where you were a suspect in an arson investigation, Joe Lopez, would *you* contact somebody to find out what was going on?"

"Yes, I would."

"If you found a transmitter on the bottom of your car and believed that you were a suspect, and you had been contacted by ATF on two previous occasions about arson fires, would you then call ATF?"

"Not necessarily."

"That wouldn't cross your mind?

"Well, we have contact with a lot of various agencies, and we might have contact with L.A. City, L.A. County, or ATF during that time period too."

"Sorry, you must have misunderstood me," Hanly said. "You are being followed. You have a tracking device on your car. And you find out that the frequency number and the PIN number belongs to ATF. And you were previously contacted by two ATF agents, one of whom just happened to leave his card. Are you going to contact ATF, and ask *why* his tracking device is on your car?"

"Most likely. Yes," the witness said.

13

VERDICT

Ironically, Douglas McCann was late for court on day five, delayed for three hours because of a fire on the freeway. And it had *not* been set by the defendant.

The first issue was facial hair. The time had arrived for the defense to introduce evidence that the defendant had a full beard in January 1987, and could not possibly have been the person with the "Don Johnson" stubble whom witnesses had chosen from the task-force mug shots. The defense had photos to prove their contention, in an album that the prosecution had not seen.

Hanly said to the judge, "I think the problem here is the fact that, *mysteriously,* a photograph shows up in this scrapbook which just happens to have 'one-seventeen-eighty-seven' written on it. It seems a little strange that all of a sudden this photograph would come up, not having been received in discovery, and just happened to have been taken the day after the January sixteenth, 1987, fires."

But prior to the appearance of Wanda Orr to testify about the photos, the defense called Conway Lu, the former employee of CraftMart in Bakersfield, where the crucial fingerprint evidence had been found. Referring to arson investigator Marvin Casey, the witness said, "The guy came in and was digging around and he says, 'Well here it is.' "

"Then what happened?" McCann asked.

"I said, 'What did you find?' And he pulled out a book of matches, a cigarette butt, and some burnt paper."

"Was he then talking to you and showing you what he'd found?"

"He explained how it worked because I asked him."

"You said some burnt paper. What color was it?"

"Yellow, if I recall."

"Did he show you the cigarette?"

"It was a cigarette butt that had been scorched."

"And he showed you a *matchbook*?"

"Yes."

"In terms of the yellow paper, was it one piece or two pieces?"

"It was two pieces that were . . . well, that looked like they should've been one piece at one time."

"But it was in *two* pieces?"

"Yeah."

This witness was perhaps the last and best hope to perpetuate the idea of a government frame-up. Marvin Casey had testified that the notebook paper was in one piece when he'd found it, and two pieces when it came back from the lab after processing. And he'd said nothing about a matchbook, which ran counter to the government's description of an unusual signature device.

Hanly's cross-examination went to the crux of the testimony: "You said that the Bakersfield fireman showed you the actual device, is that correct?"

"He kind of explained how it worked."

"And he showed you some yellow lined paper?"

"Some paper, a book of matches, a cigarette butt."

"Was it a *book* of matches or was it just individual matches and a cigarette butt?"

"If I recall, it was a book of matches."

"But are you *sure* about that?"

"It's been five years. It's hard to say."

Hanly then showed the witness Marvin Casey's photo of the incendiary evidence he'd recovered.

"Does that look like the paper you were shown on the date of the fire?"

"It's hard for me to say. It's been five years. It could be."

"So that *could* be the paper you saw on the day of the fire. Is that correct?"

"It could be."

"That's all I have, Your Honor," Hanly said.

Doug McCann tried to rehabilitate his witness with a series of short questions as to what he *did* recall.

"Do you recall there were dried flowers in the area?"

"Yes."

"Do you recall the name of the person who yelled out, 'Fire'?"

"Yes."

"There's a lot you recall about this, correct?"

"True."

"A lot of detail. In fact, you said you recalled a matchbook?"

"I *seem* to remember a matchbook, yes," the witness said.

It was time for the beard. Wanda Orr, the fourth wife of the defendant, took the stand. She was a petite woman, a few years older than John, an ethnic Hawaiian mix of Chinese and haole, soft spoken, wearing little makeup.

McCann's first question was, "Mrs. Orr, do you remember the date that you were married to John Orr?"

"November twenty-first, 1986," she replied.

And then McCann showed Wanda Orr the wedding photo of John with a beard, and asked, "Did you go on a honeymoon?"

"Yes, we did," she said.

McCann also showed a photo taken in December of that year, and the beard was there.

There was a sidebar with argument about a date written on the back of the crucial bearded photo, really about when the date was put there, the date being January 17, 1987, one day after the CraftMart fire.

When they got back to the witness, McCann asked, "What do you recognize about that photograph?"

"John, the house, the furniture on the lawn. We were having a garage sale."

"When was that?"

"I believe it was on the seventeenth."

"How is it that you remember it was January seventeenth?"

"This is from my album. I always date everything that goes into the album."

When it was time for cross-examination, Carl Faller took over: "Now, Mrs. Orr, do you recall specifically that the garage sale was on January seventeenth, 1987?"

"Yes, sir."

"How is it that you recall that?"

"Because the album states that."

"Right. But do *you* remember?"

"I remember the garage sale, yes."

"Well, do you remember the *date*?"

"It was a long time ago."

"I agree. So the only reason you are saying it's January seventeenth,'87, is because that was the date written in the album. Is that correct?"

"That's correct."

Then Faller carefully suggested that *somebody* had removed the photo from the album in order to add a date that would alibi the defendant: "Now, this particular photograph was taped into the album. Around the edges of the photograph, it appears that at one time it was *glued* into the album. Would you agree that there is residue of glue on the back around the edges?"

"Appears to be, yes," she said.

"Would it indicate that at one time it had been *glued* into the album, then removed and *taped* in the album?"

"No."

"Well, you wouldn't put both glue and tape on at the same time, would you?"

"No."

"How long did he have the beard after you were married?"

"I would just guess maybe February . . ."

McCann interrupted to say, "I don't want her to guess, Your Honor."

Faller said, "Well, he may not *want* her to, but she can give her best estimate of what she recalls."

"You may give your best estimate, Mrs. Orr," the judge said.

"February, March," she said. "I'm just guessing."

About the facial hair, the government called a woman as a rebuttal witness who allegedly had had dinner at the 1987 conference with John Orr during a time when he was "happily" married. Apparently, neither the government nor the defense cared to get into details of their evening together.

The rebuttal witness was a claims adjustor for a major insurance company. The questions to her were very brief and to the point.

"Have you had occasion to go to conferences concerning the subject of arson?" Carl Faller asked.

"I have actually only gone to one seminar," she replied.

"When was that?"

"It was in January 1987."

"Where did that take place?"

"In Fresno," she said.

"And while you were at that conference in January 1987, did you see the defendant, John Orr?"

"Yes."

"And when you saw the defendant Orr at the conference, did he have a full beard?"

"No," she replied.

"Thank you. No further questions," Faller said.

The judge said, "Mr. McCann?"

"No questions, Your Honor," said Doug McCann.

At 1:00 P.M. on the fifth day, the government addressed the jury with a closing argument. Patrick Hanly began his summation by reminding the jury that the defense agreed in opening statement that one person started all five fires: the two in Fresno on January 15, 1987, the one in Tulare on the sixteenth, and two in Bakersfield, also on the sixteenth.

It didn't take the prosecutor long to get into the defendant's manuscript, wherein his fictional arsonist started fires in a fabrics store that he called "Fabric Plus." Hanly also reminded the jury that in the novel there was a line which read, "Most of the fires started just off of the freeway," as did the actual fires.

Hanly described how the fire at the House of Fabrics fit the scenario of the fictional fabric store in the novel, and he reminded the jury that the defendant had checked out of his hotel at 6:51 A.M. on the last day of the seminar, and had all day to cruise down the freeway setting fires. With each and every point he made, Patrick Hanly would point to blowups of the text from *Points of Origin,* emphasizing again and again that the book was really not a novel but a diary.

As to the alleged conspiracy, he said, "There is no evidence whatsoever that the government had the manuscript before the fingerprint was identified. The defense has tried to paint a picture of how the government got the manuscript, and then magically, the defendant's fingerprint was discovered on the yellow piece of paper. Well, quite simply, that is not true."

Referring to the fingerprint expert from the Los Angeles County Sheriff's Department who had made the identification, he reminded them that the expert didn't know John Orr, didn't know he was writing a book, didn't know he was a fireman, didn't know anything about the case. The letters were summarized, and it appeared that they carried more weight with prosecutors than did the manuscript itself.

Some observers thought that more damaging than the letters was the testimony about the tracking device. Hanly said, "So at some point John Orr knows he's a suspect. Does he go to the police? Does he contact his superiors?

"If you recall Agent Matassa's testimony as he reread the manuscript, there was a passage about how, if the arsonist knew the government was on to him, the fires would stop. And guess what? After March twenty-ninth, 1991, they *stopped*."

The defense got its chance at 2:20 P.M., after a short recess.

"Good afternoon," defense counsel began. "As you are aware, the government gets two shots at closing argument. They will be able to respond to whatever I have to say here, and there are a couple of reasons for that. The court will tell you that the government bears the burden of proving the case beyond a reasonable doubt. And the fact that they argue twice, that's simply our system."

When he discussed his theory that the book manuscript was in the hands of the task force prior to the alleged fingerprint match, he said, "Why is Matassa so adamant that this guy was *not* a suspect until April seventeenth, 1991? It's obvious, because a week before that they have his photos in the lineup." That, in reference to the Ken Croke transposing dates on his photo spreads.

"How do we know if they had the manuscript or not? Guess what? In whatever month, it happened after the fingerprint match, according to their version."

It is possible that the defense lawyer's fervor and machine-gun oratory covered up some of the confusing syntax as to the fingerprint itself: "Because Casey comes in here and on direct testimony, talking about the yellow paper, he's looking over at the jury saying, 'I remember this. I remember that.' And I asked him some tough questions like 'Hey, there's no documentation.' He doesn't look over here. There is not documentation. Why should we say, 'Casey, you told us the truth'? Because you happen to work for the fire department? Because you happen to look like a guy who may tell the truth?"

He went on for a while about the framers of the Constitution, and the jury system, and how the witness Conway Lu told him that the yellow notebook paper looked different from what was presented in court.

And then he said, "Some yellow paper was found. This is what the government presents us, this came from that fire. Now, hold it a minute there. This thing is burnt. It looks like it came from a fire. The government can say defense counsel has not proved to you that there was a conspiracy, or that someone switched the paper. Hey, that's not our burden. It's their burden to slam-dunk it. You have the right to question if what they are telling you is true. Remember, this isn't Perry Mason. I didn't bring in the arsonist. That's not going to happen. It's not up to the defendant to bring in the actual guy."

Doug McCann portrayed the witnesses who were shown photo lineups as being uncertain or wrong, and he criticized Matassa for not showing the dissimilarities in the book manuscript along with the similarities.

As he was winding down, he returned to the fingerprint: "Total unreliability as to Casey. The guy was putting John Orr on his résumé. Are we going to believe Casey because he's a fire captain and we are not going to believe Conway Lu? Conway Lu is telling us that the paper is entirely different from what he saw. Conway Lu tells us that there were two pieces, not one piece. Casey said there was definitely *one* piece."

About the fingerprint expert, Richard Kinney, he said, "Kinney's conclusion in '89 was that there were negative results. That means a finding that the print was not the defendant's. . . . The bottom line is, the only natural conclusion is, he was not looking at the *same* latent print, because the positive match contained thirteen identifiable points at least. It was an obvious match. This taints the chain of custody again, because in the middle of all that, a guy is looking at a thing over a two-year period, and was looking at different things.

"The only natural conclusion is, he *wasn't* mistaken in 1989. He was looking at a latent print that wasn't John Orr's and he came to a conclusion that it wasn't John Orr's. He's in the same government that all these guys in suits are in.

"I'm just about finished here. The parties have agreed to certain facts that have been stated to you. . . . The government believes a man was seen at a fire scene by their witness. Defense counsel believes him. He saw the actual arsonist who was in his mid-twenties. How can you possibly say yes beyond a reasonable doubt when they are describing him in his mid-twenties? How can you say it's John Orr when the man was in his mid-twenties and he had jet-black hair? That's reasonable doubt as to Family Bargain Center, but also CraftMart. That's reasonable doubt as to all of the charges. Thank you very much."

Assistant U.S. Attorney Carl Faller wasted no time in closing arguments. He stood and said, "There's an old saying that's been around the courtrooms a lot longer than I have been, that says when the facts are against me, I argue the law. When the law is against me, I argue the facts. When they are both against me, I kind of stand up and scream like hell and then I put the prosecution on trial. I put the policemen on trial. I put the government on trial, trying to deflect attention from the evidence."

The prosecutor went point by point through Douglas McCann's closing argument, and then addressed the fingerprint evidence: "If it were a perfect world, this case should have been over in 1989, there's no doubt about that. The defendant should have been convicted three years ago, but he wasn't because Dick Kinney made a mistake."

When he got to the black bag seized on the day of arrest, Faller said, "Now, the idea, I suppose, is that the defense wants you to think that these items were here because the defendant was using them in training other firefighters, and there was some talk about one session that Joe Lopez went to where he was requested by the defendant to construct a device for one training session. Well, when you start to look at what's in here and start to realize how many packs of cigarettes this nonsmoker had, he must've been going to train every firefighter in Los Angeles."

The prosecutor reminded the jury about the tracking device, and that arsons at retail stores had stopped when the defendant was informed that the Pillow Pyro Task Force was in existence.

Referring to the manuscript, Faller said, "The Hancock Fabrics fire jumps out at you. You could see that building burning on the page. Every time we don't want to believe that an arson investigator like the defendant would be starting fires that he's sworn to put out, that he's putting the very people at risk that he's sworn to save, you keep running into another fact. And pretty soon, your common sense, your reason is just overwhelmed.

"Ladies and gentlemen," Faller continued, "the door is finally about to close. We don't care *why* he did it. All we care about, and all you can care about, is that he *did* it. And the evidence has proven that he did it. And based upon that, the only rational and reasonable verdict is that the defendant is guilty of each of the charges in the indictment. Thank you."

During recess when neither the judge nor the jury were in the courtroom, Carl Faller turned to the defense table, and referring to McCann's characterization of prosecutorial misconduct, said, "That was a cheap shot."

"Well, *you've* been making cheap shots," McCann retorted.

More words were exchanged, and suddenly Carl Faller was crossing the space between counsel tables heading for McCann. John Orr stood up, and the marshals jumped up and ran forward, getting between the attorneys.

Judge Oliver Wanger was not a big man, but he had a *big* voice. When he returned from lunch he looked like he'd just been told his egg salad was full of salmonella. "I've been told there was almost a *fight* in my court," he said, glaring at the lawyers.

Douglas McCann, who was smaller than Carl Faller, said, "He's a big man, Your Honor. It was very intimidating."

Pat Hanly interceded and said, "It was *nothing,* Your Honor."

The judge let the attorneys know that it had *better* be over.

Then the jury was brought back for their instructions from the judge as to the law and their duty.

After all of Douglas McCann's objections were made for the record, the judge addressed the jury's deliberation time, saying, "My inclination would be to let them go at five P.M."

"I agree," Faller said. "They've had a long day."

The judge turned to the defense lawyer and said, "Mr. McCann, do you have any view on that?"

"Continuous deliberations," McCann replied. "Through the night, whatever."

"Is that your preference?" the judge asked.

Douglas McCann relented: "Whatever the Court would like to do."

The judge said, "Thank you, Mr. McCann. We stand in recess."

If Douglas McCann had been completely serious about the jury not going to bed until they reached a verdict, they'd have needed a sack full of No-Doz. The jury went out on Tuesday, July 28.

Normally, the prosecution is not happy when a jury is out too long. On Wednesday at 1:40 P.M. John Orr's jury wanted to see the so-called short version of *Points of Origin*. And they indicated that they might want to see the entire manuscript as well. It provoked legal wrangling.

Pat Hanly said to Judge Wanger, "I don't want the jury to think that they cannot have the full manuscript because *we* don't want them to have it. It was the defense's request to keep the entire manuscript out."

McCann did not agree: "Your Honor, I'm afraid for the jurors to read about a rape scene. But I'm willing to agree to let it in if they want to redact it."

It may have been pride of authorship, but the defendant disagreed with his lawyer and wanted the jury to read his work as he wrote it, erections and all. The judge disagreed.

Pat Hanly eventually sat down with five task-force people. Each took thirty pages and highlighted sexual references. Every time the fictional arsonist looked at a fire, touched his member, and it got hard, somebody would redact "hard." On the following day, the jury spent its time reading about arsonist Aaron Stiles redacted, but not erected.

Finally, on Friday, July 31, 1992, after three days of deliberations, the jury returned with a verdict.

The courtroom was packed with media and spectators. Mike Matassa was not there, nor was Glen Lucero, two who had worked so long on the Pillow Pyro Task Force. Lucero had been missing his wife, Martha, and had been driven home by Matassa, who thought that deliberations might go through the weekend.

The verdict for the five counts was on two pages and in the hands of the jury foreman.

"Has the jury reached a verdict in this case?" Judge Wanger asked.

"Yes, sir, we have," the jury foreman replied.

"I'm going to ask that the clerk read the verdict," Judge Wanger said.

The clerk was a tall blonde named Candy. Pat Hanly saw her hands shaking when she took the two-page verdict form and began to read: "We the jury in the above-entitled case find, as to the defendant, John Leonard Orr, the following verdict: Count one, eighteen U.S.C. eight-four-four-i, arson, on or about January fifteenth, 1987, at Hancock Fabrics, five-one-seven-nine Blackstone Avenue, Fresno, California . . ."

Hanly heard her audible gasp as she read, "Not guilty."

The clerk continued to read, "Count two, eighteen U.S.C. eight-four-four-i, arson, on or about January thirteenth, 1987, and on or about January thirtieth, 1987, at House of Fabrics, five-two-six-five North Blackstone Avenue, Fresno, California . . . Not guilty."

That was the arson count where the incendiary device had not been found until two weeks *after* the first arson, accounting for the separate dates.

Both John Orr and Prosecutor Pat Hanly later reported to have had the same thoughts: that both sides had *stipulated* that all five arsons were committed by the *same* person. It looked like a clean sweep for the defense!

Pat Hanly hardly heard her read, "Count three, eighteen U.S.C. eight-four-four-i, arson, on or about January sixteenth, 1987 . . ."

Pat Hanly thought: My first huge trial! My career is *over*!

While the clerk continued: "Family Bargain Center . . ."

Hanly looked over at Douglas McCann and John Orr and he thought he saw them rising up in triumph, as the clerk read: "One-one-six-seven North Cherry Avenue, Tulare, California . . . Guilty."

There were more than courtroom murmurs when she got to count four, the CraftMart arson in Bakersfield where Marvin Casey had found and collected the famous latent fingerprint. She said: "Guilty." And "Guilty" again on count five, the Hancock Fabrics fire in Bakersfield.

And after the jury left the courtroom, and everyone caught their breath, Carl Faller rose and asked that the defendant be remanded into custody pending sentencing. He said, "This being a crime of violence providing for the potential of great injury and loss of life, potential damage to property, and damage to persons, pursuant to the section, the Court must remand the defendant."

Douglas McCann opposed the motion, arguing that the defendant had been under house arrest and electronic monitor since December, and he didn't believe there was a danger issue. Furthermore, he pointed out that since John Orr faced another trial in Los Angeles, it was critical that he not be in custody.

"The crime itself, as a matter of law, is one that is a crime of violence under the code section," Judge Wanger decided. "The government has made the motion pursuant to the law . . . I must and do remand Mr. Orr to custody."

Monday, November 2, 1992, was the date of sentencing. But before sentencing began, Douglas McCann cited several instances of what he believed were examples of prosecutorial misconduct, and he made motions for a new trial. Then McCann asked that John Orr be allowed to read a prepared statement prior to the defense lawyer's plea for leniency, and the Court granted the request.

John Orr stood and addressed the Court: "Thank you. As the Court is aware, I have proclaimed my innocence of these charges since the day I was arrested, December fourth of 1991. This proclamation was immediate before I ever saw any information contained in the affidavit, or had any idea what the evidence was. I knew I was innocent of any wrongdoing, and told investigators of that unequivocally at that time.

"The U.S. Attorney's Office was repeatedly advised of that fact and were offered an open interview with me which they refused. The U.S. Attorney's Office was also offered a polygraphic and psychological exam, and all of these offers were refused as well. Your Honor, the U.S. Attorney's Office was listening, but they weren't hearing.

"To coin a phrase that the U.S. Attorneys proclaimed as my admission of guilt uttered by me at an interview: 'I won't close the door on that.' I *didn't* close the door then and even now I welcome any discussion with their investigators about this case.

"The Los Angeles U.S. Attorney's Office has taken a similar closed-door policy, and they would surely be surprised at irrefutable information they could have accessed months ago, which could have saved them thousands of hours of investigation. This information proves my innocence in Los Angeles, but was overlooked in haste after reading the manuscript.

"There was never any presumption of innocence. The presentation of my manuscript as a journal of my fire-setting activities is fictional, just as *Points of Origin* is fictional. In the manuscript there are twenty-nine fires described. Only three bear any resemblance to the actual series of fires that occurred in Fresno in 1987. Only three out of twenty-nine occurred in retail establishments. The rest are brush fires set in alleys and garages, the more common targets of the type of arsonist I portrayed in the book.

"The uncanny similarities that the U.S. attorneys portrayed as evidence against me are merely facts that were passed along among investigators in meetings in 1987 and subsequent to that date, and later inserted into my manuscript. Simple research. As I stated in solicitation letters I sent to publishers: *Points of Origin* is simply fact-based fiction.

"I believe the Court's and the U.S. attorney's perception of me is that I'm a reasonably intelligent man, respected in the fire service with an unblemished record until December of 1991. Certainly not the kind of person that would create havoc-by-fire in the San Joaquin Valley, and keep a journal of fire-setting experiences, write a manuscript chronicling the events, and then attempt to have it published. The *National Enquirer* couldn't have come up with a more ludicrous story. I'm not a fool.

"The fingerprint issue. Why was it that out of the charges against me, only in that one was the chain of custody a serious problem? Exculpatory evidence was discarded shortly after discovery, expert witnesses could not tell what they compared, and the print was clearly not mine in the 1989 comparison. Assuredly there is reasonable doubt as to its value in 1992.

"I was found not guilty of two counts, one of which was an attempted arson that occurred two weeks after the conference in Fresno. This certainly substantiated the fact that these fires were perpetrated by the same person, possibly someone local.

"Your Honor, my life has been dedicated to the fire service and law enforcement for over twenty-two years. I have personally been trapped by fire and smoke on three occasions. I know the panic, the terror, and the helplessness that even a well-equipped professional firefighter can experience as a fire advances uncontrolled.

"I know how those witnesses felt. My heart went out to them. I don't wish that kind of experience on anyone, and I feel helpless and frustrated because the person responsible remains at large. I have fought fires, performed rescues, and carried the bodies of men, women, and children who have died as a result of fire and smoke.

"I have been devastated by this misguided investigation. But beyond that, the fire service has suffered with the perception that they were betrayed by one of their own. Your Honor, they have *not* been betrayed. They and I have been victimized by a total lack of communication and overzealous investigators. My personal reputation, my entire career speaks for itself and I stand by it. I truly hope that justice will ultimately prevail at least for the sake of the fire service.

"Your Honor, thank you for the opportunity to be heard. Whatever your decision is on my sentencing, I will continue to abide by the Court's orders as I have from the beginning of this personal nightmare, and continue to fight to prove my innocence."

When Douglas McCann had the opportunity to plea for his client, he said, "I saw a jury convict Mr. Orr. It's not surprising that they convicted him, because of the fingerprint evidence. That was the entire case. . . . I don't know if I stand here next to a man who did not commit these fires. You have just heard from him telling you that he didn't start the fires. . . . If John Orr was telling the Court that he was responsible for the fires, I could say he's accepting responsibility, showing remorse, should receive something other than the maximum. He has no prior record. . . . But I'm not in that situation right now.

"In terms of the psychiatric report, the doctor never really performed an evaluation, a psychiatric diagnostic study. He just basically said, 'If this man is guilty of these fires, given everything I know about the case, he's obviously troubled. He obviously has a mental problem. He obviously would benefit from some type of care.'

"I don't know how in the world this Court can overlook that. I think the position of the U.S. attorneys here in Fresno is to treat him like a common criminal. . . . In sentencing we always need to consider motive.

Here I am talking with an assumption that he did it, and I'm standing next to a man who told the Court he *didn't* do it. It's a difficult argument for me to make. I can simply say that he's got no prior record.

"Joe Lopez testified that he went out and bought food for John Orr's family. That's a reflection not so much on Joe Lopez, but a reflection on John Orr, that there are people who *care* about this man.

"In fact, there are fire investigators here to observe his sentence. It actually turns one's stomach. I don't know why they are enjoying it. When the jury came back with the verdict of guilty, was that a day of celebration? That was a very sad day for everybody involved."

Judge Wanger interrupted the defense lawyer's plea at this point to say, "It is a public forum. These proceedings are open to all."

"I have no objection to them being here," McCann continued. "I anticipate the U.S. attorney asking the Court to give John Orr the maximum sentence. To max him out for as long as possible with no inquiry as to why this happened. In fact, Mr. Faller said, 'We don't *care* why it happened. We got our guy.'

"Motive *is* a factor that should be considered if the Court is going to assume that he's guilty based on the jury's finding. We have to ask ourselves, why did these fires start? Did John Orr get any benefit out of these fires? If there's no motive then we have to look to the psychiatrist who said that if you make that assumption, then there's only one conclusion: that you have some type of pathology.

"One other small point: The probation officer indicated that John Orr has nothing redeemable about his life because he's been living a fraud all these years. Because he's an arsonist. As the Court is aware, he has been a well-respected arson investigator and instructor. At least on that level, there are people that benefited from knowing him." McCann suddenly looked to his client, then said to the court, "One second."

When John Orr and Douglas McCann finished conferring, McCann said, "I would submit it, Your Honor."

The defendant decided that his lawyer had said enough.

Patrick Hanly said to the court, "Your Honor, it is the government's position that the Court should follow the probation report's recommendation, and sentence Mr. Orr to the thirty-year maximum sentence, ten years on each count, which means that Mr. Orr will be eligible for parole in as little as ten years.

"All the Court has to do is remember Mr. Orr's own words about the panic, the terror, and the helplessness that is felt by the victims of arson fires. Who better than this man right here to know the danger that an arson fire creates, then come into this court after a jury has found him guilty, and proclaim his innocence. And proclaim that he has been set up by the government. It's ludicrous. He should get the maximum sentence, thirty years. He should be sentenced under four-two-oh-five-a, which requires him to spend a minimum of ten years, and the Court should order him to pay a fine.

"And it's the government's understanding that he has now sold the rights to his novel, I believe to HBO, and I would like the Court to order restitution to be paid by the defendant."

Hanly was referring to a sale for which John Orr was paid fifteen hundred dollars against fifteen thousand dollars if it was ever produced.

"And furthermore, Your Honor," Hanly continued, "this *is* somewhat of a day of celebration because a very dangerous man is no longer on the streets. And law enforcement *does* celebrate on the day when dangerous criminals are convicted and put away, as required by the law. Thank you."

When Judge Wanger was ready to sentence the defendant, he said, "I have read very carefully all that you have written, and analyzed what you have said. I know that you stand here absolutely maintaining your innocence. I believe in the jury system, and I believe in the jury. In this case, there was sufficient evidence to convict you, as the jury did.

"You chose in your own defense not to proclaim your innocence personally. That was a strategic decision and a choice you made *not* to tell the jury, 'I didn't set these fires.' That choice was yours and it's respected. However, the evidence was substantial, and the evidence was sufficient to convict you.

"You are guilty of each of these counts, and what I must say to you, as a sworn law-enforcement officer, is that the proof of your guilt and the fact of your guilt then establishes that you betrayed the highest trust that was placed in you to protect the public from the terror that you have described, and to care for them, and to use the great skill and the respect that was afforded you in your profession to do the right thing and not the wrong thing.

"I do find that you are a danger to the community and that you are someone who must be incarcerated, and there must be an example made in this case. . . . It is the judgment of this Court, Mr. Orr, that as to counts three, four, and five, you are hereby committed to the Bureau of Prisons to be imprisoned for a term of ten years as to each count, each count to run consecutively with the other. I'm sentencing you pursuant to eighteen U.S.C. section four-two-oh-five-a for a total of thirty years. You shall pay restitution in the amount of two hundred twenty-five thousand nine hundred seventy-one dollars to the victims in this case as will be specified by the probation officer."

Many observers expressed the wish that when the judge was proclaiming his belief in the jury and the jury system, he would've enlightened them as to how the defendant could have been acquitted of two counts and convicted of three, after both sides stipulated that the same fire setter had committed all five arsons. Some said that the verdict validated those who had been calling for a new system composed of professional jurors.

Douglas McCann asked for bail, which was denied. The defense counsel then said of an appeal, "Let the Court know I will be filing the notice for him, and I will no longer be on the case after that. It will be a *pro per* notice."

John Orr later wrote, "There was bitterness on Doug's part. We'd been through a lot and he thought I was disloyal. He wanted to be part of the L.A. case, but I fired him."

Douglas McCann had expressed revulsion at the joy he saw in the faces of task-force members who were there in court for John Orr's sentencing: Glen Lucero, Mike Camello, Tom Campuzano, firefighters all, they were there. Mike Matassa was there representing ATF, along with Special Agent Chuck Gaylan of Fresno, who had helped Marvin Casey secure the ten fingerprint cards examined by Richard Kinney at the Department of Justice.

There had been another man there in court during the defense's case, perhaps unnoticed by John Orr and his lawyer. He was very interested in the defense strategy *and* in government mistakes like the one made by the fingerprint expert. This man was considering ways that he could deal with a law-enforcement error even more egregious. He was hoping one day to prove to a jury of twelve Los Angeles citizens that a catastrophic fire long ago, deemed an accident, was actually an arson. A fire that had killed four human beings, including a small child.

Deputy District Attorney Michael J. Cabral was there contemplating prosecution that could put John Leonard Orr on death row and take away his *life*.

14

STRANGE FISH

The convicted arsonist had experienced severe depression after his sentencing. "Utter devastation," he called it. However, the federal facility to which he was sent, Metropolitan Detention Center in downtown Los Angeles, was about as comfortable as such places get. There were pool tables and other recreational facilities, the food was okay, and it wasn't overcrowded. He'd been there for a short time just after his arrest, and some of the inmates he'd met then were still present to welcome him back.

The only frightening moment came not from an inmate but from a barber, a student barber in the prison barber shop. The prisoner had been told that his beard would have to go, and he had to face a shaky kid with a straight razor who had never shaved a beard and couldn't grow one. The senior barber saved bloodletting by doing the job himself.

Inmate Orr had to spend some time in the hole after his arrival. As a former law-enforcement officer, he was required to sign a waiver before they'd release him into the general population, and he was quick to sign. He figured if he hadn't gotten his throat cut in the barber shop, he might as well risk it in the yard.

Since he was so near home, he received plenty of visitors, and because it was such a good facility, his depression gradually began to abate. His appeal gave him hope. His primary concern had to be in choosing a lawyer to represent him in the coming indictment for the Los Angeles arsons. If his appeal failed he couldn't afford another conviction, not if he hoped to be paroled in his first year of eligibility—the year 2002.

It had been with trepidation that Assistant U.S. Attorneys Stefan Stein and Walter Brown submitted their brief to the U.S. Court of Appeals for the Ninth Circuit—"the infamous Ninth Circuit," as it was called by law-enforcement officers who believed that it was packed with liberals and had a defense bias in criminal matters.

Stein and Brown were at last appealing the decision of District Judge Edward Rafeedie for excluding John Orr's novel and his letters to publishers and agents, because the prejudicial effect outweighed their probative value.

There were three Ninth Circuit judges sitting on the panel when Stefan Stein stood before them with an opening he'd rehearsed aloud until even Mike Matassa could've delivered it. He wanted to point out, in effect, that the purpose of evidence *is* to prejudice a jury. One of the judges on the panel was Steven Trott, a former member of the Highwaymen, the sixties singers who'd had a couple of big hits, including "Michael Row the Boat Ashore."

As Stefan Stein stood before the appellate panel, preparing to row his own boat, Judge Trott said, "Sit down, counsel."

They didn't want argument. Their decision read:

> We respectfully hold that the district court abused its discretion in excluding this evidence. . . . The manuscript and letters are highly probative of modus operandi and thus the identity of the arsonist. . . . Therefore, having carefully evaluated all of these factors, we hold that the evidence . . . was properly admissible because it was so highly relevant to proof of modus operandi and identity. REVERSED.

It meant that Stefan Stein could look forward to trial. After having had his case "yanked away," as he put it—after having "his world turned upside down" when John Orr went to Fresno—after all that, he was finally going to trial in Los Angeles. His colleague Walt Brown would not be there for it, having gone on to another assignment, but Brown had been replaced by another bright and energetic young prosecutor, Debra Yang.

The Pillow Pyro Task Force was kept as busy as ever after the Fresno trial was concluded, for now it was time to prep the L.A. witnesses and get them ready. Mike Matassa had been promoted to resident agent in charge of the Riverside office of ATF, and had to split his time between there and assisting with Pillow Pyro business. And there was a lot of business to do, even through the holiday season and into the new year of 1993.

The assistant U.S. attorneys had decided to take eight counts of arson to the federal grand jury: three from the Central Coast fires of 1989, the rest from the Los Angeles series. The three on the Central Coast were those that took place on the same street in Atascadero on March 9, 1989, during a three-hour spree: Pacific Home Improvement Center, Cornet Variety, and Coast to Coast Hardware.

The remaining five counts named the fires at People's Department Store in Los Angeles; Builder's Emporium in North Hollywood; D&M Yardage in Lawndale; and Stats Floral Supply and Thrifty Drug and Discount Store, both in Redondo Beach.

Stefan Stein and Debra Yang had studied the transcript from the Fresno trial and had their own strategy planned, with some improvements. They were preparing the witnesses for what would surely be a media event even bigger than it had been in Fresno, because John Orr was a local figure in both the fire-fighting and law-enforcement societies.

There were stories and TV coverage about the coming trial. *People* magazine ran a story on John Orr with a photo of him in court. On the opposite page was one of him in action at the scene of a building fire.

His wife Wanda told *People*: "He's never been anything but a kind, loving and trustworthy person."

Peter Giannini came highly recommended to John Orr by several people familiar with Los Angeles criminal defenders. He was a forty-five-year-old trial lawyer with nineteen years of legal experience. But lawyers like Giannini did not come cheap, and Wanda had to mortgage her home to pay his sixty-thousand-dollar fee. The defense lawyer spent more than a month examining the eight counts of arson facing his client, then came to him and warned, "If we fall even on one count it could double your sentence. Right now you're facing ten years behind bars."

The matter seemed straightforward to Giannini. His client would plea to the three arson counts in Atascadero, which had no significant damage involved, thus no civil liability for restitution.

The defendant's version of the plea bargain differs from that of his attorney. John Orr maintained that he'd paid his lawyer and wanted to go to trial to make him earn it. He claimed that when the lawyer broached the idea of a plea bargain that might not increase his time served by one day, John Orr said, "Fuck that! I'm not taking a plea bargain!"

The defendant remembers his lawyer saying, "I see no chance of a successful appeal on the Fresno case. Take the deal instead of rolling the dice with the jury. It's the plea bargain of the century."

As it happens, it might have been just about impossible to find a lawyer who would have disagreed with the logic at that time. Even John Orr later admitted that pleading guilty to a few counts of arson had started to seem sensible. He told his wife: "I'd do ten years for a crime I didn't commit before I'd see you lose your house for attorney fees or for expenses."

He reported that for those reasons, he would take the deal even though he was an innocent man and the victim of a government frame-up.

Four days before trial was to commence, Peter Giannini contacted the U.S. Attorney's Office to speak about a plea bargain. Stefan Stein was astounded. It was one of those moments when one doesn't know whether to laugh or cry. He probably wanted to cry after all the hard work, after the disappointment of having his case yanked away and sent to Fresno, and after his successful appeal to the Ninth Circuit.

But there were other considerations. The task force was happy when they heard about the offer. The man who accused them of conspiracy, of a government frame-up, would now plead guilty. It was their vindication.

And if they turned down the plea, went to trial, and convicted him of more counts, what was Judge Rafeedie likely to do when it came to the imposition of sentence? The U.S. Attorney's Office believed that whether the defendant pled guilty or was convicted at trial, the sentence would most likely run concurrent with the sentence he was serving. In other words, his actual prison time would not be increased by one day, so why go through a fruitless and expensive exercise?

It made sense to Stefan Stein, who'd sweated for weeks over a beautiful opening statement that made the task force proud. It made sense, yes, but he'd done so damn much *work*.

The U.S. Attorney's Office made its decision within twenty-four hours. They would accept a plea bargain to three counts of arson with certain conditions attached. Stefan Stein wanted the defendant to plea to at least one count of arson in his own backyard, which meant one from the Los Angeles series.

Stein was impressed by John Orr's attorney, although he didn't know much about this trial lawyer who mostly practiced in state courts. Stein found Giannini to be open and reasonable, and Stein was willing to accommodate the defense in choosing one count of arson from the L.A. series that wouldn't involve restitution. The defense chose Builder's Emporium in North Hollywood, where an incendiary device had been found, but only sixty dollars in damage had been done.

Peter Giannini could not have known it at the time, but that choice would return to torment him in a few years. Or, as he himself put it: "Builder's Emporium came back to bite us in the ass."

At the time of the plea bargain, the defense had heard rumors that Michael Cabral, an arson specialist at the DA's office, was conducting an investigation into the College Hills fire of 1990 as well as the Ole's Home Center fire of 1984. Giannini spoke with his client about that information, but John reassured his lawyer that there was absolutely nothing to fear from such an inquiry. Nothing at all.

Just to be sure, Giannini tried phoning Michael Cabral to see if he could learn whether or not there was any possibility that the DA might seek to prosecute his client at any time, but he said that Cabral did not return his call. John's lawyer later said that if he'd had any serious notion that the DA was going to file a state case, he would have made him sign off explicitly before pleading his client on the federal arson counts. Neither he nor John Orr was much worried about Michael Cabral's investigation.

He took John Orr at his word.

On May 12, 1993, U.S. District Court Judge Edward Rafeedie imposed the following sentence and conditions upon John Leonard Orr for his guilty plea to three counts of arson:

He was to serve ninety-six months on each count, to be served concurrently to one another, this sentence to be served concurrently with the thirty-year sentence previously imposed on the defendant in the Eastern Judicial District.

The defendant and his lawyer were more than satisfied. The concurrent sentence meant that based on Federal Bureau of Prisons guidelines, John Orr would probably be paroled in the year 2002, when he'd be fifty-three years old with a lot of life ahead. The defendant was to serve his sentence at the Terminal Island Federal Correctional Institution in San Pedro, the southernmost area of Los Angeles.

As far as most observers were concerned, it had, indeed, been the deal of the century for John Orr.

Of all the stratagems and machinations common to the world's most esoteric profession, the plea bargain is one of the most serpentine. Without it, American courts of law would be overwhelmed and immobilized, they say. Yet to observe it in practice is to cause the uninitiated to gape, bewildered by the strange school of fish that swims in these litigation tanks.

On March 24, 1993, John Orr had stood before Edward Rafeedie and uttered the word "Guilty" to a subjective and somewhat arbitrary choice of three arson charges that satisfied lawyers on both sides. There were no questions asked of the defendant to determine if a man insistent that he was innocent had experienced a road-to-Damascus conversion. There were no attempts to determine if the defendant would accept psychiatric help. There were no questions designed to see if there might at least be a willingness to reveal information that would prove invaluable to understanding the obsession that grips serial fire setters. There was not an attempt on ethical or moral terms to ascertain if this prominent arson investigator had ever experienced *any* regret for indulging the fearful compulsion to terrorize and destroy all that he had sworn to protect.

In short, there were no questions on *any* level—psychological, social, ethical, or moral—directed at a unique defendant at a unique time of exposure and vulnerability. The task force was waiting for such questions, longing for answers from a man who had been a respected and notable member of the fire-fighting fraternity and the law-enforcement community of investigators.

Never in crime-fighting history had there been such an opportunity to trade something of value with an organized serial arsonist, that most rare and elusive of all violent serial offenders, about whom so little is known. And this one, this very special convicted serial arsonist, was considered by lawmen to be perhaps the most organized and most proficient of any in the annals of U.S. crime. Instead, at the end of the day there was just a seven-page document written in legalese to satisfy lawyers.

There was not an attorney associated with the prosecution or defense of John Orr who did not use the word *strange* in describing him. But there wasn't a bubble of common curiosity that one could discern floating to the surface of the isolated tank in which these *other* strange fish swim.

The defendant was not even asked a probing question to ascertain if his plea was merely a device to manipulate the sentence. His former partner, Joe Lopez, who was there in court, said that while John Orr was saying the word *yes* to his guilty pleas, he was shaking his head *no*. But no one wanted to risk sabotaging the contrivance and clouding the water in the litigation tank. John Leonard Orr, the arson catch of the century, simply stood before Judge Edward Rafeedie and uttered the word "Guilty" to a subjective choice of three charges that satisfied all of the strange fish swimming in that tank at that moment on that day.

They called him "The Bulldog." When John Orr began serving his sentence in the U.S. penitentiary at Terminal Island, Mike Cabral had been with the Los Angeles District Attorney's Office for seven years, specializing in arson prosecution for three of those. He was a career prosecutor in every sense of the word, having been a law clerk in that office for two years prior to becoming a member of the bar.

Cabral was raised in Fremont, California, and had attended Chico State College and San Jose State College before moving south. Both sides of his family were of the Portuguese working class, and he'd graduated from Southwestern University School of Law in Los Angeles, a workingman's law school, fulfilling an ambition he'd had since the age of thirteen.

In August of 1993, he celebrated his thirty-fourth birthday with his wife, Margie, and his three children. In order to provide the best housing his salary could afford, Cabral lived in Moreno Valley, sixty-five miles east of Los Angeles, and in order to avoid the freeway traffic, he arrived in his compact car at his office by 5:30 A.M. He worked an average of nine and a half hours a day, unless trial work bled into the peak traffic hours, and then he'd just stay and work some more until the freeway unclogged.

The prematurely balding young prosecutor was built like a refrigerator, the side-by-side, double-door model. Five feet eight inches tall, he admitted to wearing a size 50 suit, but was quick to say, "It's all in the shoulders."

His courtroom style reflected his look: never eloquent, but polite, seemingly relaxed but inwardly intense. His kind of prosecutor could be effective with downtown jurors, people not high enough on the social ladder to have avoided jury duty in the first place. Mike Cabral looked like someone who couldn't have avoided jury duty either, a working-class guy whom an inner-city juror might intuitively trust. He fared well against glib and smooth lawyers who dress to impress and wouldn't be caught dead in an off-the-rack garment-district special.

From his earliest assignment with the Major Frauds Unit, Cabral had liked doing arson cases, and he'd attended a one-week course ambiguously called Advanced Arson for Profit for Prosecutors at the Federal Law Enforcement Training Institute in Georgia. Cabral also had been invited to attend a car-fire-arson session at the Glendale Training Academy by the host, Captain John Orr.

Cabral's District Attorney's Arson Task Force, as it was called, had officially been up and running since February 1992. Cabral had set it up in a conference room on the eighteenth floor of the Criminal Courts building but eventually was given space in the Hall of Justice, the old court and jail facility that was soon to be shut down permanently. Most Americans had seen that ancient block of granite in films and TV shows. Nothing in Los Angeles looked so foreboding and grim. It had housed many notorious criminals, including Charles Manson and his followers.

Cabral's task-force "headquarters" was a room barely large enough for a conference table and six chairs. There was one phone, a few maps on the wall, and boxes full of evidence and reports, including ten thousand photos and more than one hundred thousand pages of discovery that would be provided to the defense if the task force could get a case together.

Cabral's investigators were Walt Scheuerell, a sergeant with the Los Angeles County Sheriff's Department Arson/Explosives Detail; Rich Edwards, the deputy sheriff who'd monitored the Teletrac at the Warner Brothers Studios fire; Tom Campuzano, the L.A. Fire Department arson investigator who'd also worked with the Pillow Pyro Task Force; and Bill

Donley and Chris Loop, of the Glendale Police Department. A short while after the task force was formed, they were joined by Steve Patterson, the arson investigator from the Burbank Fire Department who had called John Orr for assistance with the Warner Brothers fire.

Everyone except Cabral wore very casual clothes: polo shirts, T-shirts, jeans, and tennis shoes. This task force was not working under the same pressure as the last one, since their quarry was in prison and no longer a danger to the public, but they had other pressures. If they were going to go to trial they had to stay ahead of the statute of limitations that was running out on the Kennington, Hilldale, and San Augustine fires. Ole's Home Center—if indeed they could ever prove it was an arson—posed no time problem, since there is no statute of limitations on murder.

After John Orr's conviction in Fresno and his guilty plea, Mike Matassa had phoned Mike Cabral to kid him by saying, "We served you a softball, now hit it over the fence."

But Cabral knew that this softball was a dancing knuckler that maybe nobody could hit, particularly in regard to the Ole's "accidental" fire, where the insurance companies had shelled out four million dollars to the families of victims and their lawyers. It was a wound that nobody was eager to reopen, including the L.A. County Sheriff's Department, which had called it an accident and was now facing inquiries from its own people, Scheuerell and Edwards, who were trying to prove it was *not*.

From the beginning there was a feeling of competition between this task force, who'd felt nearly excluded on the periphery at John Orr's arrest, and the Pillow Pyro gang. And Cabral confessed to having been upset with the U.S. attorneys who'd allowed John Orr to plea bargain on the L.A. arson series. He thought that guilty verdicts on most or all of those would have been enormously important with his own attempts to convict solely on circumstantial evidence and modus operandi. But after Cabral had heard from the U.S. Attorney's Office that a concurrent sentence was probably in the cards whether or not they'd gone to trial, Cabral called their decision "justifiable."

And when John Orr and his lawyer chose the Builder's Emporium arson attempt for the plea bargain—a fire where a "signature" incendiary device had been found, a hardware store that was exactly like Ole's—Deputy District Attorney Mike Cabral was more than content with the plea bargain.

"They pled right into my case," he said of John Orr and his lawyer. "Right *into* the Ole's fire. And it'll *burn* them."

There was an inescapable fact confronting the District Attorney's Arson Task Force. They were not looking at months of work, they were looking at *years* of work. The Ole's fire alone presented staggering problems. Ole's corporation had been bought out by another hardware retailer and that one was no longer in business either. Finding all of the former-employee witnesses was nearly impossible.

Trying to legally reconstruct Ole's was daunting. The building that had housed Ole's Home Center had formerly been a Thrifty Drug Store that had shared the space with a food market. Escrow information didn't even exist anymore, but they had to secure blueprints from the original building as well as from the major remodeling for the drugstore chain, especially concerning work that had been done when they'd installed a dropped, T-bar ceiling. That meant that they must find the people who'd actually done the work.

Mike Cabral had to thoroughly study this attic in order to prove that a fire originally called an "undetermined fire" probably originating from faulty wiring in the attic could not have happened that way. The task force had to demonstrate that the Ole's conflagration, which had moved so fast that people could not outrun it, was not consistent with any sort of attic fire that had dropped smoldering material down into the main store.

One of the less arduous jobs, but still enough to keep an investigative team busy for a year or so, was the need to look at incidents of brush fires, potato-chip fires, and arson fires in retail establishments during business hours over the ten-year period preceding John Orr's arrest. They found only seventy-eight in retail stores in all of California, and they believed that most of those had been set by John Orr.

Of the brush fires, they determined that in the foothill communities of Glendale, Pasadena, and La Crescenta—as well as portions of Los Angeles near John Orr's home—there had been hundreds during the period they were studying. Rich Edwards had personally done some work on those arsons before John Orr's arrest, and at one point had been trying to put together a kind of arson task force called "Firestorm." He'd had the idea to install pole cameras to see if he could get photos of the areas where the fires occurred repeatedly, hoping to snap a photo of a suspect.

Edwards recalled that while his first pole camera was being installed, Captain John Orr just happened to be cruising by and spoke with the deputy sheriff who was monitoring the installation. There were no more fires in *that* area, but multiple fires broke out on the same day in other canyon locations where there were no cameras.

Mike Cabral's task force came to believe that John Orr was responsible for the vast majority of all the arsons they were studying, and by way of unverifiable proof, they pointed to the astounding statistic that showed a 90 percent drop in brush-fire activity since his arrest. In the county foothill area, brush fires had averaged sixty-seven a year clear back to 1981. After his arrest the average had dropped to *one* per year.

For the career law-enforcement people on the task force, like LASD's Scheuerell and Edwards, their next assignment was an eye-opener. Mike Cabral instructed them to interview all of the Glendale firefighters who'd worked with John Orr at any time in their careers. The lawmen reported that they'd had no idea how close and insulated was this firefighting band of brothers.

They set up interview teams and divided the workload into groups. Rich Edwards found the experience fascinating, especially the emotional swings in the men he interviewed. It varied, he said, from those who offered complete cooperation to the others still in denial that their former colleague could have committed the offenses for which he'd been convicted.

Some of the firefighters evinced shame and anger, and would point their fingers at the cops and say, "You better be *right*, by God!"

Edwards reported that during one interview a veteran fire captain said, "This man you're describing isn't the John Orr I know. And if he set the Ole's fire and killed those people, then he needs help. He's a *sick* man if he did it, and a sick man shouldn't be in jail. And I'd still work with him today!"

Rich Edwards later said, "I thanked him for his candor after I picked my chin up off the table."

Edwards's investigation led him to believe that some of those brush fires were fashioned so that if they had been attacked properly by an engine company they could have been handled. But if the firefighters were out grocery shopping, and didn't get to the scene in a timely manner, the fire would turn out to be significant. Edwards was convinced that

John Orr had set some of them so that Glendale wouldn't lose an engine for budgetary reasons.

And then there were brush fires set when he was associated with a brush-clearance company. "If you didn't clear your brush as ordered," Edwards said, "you'd get a *fire*. John's a very complex person."

The D.A.'s task force also discovered some possible offenses they hadn't been looking for, such as embezzlement of FIRST funds. It turned out that the funds taken in from the FIRST-sponsored classes at the Glendale Training Center were supposed to go to FIRST and the city on a sixty–forty split. John Orr, the treasurer, had signatory authority, and they suspected he'd diverted some of the money to buy Vegas World gift certificates on a FIRST credit card that nobody else knew existed.

As soon as John heard rumors that Mike Cabral's task force was investigating those activities, he phoned Cabral.

"I resent being called a thief!" he informed the prosecutor.

The alleged embezzlement amounted to no more than two thousand dollars, and Mike Cabral, who was trying to build a case of capital *murder,* said, "John, I think I can promise that I'll never charge you with theft."

When he'd arrived in 1993 at Terminal Island Federal Correctional Institution, John was given a perfunctory interview by a twenty-something psychiatric intern who asked the same question he'd been asked over the years by older shrinks during preemployment interviews.

With her glasses slipping from her nose and her pen pointed at heaven, she said, "Please describe your early family life for me."

He gave the response he'd always given to the more experienced practitioners of her art: "Ozzie and Harriet."

A bit taken aback, the young woman studied the new inmate and said, "Are you referring to Ozzy Osbourne?"

John later described a feeling of utter despair. His future was being directed by some kid who'd confused Ozzie and Harriet with brain-bashing rockers in Jivaro war paint who bite the heads off bats!

John Orr was only forty-four years old, but he felt old, older than fire.

15

MARY DUGGAN

T erminal Island was not such a bad place as prisons go, and federal prisons at their worst were better than the hell-on-earth that is the state prison system. The cons who had done hard time in state institutions such as Folsom or San Quentin referred to facilities like Terminal Island as "Club Fed." There were no walls, just a fifteen-foot chain-link fence topped with razor wire. The prisoners could even see the luxury liner *Queen Mary* and watch power boats and Jet Skiers roaring by.

John Orr tried to avoid the chow hall, where inmates smoked, littered, and spit, prisoners who were usually sick from some virus or another. When he could afford it he preferred to live on soup and canned items from the commissary. He'd wangled the job of prison librarian, which carried a bit of prestige and comfort, and he was settling in, hoping that something would come of the appeal that had been filed by the Office of the Federal Defender. An argument on appeal was that the jury in Fresno had been allowed to hear about a series of fires in retail stores, and about "lists" of incidents beyond what were expected to be allowed as "uncharged acts." The federal defender believed this to be "impermissible bootstrapping." John considered it to be just plain confusing, but he was not a man to give up easily, and he had some confidence in his appeal. It would take time, but he had plenty of that.

A colleague to whom John Orr wrote after his confinement was Captain Steve Patterson, the Burbank Fire Department arson investigator who was part of Cabral's arson task force. The man whom Steve Patterson considered "a mentor" said in his letter that he hoped Patterson still believed in him, and didn't think that he'd started the Warner Brothers Studios fire that they'd investigated together just prior to the arrest.

Patterson had attended the Fresno arson convention, also attended by Rich Edwards and Walt Scheuerell, who'd known that John Orr was the target of the Pillow Pyro investigation when Patterson did not. John had arrived late that evening and Patterson invited him to sit at their table. He wondered if that small kindness had motivated John Orr to write to him.

Steve Patterson was five years older than John and had been a firefighter longer, but he didn't have nearly as much investigative experience, certainly not as much as all the cops on his task force. Patterson had receding gray hair and soft blue-gray eyes, usually wore a little smile, and talked slowly. He was facing his fiftieth birthday, but looked fit. This fireman had a gentle face without a trace of the cynicism that one would expect from task-force colleagues who'd served in the police service for a similar period. And even though he was an arson investigator Patterson had never aspired to be one of the cops, as John Orr had. He approached his task-force role with humility and a willingness to learn from the others.

One of the more spectacular fires in the L.A. series that Mike Cabral's task force had been looking into was Mort's Surplus in Burbank. Steve Patterson, who'd asked for and received John Orr's help with that particular investigation, was very surprised to learn that among the evidence seized during John's arrest was a video of Patterson arriving at the scene while the building was burning. John had never told Steve Patterson that he'd also been there *during* the blaze, videotaping it.

It may have been that all of the cops on the D.A.'s task force had decided to throw their least experienced investigator a bone. They gave Patterson the job of interviewing wives and girlfriends to see if raw gossip could be refined into usable evidence. Patterson was exactly the right guy for the job he was given. He was a quiet-spoken family man with that guileless expression, just the ticket for John Orr's women, if they had anything to offer. And they did. Steve Patterson was about to get an education.

One of the women Patterson interviewed sat in her living room on a sunny afternoon, looking a bit apprehensively at the kindly face of Steve Patterson. This one might've been waiting for someone like Patterson. Among the first words out of her mouth were: "You don't have to ask. Yeah, I think he did it. He had a dark side. A weird side."

When Steve Patterson asked how dark and how weird, she recalled a moment at a party when John was hitting on one of her girlfriends so she threw a drink in his face and said, "You better cool off."

Patterson thought he was going to hear a lot of ordinary complaints like this, until she said, "And he liked unusual sex. I went along, but I'd always maintain control. Until one time he got carried away, and put a pillow over my face. And he put his gun up to the pillow and said, 'I'm gonna blow your fucking head off!' "

Steve Patterson felt the hair on his neck tingling. This was close to what the fictional arsonist in John Orr's novel does to the girl named "Trish."

After that interview Steve Patterson began reading the manuscript of *Points of Origin* as a journal. Because the protagonist in the novel was interested in a female emergency dispatcher, Patterson made discreet inquiries to find out if John Orr had ever dated women at the dispatch center. And before long he found himself having a private chat with one of them in her home.

She started out by describing John Orr as a "gentleman" who'd liked to stay home and watch TV. But the more she talked the less gentlemanly he seemed. Soon she got to the part where he made her wear old clothes because his idea of foreplay was tearing them from her body, after which she'd have to submit to mock rape.

The bodice ripping got a little tiresome, not to mention expensive, so she'd dumped him, but he kept showing up at her job until she threatened to bring harassment charges. She also confessed to Patterson that he'd once offered to torch her car for the insurance money, but she'd declined.

When Patterson got back to the Hall of Justice he had some stories for the gang, who decided that John Orr's girlfriends probably had to shop at the Salvation Army or the Goodwill Store so they wouldn't use up their whole clothing allowance on one of those "dates."

Then there was the investigator whom John had dated for a period of time. She had definitely fallen out of love and used words like "angry, vindictive, and narcissistic" to describe him. She broke off the romance because during one of their lovemaking sessions he'd handcuffed her to the bed and *left* her there. And he'd also given her a little of what Rich Edwards and Wally Scheuerell had come to call "tough love," by sticking a gun in her face.

Well, riding crops and monocles might be one thing, but guns and handcuffs were something else again. Steve Patterson's neck hair was putting out enough electricity to light up Burbank when he got back to the "diary." The fictional arsonist also binds Trish at gunpoint during the rape scene. So if everyone on the task force was matching the exploits of the fictional arsonist with John Orr's real-life fire setting, what about the scenes with women?

John Orr's last girlfriend was named Chris, as is a girlfriend of his fictional protagonist. In the Ole's fire, four people had died, including a two-and-a-half-year-old boy named Matthew. In the fictional "Cal's" fire, five people die, including a three-year-old boy named Matthew. Some of the task-force members wondered: Where's the fifth victim? Could he have inserted that fifth victim in an otherwise identical portrayal of a real event in order to taunt, or to fulfill a dangerous fantasy by putting himself at risk? He was a man easily bored, as are all violent serial offenders, so obviously he *loved* to take risks. What if the girl in the book who experiences a violent sexual attack mirrored one from John Orr's secret life? At that stage of the task-force investigation, Steve Patterson had normal blood pressure, but it was about to change.

Points of Origin was studied like a text for a promotional exam. Patterson kept turning to the passages involving Trish. Both the fictional arsonist, Aaron Stiles, and the arson investigator, Phil Langtree, are attracted to that teenager—Langtree "uncomfortably" so, because he is the good firefighter, Stiles in an obsessive way, because he is the bad firefighter-arsonist. Stiles first encounters Trish in a 7-Eleven store when he sets an incendiary device that is spotted before much fire damage is done. The fictional arsonist can't stop thinking of her. She becomes confused in his head with his fire-setting fantasies.

Steve Patterson began to make notes, first about the 7-Eleven store. That convenience-store chain had figured prominently in John Orr's life.

One of his ex-wives had worked there and so had he. In the novel, Trish spurns Aaron Stiles's advances at the 7-Eleven store. As his obsession progresses, the fictional firefighter decides to commit his first violent act apart from his fire setting. He decides to rape Trish.

Stiles stakes out the apartment where the girl lives and sets a fire nearby at a travel agency. The fire thrills him enormously, and Trish is one of many people who leaves the apartment building to watch. Later, he knocks at her door, and when she opens it, he shoves his gun against her face and forces his way inside.

The firefighter arsonist rolls the girl onto her stomach and straddles her with his gun at her face, saying, "I will fucking put a bullet in your head." Aaron Stiles then rips the girl's T-shirt down, restraining her at the elbows. He grabs a nearby bathrobe and ties her wrists behind her back. He gags her and rips off her shorts and tries to mount her from the rear, but his erection dies.

Stiles is flaccid and furious. He slaps the girl and ties her at the ankles with remnants of the bathrobe. Then, bound at the wrists and ankles, she is dragged into the kitchen and tied to the kitchen drain pipe with panty hose. He reenters the living room and sets an incendiary delay device in her sofa, one that will give him time to rape her and escape while she burns to death. The girl is saved by a passing Samaritan who phones the fire department from the 7-Eleven store. She has not died because the sofa is an old one with very little foam stuffing, and the fire has vented through an open window.

When Patterson was finished, the cross-comparisons between fiction and reality were blurring. He believed he was burrowing into something dark, something evil.

When Steve Patterson got back to task-force headquarters he found that his work and his theories exacted a lot of blank stares, quizzical smiles, and raised eyebrows. He received encouragement from nobody. All of the task-force cops, with their cop cynicism, sort of patted the fireman on the head and said, in effect, Nice try, but we're buried in paperwork and swamped by Cabral's need to find long-vanished witnesses and cross-eyed from looking at reports from fires that may or may not involve John Orr.

And it hadn't helped that arson profilers from the FBI Academy had made off-the-record estimates that John Orr may have committed a few *thousand* arsons in his lifetime, but who the hell was counting? So, thank you very much, Steve, but we don't have time for Hollywood-type murder mysteries; if that's what *you* want to do, good luck. That was more or less the message that Captain Steve Patterson of the Burbank Fire Department got from his task-force colleagues.

One former girlfriend of John Orr didn't square with anybody in the novel, as far as Patterson could see, but she certainly was the living embodiment of John Orr's conflicted feelings about police in general. She was the female cop who told Cabral about John wanting to make it with her in a fire station. And how he'd always try to touch her and kiss her when she'd don her uniform. But at the same time he'd tell her how stupid cops were and how much smarter he was. There was just too much symbolism there about power and control and authority and handcuffs.

Then Steve Patterson would have to chill and remind himself that these other guys were more experienced investigators. They were police officers, and he'd spent most of his career fighting fires. Maybe he *was* getting carried away. Maybe he'd seen all this in a movie sometime.

But then he'd stop and think, No, goddamn it! I've never seen a movie like *this*. Not ever. And there was another thing: John Orr had liked to shoot nude photos of his women, just as he'd liked to shoot photos of his fires, just as most violent serial offenders have a need for mementos, to relive those *moments*.

Maybe for John Orr sex and fire had *fused*.

Task-force duties actually increased in 1994. They were meeting three times a week and reporting anything significant to Mike Cabral, who intended to indict John Orr not only for multiple murder in the Ole's fire, but for the College Hills disaster, the Warner Brothers Studios fire, and the brush fires known as the Hilldale fire in La Cañada and the San Augustine fire in Glendale. However, the statute of limitations on the latter arsons would run out on November 23.

By this time Steve Patterson was up to his eyes in *murder*. He needed help from police detectives, but no cop could take seriously such a half-baked idea. There is nothing that disgusts police investigators more than amateurs offering investigative advice that *always* sounds as though it's from a made-for-TV movie.

It came to a head when Steve Patterson phoned one of the detectives
he knew at the Burbank Police Department and asked, "Do you have any
unsolved murders on the books? Going back, oh, ten years?"

The detective said, "Yeah, we have three."

"Don't tell me about them," Steve Patterson told the detective. "Let
me take a crack at one of them. Was she a young woman? And was she
tied up?"

"Yeah, we got one just like that," the detective said. "Her name was
Mary Duggan. A 1986 case. She was found in her car, raped and suffo-
cated."

Steve Patterson's obsession grew exponentially. Thus began a years-
long quest to solve the murder of Mary Susan Duggan.

She had been the cheerleader type in high school but had gained
weight after graduation, perhaps losing some self-esteem in the process.
Her parents lived in the San Fernando Valley and she'd worked at a bank,
which, Patterson quickly noted, was a few blocks away from the private-
investigation business owned by John Orr's former housemate and part-
time employer.

Patterson thought that she and John could've met in or around the bank.
John had a nose for vulnerable women, and a line that prompted casual
conversation which sometimes went somewhere. Moreover, in the novel,
Trish's mother had worked at a bank, which Patterson saw as another link.

Mary Duggan had been seen last at a pizza parlor all alone, around
midnight. Whether or not she'd been waiting for someone would never
be known. A Burbank cop on patrol had spotted her silver Ford Mustang
in a parking lot, and when he saw the car again the next night he noticed
that the window was broken on the driver's side. He got out to check,
and found Mary Susan Duggan—listed that night as Jane Doe #39 by the
L.A. County coroner—in the Mustang, covered by newspapers and a
"tanker" jacket.

Steve Patterson's neck hair started swaying when he learned that she
had ligature marks on her ankles and wrists, like Trish in John Orr's
novel. She hadn't been gagged with a bathrobe as in the novel, she'd been
gagged with tissue that forced her tongue back in her throat, suffocating
her. Mary Duggan had been barely twenty-two years old, three months
older than Steve Patterson's daughter, Jill. Patterson drove to the place
where she'd been found. Just three hundred yards from a 7-Eleven store.

But his colleagues said, So what? There're 7-Eleven stores everywhere. And rapists often bind their victims. So what?

Steve Patterson returned to the novel. In *Points of Origin,* the owner of the 7-Eleven store, a Pakistani, spots a fire that the arsonist Aaron Stiles has set with a delay device, and he hits the store's robbery alarm to summon help. He extinguishes the small fire and is warned by the arriving police never to use the robbery alarm as a signal to the fire department.

Patterson's former arson partner, a detective with the Burbank police, pulled old reports from the 7-Eleven store near the place where Mary Duggan's body was found. The store owner, a Pakistani, had also experienced a fire and had hit the robbery alarm to summon the fire department.

Steve Patterson contacted his colleagues, including some from the Pillow Pyro Task Force, and said, "See? John Orr was in that store! It's *not* fiction!"

The task-force cops said, So what? There're more Pakis running 7-Eleven stores than there are milking opium poppies in Islamabad. And half of them improperly use their robbery alarm at some time or another. So what?

Steve Patterson asked, "What's John Orr gotta do? Send us smoke signals? He's telling us in his book what he *did!*"

Cops on the task force would roll their eyes and snicker and barely keep their sneers under control. Ditto with others on Mike Matassa's task force when Patterson called them for moral support and encouragement.

The attitude said it all: *Firemen.* You can't make cops out of firemen.

Steve Patterson persuaded LASD's Rich Edwards to request information from the coroner's office, where John Orr had yet another former girlfriend. Patterson wanted to know if John had ever ordered any reports on Jane Doe #39, Mary Susan Duggan. The coroner's employee remembered that some years prior, he'd asked for reports on a coroner's case, but she had no memory of the name or what it was about.

When Steve Patterson inquired of Burbank detectives whether or not there had been DNA found, he was told that in 1986 there was no DNA analysis. So-called genetic fingerprinting was unknown to American law enforcement at that time.

"But since then," Steve Patterson wanted to know, "has anyone DNA'd whatever was found?"

He couldn't get a direct answer. It was an old case.

"Mary Duggan just seems forgotten," Steve Patterson complained. "A girl my daughter's age. Just *forgotten.*"

What he did find out was that vaginal swabs taken back in 1986 had revealed a trace amount of semen on her legs and buttocks, indicating that the killer might have ejaculated prematurely. In *Points of Origin*, after the arsonist goes flaccid he sets an incendiary device. Moments from flaming ignition where he might be trapped, he achieves his erection but ejaculates prematurely.

There was no stopping Steve Patterson then. He persuaded a Burbank detective to show him other evidence found in Mary Duggan's car, like the tanker jacket that had covered her body.

Steve Patterson asked the detective, "Has anyone checked the pockets?" And he was given one of those do-we-look-like-idiots? snorts of disgust.

"Can I look in the pockets?" Patterson asked, and got a let's-get-it-over-with, shrug.

He found in one of the pockets a toothpick and a chocolate mint. "Nobody seems able to tell me much about the lab evidence," Patterson said, "but isn't this toothpick something that could be sent in for a DNA test?"

The detective told Steve Patterson to put it back in the pocket and he'd check on it if he had time.

When Patterson got back to his task-force mates and tried to point out the importance of the toothpick for DNA analysis, he was met with more glazed expressions. They pointed out that lots of guys carry toothpicks, but when people pick their teeth they throw the toothpick away. They don't save it as a keepsake.

"In the book, chocolate mints're placed on their hotel pillows at the arson convention," Steve Patterson argued.

"Chocolate mints are everywhere!" he was told. "So what?"

It was always: So *what*? Steve Patterson went back to his copy of *Points of Origin* because he was sure there was something else. . . . And then it hit him!

At the beginning of the terrible description of the "Cal's" fire, he read: "While standing in the parking lot sharing a chocolate mint cone, she decided to entertain Matthew further by walking through Cal's."

If his neck hairs had swayed before, now they were break-dancing.

There were other duties that had the potential of getting Steve Patterson into trouble, aside from his quest to solve the murder of Mary Susan Duggan. He had occasion to interview an uncle of John Orr who had a business near an area where brush fires had broken out frequently. After a routine chat, the uncle called his wife, who called the Glendale fire chief, who called the Burbank fire chief, who called Steve Patterson and said, "You leave John Orr's family alone!"

The Glendale and Burbank fire departments had a close relationship, and there were still firefighters who did not want to believe that Captain Orr was a serial arsonist.

Steve Patterson later said, "I was like a dog on a leash. I was constantly being jerked backwards by my masters."

He tried working on other leads. John Orr's first wife and two daughters lived in Orange County, and John had gone to visit them for Christmas in 1990. A Thrifty Drug Store in their neighborhood burned on the very day he'd visited. Steve Patterson learned of other Thrifty Drug Store fires in Orange County, in addition to the pair of Thrifty fires in March of 1991 that they were sure he'd set. Patterson and Bill Donley went to the home office of Thrifty Drug Store in Hollywood and discovered that a secretary there *knew* John Orr.

It was always sex and fire. That brought Patterson back to Mary Duggan. He discovered that her former place of employment had experienced a fire while John Orr had been doing insurance work for his PI friend, so could he have met Mary on *that* occasion?

It wasn't difficult for Patterson to see that some of the cops were really getting sick and tired of his hunch and his theories. He'd hear remarks like, "We're trying to put together a capital murder case! What *more* do you want?"

To which Steve Patterson had an argument: "What about Mary Duggan's family? And how about Mary Duggan *herself*?"

When he'd be challenged with, "Do you think you're smarter than the detectives, Steve? Is *that* it?" He'd say, "I'm *not* smarter than the policemen. I'm *not*. I'm just a fireman, but . . . it all seems to *fit!*"

He'd unwind by working in the yard. He figured that during those days he'd mowed more grass than the grounds crew at Lakeside Country Club.

There was, however, a bit of task-force work done on Steve Patterson's Mary Duggan theory. Rich Edwards and Walt Scheuerell did look at car fires where women's bodies had been found. The victims were hookers, a few in Los Angeles and one in Pasadena, but nothing matched up with the murder of Mary Duggan.

Steve Patterson wanted more. He was frustrated to learn that nobody had ever checked with the cab companies to see if they'd picked up anyone in the vicinity of the 7-Eleven store on the night that her car and body had been left there. And he wanted *very* much to talk to the Duggan family.

Because of his badgering, a detective did call her family to ask: "Did she ever date a lawyer? Did she ever date a policeman? Did she ever date a fireman?"

But they had no answers. Steve Patterson wanted to come right out and ask it: "Did you ever hear Mary mention the name 'John Orr'?"

Finally, Steve Patterson could not contain himself. He had to interview the family of Mary Duggan, and that request found its way to the Burbank detectives. Patterson was called into the office of his boss at the Burbank Fire Department, and there waiting for him was not his boss but a detective lieutenant.

There was no debate, no explanation, no desire to know what Steve Patterson had learned. The detective lieutenant said, "Take your fucking nose *out* of police business and stick it somewhere else!"

The "discussion" was over. The detective left him there, fuming. But now his chain had been jerked and cinched up tight.

Mike Cabral told Steve Patterson that being a young prosecutor he did not have the gravitas to take on the Burbank Police Department, that maybe Patterson better just forget Mary Duggan for now and get on with the work they *must* do.

But just when Steve Patterson knew that he could go no further with his pursuit of the murderer of this girl who was his daughter's age, this girl who'd suffered such a cruel death—just as he was talking himself into getting over it now that it had turned into a pissing contest between the Burbank PD and an upstart fireman—Wally Scheuerell, the elder statesman of the task force, asked Patterson if he'd ever noticed what John Orr had written on page 272 of his novel in regard to one of the book's leading characters.

When Steve Patterson turned to the page in question, he found a discussion in a Fresno hotel during an arson conference, between the protagonist, arson investigator Phil Langtree, and his lady love, Chris. Phil Langtree describes to Chris the arsonist's attack on Trish, how he'd tied her up and tried to murder her, and that he must go back and investigate. Chris picks up the hotel phone to arrange a flight from Fresno to Burbank Airport, and for the first and only time in the novel, Chris gives her surname, which Steve Patterson hadn't noticed before:

"This is Chris Kilmary, room 432, would you please call the airport . . ."

For an old movie buff, it felt as though every hair was standing electrified, like the Bride of Frankenstein!

Before he could say anything, the old detective said to him, "I already checked with DMV. There's not a single last name like that in all of California's motor vehicle records. Why would he choose *that* name?"

All that Steve Patterson could do was repeat it: "Kilmary. Kilmary. *Kill Mary.*"

There was one day remaining before the statute of limitations was to expire on the brush-fire arsons when Deputy District Attorney Michael J. Cabral presented a twenty-five-count indictment of John Leonard Orr before a Los Angeles grand jury on Monday, November 21, 1994. It charged four counts of murder and one count of arson for the Ole's fire; one count of arson for the fire at Warner Brothers Studios; three counts of arson for the brush fires that burned homes on Kennington Drive in Glendale, Hilldale Drive in La Cañada, and San Augustine Drive in Glendale; and sixteen counts of arson for some of the homes burned in the College Hills fire of 1990.

That was a moment in time that John Orr would never forget. He was in his cell at Terminal Island listening to the radio when the program was interrupted by a commercial sponsored by the ABC affiliate, inviting the radio audience to tune in to the five o'clock news.

"The top story tonight," the announcer promised, "involves a fire captain indicted for murder."

Peter Giannini, the attorney for John Orr, told reporters that he was stunned, particularly in reference to the Ole's disaster.

John stayed away from the television all that evening, and phoned his wife as soon as he could.

Wanda Orr was contacted by Peter Giannini, who offered his services, explaining that they would not have to pay for the defense, which he knew would be impossible. He said that he could represent her husband and be paid by the state of California through a court appointment.

Wanda Orr contacted the prisoner, who reported a feeling of numbing despair. He agreed to retain Giannini, and wondered how long he would be permitted to remain in the relative comfort of Terminal Island. His answer came surprisingly fast.

Mike Cabral writted him out of Terminal Island and had him transferred to the L.A. County Jail in a matter of days, into the Protective Custody Unit in the old jail, where they kept the "high-power tank" for the high-profile prisoners. John later described his early weeks in the county jail as "sleep time." He said that he never had nightmares when he slept, and the only way to escape daytime horrors was to go to sleep.

His days in the high-power tank consisted of walking to and fro in a nine-by-nine-foot cage. Every other day he'd get to use the phone for a half hour. The prisoners were allowed to exercise once a week, and that year the only real entertainment was provided by hearing O.J. Simpson getting the word of the Lord from former football player turned preacher Roosevelt Grier when he came to visit.

Once, O.J. yelled, "I been covering up for that bitch for twelve years!"

The jail authorities insisted to the media that O.J. Simpson was being treated like any other prisoner. The inmates said, Right, if any other prisoner happens to be a pope.

John told his attorney that they had to get their case to court as soon as possible. Just after New Year's Day of 1995, the prisoner said that he didn't see how he'd survive more than a few months in that cage without trying to kill himself.

Steve Patterson was sent back to the firehouse, where he looked forward to retirement in a few years. There was no point obsessing over the Mary

Duggan case, making himself sick. Everybody seemed willing to forget her. It was as though she'd never lived.

But there were statistics, interesting statistics to which both of the task-force groups had access. The profilers at the FBI Academy had estimated that 70 percent of serial killers had been fire setters at some time in their lives. The incessant need for risk and excitement drove them to games of higher and higher stakes until "possession" of a fire wasn't enough. Then came the compulsion to "possess" human beings.

Even though they'd discovered John Orr's predilection for "tough love," nobody wanted to entertain the notion that his compulsion could have gotten out of hand. Steve Patterson had run up against the same kind of cynicism that another fireman had faced, a man Patterson had visited after the Fresno trial, when the district attorney's task force was re-interviewing all potential witnesses. Marvin Casey had faced that wall of blue ice. That cynicism which had killed more cops than all of the guns, knives, clubs, bombs, and cars combined. Cop suicides, the quiet statistic, outpaced killed-on-duty numbers just about every year in every major police agency.

Firefighters were not cynics, and the reason was simple: everybody *loves* a fireman. Gradually, Steve Patterson's hypertension decreased and so did his time behind a lawn mower. Life back in the firehouse offered camaraderie and the old familiar comforts. But he never quite got Mary Susan Duggan off his mind.

Walt Scheuerell and Rich Edwards respected Mike Cabral for "having a vision" that was about to be given a unique test. Nobody had ever been convicted of arson without the prosecution eliminating the probability of accidental fire. And the two LASD investigators were up against a case where one of their own, a crack arson cop, had declared Ole's an accidental fire.

After Scheuerell and Edwards talked with Sergeant Jack Palmer, their proud retired colleague, Scheuerell referred to Palmer as a "tired investigator" who just hadn't interviewed enough witnesses at the Ole's calamity of 1984. But finally, Palmer told them that if they came up with a different conclusion, they had to go with it.

Scheuerell said that he and Edwards, and others like them who investigated arsons for the Lean Green Machine, were the "stepchildren" of the L.A. Sheriff's Department investigators. And their homicide detectives were a bit embarrassed about Ole's. They were betting against Cabral's efforts to stoke the ashes of that long-dead conflagration.

The defense had to be given an inordinate amount of preparation and investigative time, given the complexity of the capital murder case that the district attorney had filed, so Scheuerell and Edwards were left with the mop-up assignments, even though they'd mostly returned to their routine duties as LASD arson investigators.

Scheuerell was fifty-five years old in 1995, and Edwards was ten years younger. The senior citizen of the task force had a street cop's suspicion of feds, and in dealing with the Pillow Pyro Task Force he'd always suspected that he hadn't learned all there was to know, but wasn't sure what was left. When John Orr had been arrested, he and Edwards were kept on the "arrest periphery."

In 1996, Sergeant Walt Scheuerell had open-heart surgery and retired from the L.A. County Sheriff's Department, where he'd served for thirty-five years. Although Scheuerell had been a "bit standoffish," according to firefighters in the task force, always expressing his opinions as tersely as possible, the firemen might've been comforted to know that he was one old cop who'd never been scornful of their efforts.

Scheuerell said that he had wanted Steve Patterson to find a "fifth victim" somewhere, believing that there might have been a psychological need for John Orr to have cremated *five* people in his fictional version of the Ole's fire. And he was the only career law-enforcement officer on either task force to say that the man who deserved the most credit for resolving the John Orr saga was not a cop but a fireman: Marvin G. Casey of the Bakersfield Fire Department.

After O. J. Simpson had been freed, the other prisoners got to go up to the roof twice a week for air and exercise. The Protective Custody Unit was a twenty-four-hour-a-day-lockdown experience. John Orr had occasion to complain in writing to the senior supervisor that his *Playboy* and *Penthouse* magazines had been stolen by deputies. And he believed that was what prompted a random search of his cell for contraband. He was stripped, handcuffed, and forced to watch as they tossed his cell.

His neighbor in the high-power tank was a forty-five-year-old Vietnamese cocaine trafficker who had supposedly fought in the war. The resourceful Asian figured out a way to turn a recessed light fixture into a little stove for boiling water, a luxury which he traded for instant coffee and candy bars. He gave bags of hot water to John Orr in exchange for letter-writing services, and it made John's life more bearable. His wife had divorced him in 1996, so it was a particularly miserable Christmas.

Death-penalty cases had been starting to wear down attorney Edward Rucker. He had done eight by the time he was asked to join the John Orr defense as a court-appointed counsel, specifically defending against those four counts of murder. Only one of the defendants whom Rucker had represented ended up on death row, a man who'd shot down a cop during a traffic stop and then executed the fallen officer, a difficult death verdict to overcome.

Each death-penalty case had taken a toll on the lawyer, who recalled having watched a TV documentary that featured John Orr. It gave him an idea of how his client would be targeted by law enforcement for his betrayal of the profession. By the new year of 1997, Ed Rucker was fifty-four years old, and had been practicing law since 1967. He was a former basketball player for the University of California at Berkeley, where he'd also gone to law school. Six-foot-seven-inch attorneys have to be particularly aware during trial, careful not to get too close to the jury and intimidate by size. It may have contributed to his laid-back, courteous style in a courtroom.

When he agreed to occupy the second chair at the defense table he was given stacks of boxes full of discovery material that had not been indexed or organized. It just lay there, all for him. And the defense had already had the case for two *years*. He knew that the court would step in one day soon and put a stop to any further delay. Rucker wasn't sure if his cocounsel would be on the winning side when it was over, but as he pored over some of the Ole's material he thought that he had a shot with his part of the case, by creating doubt as to whether the fire was arson or an accident.

Upon being approached by Rucker about the death-penalty decision, prosecutor Mike Cabral said he didn't care if John Orr's life was spared, he only wanted him off the streets for the remainder of his days. It led to an off-the-record offer. Rucker reported that Cabral would be amenable to a guilty plea and would not seek the death penalty if John Orr would do what serial-arson profilers desperately wanted him to do: speak freely about this and all of his arson crimes, starting from childhood.

All death-penalty lawyers remembered the time when America's most notorious violent serial offender, Ted Bundy, had wanted to do some life-and-death trading. After he'd had such a great time representing himself at his trial, giving interviews and fielding marriage proposals, it all had stopped. When he was just days away from his appointment with the Florida electric chair, he offered to locate his victims' bodies if the governor of Florida would commute his death sentence to life without parole. But the authorities told him, in effect, Too late, Ted. You got a date with Ol' Sparky, and Satan is waiting for his number-one draft pick.

So timing was everything. When Rucker told his client about the district attorney's interesting off-the-record offer, John was unimpressed and adamant. He would not plead guilty. He insisted that he was *not* guilty. And of all the crimes that John Orr had been charged with, both in Cabral's prosecution and those by the U.S. attorney, Ed Rucker believed that perhaps he truly had *not* committed this one.

But Rucker was never under any illusion about himself and Giannini trying to convince a jury, that, yes, he'd pled guilty to *some* arsons, but he didn't commit *these* arsons. His only shot was at persuading the jury that Ole's had been an accident. They'd try to litigate his guilty plea out of the state trials, but if they couldn't, it would be like sitting in the courtroom with the eight-hundred-pound gorilla, or more aptly put, a giant raging Fire Monster, perched behind the defense table, hissing like burning polyfoam.

Unfortunately for the defendant, page 6 of the U.S. attorney's seven-page plea agreement contained the following language:

> Except as expressly set forth herein, there are no additional promises, understandings or agreements between this office and you or your counsel concerning any other criminal prosecution, civil litigation or administrative proceeding relating to any other federal, state or local charges that may now be pending or hereafter be brought against you, or the sentence that might be imposed as a result of your guilty pleas pursuant to this agreement.

This agreement is not contingent in any way upon the out-
come of any investigation, proceeding or subsequent trial.

It would be extremely difficult to keep the Fire Monster out of the
courtroom while John Orr's attorney was fighting for his client's life.

By 1998, the high-power tank was loaded with crazies, and walking on
the tier was dangerous. John could not believe that his guilty plea to the
Builder's Emporium arson attempt in North Hollywood would be used
by the district attorney to prove that an identical fire in an identical store,
Ole's Home Center, had indeed been set by the defendant.

John claimed that the legalese in his plea agreement had confused
him, but that he'd been verbally assured by Giannini that it could never
be used against him in the unlikely event of a future state prosecution.
His attorney said, not true, that the plea agreement spoke for itself, and
that his client had assured him that he'd had nothing to do with any of
the crimes that the state had been investigating, especially the Ole's fire.

John's fourth ex-wife, Wanda, had been put into near bankruptcy. All
of his legal fees totaled $110,000, and she'd come very close to losing her
home. The only one of John's women who had stayed in his life was his
last girlfriend, Chris. She ran documents back and forth from Giannini's
office to the county jail.

The defense had taken so long preparing its case that John Orr was
numbed *past* suicidal thoughts. He alleged that Giannini would not
return his phone calls and had thus become another of the lawyers that he
hated. The only attorney left that he liked was Ed Rucker, but he claimed
that he had not seen Rucker face-to-face for over a year.

And at last, at long last, the court would not tolerate any more delay.
The trial of John Orr was set for May 1998, and there would be no further continuances granted.

In April of that year, Steve Patterson retired from the Burbank Fire
Department after twenty-nine years of service. And it seemed that Mary
Susan Duggan had nobody left to seek justice for her. It appeared that she
had lost her champion forever.

16

THE FIRE MONSTER

On Wednesday, May 6, 1998, in Department 104 of the Superior Court of the State of California for the County of Los Angeles, Judge Robert J. Perry had a question for the prosecution and defense teams standing at the bench.

He said, "We have a request from the *L.A. Times* for a still-camera photographer to be present in the back of the courtroom. He'll be shooting pictures of the attorneys during opening statements. Anybody have any objection to that?"

Deputy District Attorney Michael Cabral, speaking for himself and his assistant, Deputy District Attorney Sandra Flannery, said, "The people don't."

Edward Rucker, who stood a foot taller than the other lawyers present, with a crop of gray hair that made him look even taller, said, "I would object to it. I don't see where publicity really advances what we're doing here."

Peter Giannini said, "I think it's distracting for opening statements."

The judge said, "You've persuaded me. I'm going to deny the request."

Thus began the murder trial of John Leonard Orr, with defense counsel demonstrating that they were not grandstanders and were fully aware that they were fighting for their client's life.

The sinewy jurist, a devoted jogger, read, through gold-rimmed glasses, the jury instructions that John Orr would never forget. He talked about reasonable doubt and the presumption of evidence. The part of his reading that produced fear in the defendant was when he said, "Evidence will be produced for the purpose of showing that the defendant committed crimes *other* than those for which he is on trial. This evidence, if believed, may not be considered by you to prove that the defendant is a person of bad character or that he has a disposition to commit crimes.

"It may be considered by you only for the limited purpose of determining if it tends to show a characteristic, method, plan, or scheme in the commission of the criminal acts, similar to the method, plan, or scheme used in the commission of the offenses in *this* case.

"Now, if there is evidence that the defendant set a different fire—not one charged in the twenty-five counts, but other fires which are *not* charged in the indictment—you can't say, well, he set those other fires, therefore he must have set the fires charged in the indictment.

"Evidence of the uncharged fires may be considered only if there is a uniqueness in the characteristics of the uncharged fires which helps identify the person who set the charged fires, if indeed a charged fire was set and not caused by an electrical short or some other accidental condition. We will be talking about these issues during the trial. If you are a little confused, don't worry about it. I am sure the attorneys will straighten you out."

Sometimes on downtown jury panels you were looking at people you wouldn't dare make eye contact with if you were out on the street. And you only did it in the courtroom because there was an armed bailiff standing by. But none of these jurors looked like they might have a gun in their glove box. In fact, one of them was a lawyer who'd once worked for the City Attorney's Office as a prosecutor. And there was also a retired deputy sheriff on the jury. The defense apparently believed that these two potential enemies would go out of their way to be fair, and could explain complicated legal issues. John Orr didn't agree.

Except for the lawyer and the cop, the jury was an ethnic mixed bag of working folks, as one might expect to find on a downtown Los Angeles jury. And after hearing all that stuff about uncharged crimes, they probably thought: Confusing, Judge? Not at all.

If you're a fish, a *strange* fish.

Most who saw John Orr at this trial, at this time of his life, were looking at a man who'd aged. Three and a half years in a county jail cage does that to a person, any person who's had virtually no exercise or recreation. The defendant had lost the vigor that had been there at the Fresno trial. And now, wearing a mustache but not the beard that made him look professorial, he looked pale and soft and seedy.

The prosecution's opening statement was given by Sandra Flannery, a slender, articulate prosecutor with shoulder-length auburn hair. She was Cabral's age but had limited trial experience.

"A devastating fire was set on the evening of October tenth, 1984," she said. "It stole the lives of twenty-eight-year-old Carolyn Krause, seventeen-year-old Jimmy Cetina, fifty-year-old Ada Deal, and her two-year-old grandson, Matthew Troidl."

She went on to describe Ole's Home Center and the community of South Pasadena, with its one fire station only two blocks from Ole's, stressing how quickly the fire department had arrived. She described how Captain Eisele, needing help desperately, learned that another engine company from Alhambra was being sent to a different fire several blocks away at a Von's Market, a diversionary fire. And she said that yet another diversionary fire had been set at an Albertson's Market in Pasadena.

Sandra Flannery told the jury that 125 firefighters were needed to extinguish the Ole's blaze, too late for the victims trapped inside, and that ten minutes after the first engine had arrived, Glendale arson investigator John Orr was standing by the fire truck with a thirty-five-millimeter camera around his neck, asking for permission to shoot photos.

The jury was told that within twenty-four hours after the fire, the defendant had told Karen Krause Berry, sister-in-law of one of the victims, that the fire *was* an arson, and he later told her it had been started by an incendiary device placed within polyfoam products.

Sandra Flannery said she would present evidence of another uncharged act, the arson attempt at the CraftMart store in Bakersfield, where a fingerprint had been recovered. And that the prosecution would present evidence that a time-delay incendiary device had been used to set fires in Atascadero, as well as at Builder's Emporium in North Hollywood. And that the defendant had admitted to placing an incendiary device at each of those locations.

There it was, those guilty pleas. The hissing Fire Monster was glaring at the jury, and John Orr's lawyers knew it.

"These uncharged acts will be presented to you," she said, "to show that the Ole's fire was set as part of a common scheme, a modus operandi by which a distinctive time-delay incendiary device was used to set fires in similar types of materials at similar types of locations."

Mike Cabral, when it was his turn, addressed the jury to explain that the remaining counts of arson, counts five through twenty-five, mostly involved the homes that had been burned in the College Hills fire. He explained that they had finally charged the defendant with torching sixteen of the sixty-six, only those that had been burned to the ground.

After recess, the jury heard from defense counsel Ed Rucker, whose job it would be to convince the jury that the Ole's fire had been rightly called an accident. The towering defense lawyer immediately established that he was going to distance his arson count from the others that were being handled by Peter Giannini.

He said to the jury, "You're going to be presented with evidence of numerous fires. In an attempt to assist you in that, Mr. Giannini and I have divided the case up, so that I will speak to you *only* about the fire at Ole's on October the tenth, 1984. If I question a witness, it's going to be *only* a witness that has to do with Ole's. And this is a fire that took place fourteen years ago."

John Orr described Ed Rucker's style as "understated and gentlemanly." A great deal of delicacy was required when he said, "The Ole's fire was a tragic, tragic, fire in which four people lost their lives: a very young boy, his grandmother, and two young people. Tragic. If Mr. Orr is found not responsible for the Ole's fire, we don't get to the penalty phase, it's not a death-penalty case. So, no matter what you decide on the *other* fires, it's *only* the Ole's fire in which we're dealing with capital punishment, if you find Mr. Orr responsible for it.

"We're going to put on a defense. We're going to call witnesses. And we will attempt to show you that Mr. Orr is not responsible for this fire. In fact, *nobody* is responsible for this fire. Ole's fire was *not* an arson."

And then Rucker had to directly call attention to that hissing thing behind them.

"You're going to hear that Mr. Orr has *admitted* that he set fires. Now, this is a shameful thing. You'll hear testimony that he admitted in federal court that he set *three* fires, and was sentenced to thirty years. This is where your oath as a juror is challenged. Are you going to make the system work?

"We will present evidence that the Ole's fire was an accidental fire that started up in an attic area. This is not the first time that the Ole's fire has been litigated in court. There was a civil suit filed on behalf of the families of the deceased, and the case was tried, and what did they conclude? Nobody testified that this was an arson fire. *Nobody.* They all agreed that this was a fire started by accident, probably through some bad wiring up in the attic area."

Rucker gave the jury an idea of how attic fires start and smolder, and drop down through the ceiling. He said that when oxygen is introduced there can be an explosion, also called a flashover. He talked about the sprinkler system, and the fire doors, and the general contractor, and circuit breakers. It became quickly apparent to the media that this long and technical dissertation on fire cause and origin was just a prelude to what was coming.

Rucker concluded with, "You're not going to hear from a single witness who saw John Orr inside that store that night. In fact, you're going to hear evidence that at the time this fire was first seen, John Orr was talking with another fire investigator concerning another fire. And I think the evidence is going to show you that this is not arson. And I think you're going to be confident to return a verdict of not guilty on this fire."

When Peter Giannini had his turn, the jury got to hear that voice, fathoms deep, a voice that Stefan Stein said was a trial lawyer's dream voice. He began by reminding the jury that his client was not a common criminal.

He said, "One of the things that you know is that John Orr was an arson investigator. Whatever else he may have done, he was an arson investigator. He was highly respected in his field. He was a teacher of arson-investigation techniques, and he was at a lot of fires. He was at thousands of fires."

Peter Giannini couldn't have appeared more unlike Mike Cabral unless he'd grown as tall as Rucker. He was slim, with dark hair combed straight back, resembling one of the bosses in *Godfather II,* but with an even better tailor. He looked like what he was, a prosperous attorney with a practice in Century City.

Both he and Rucker were older and more experienced than the thirty-eight-year-old prosecutor, but both were about to learn why they called Cabral the Bulldog. It was not just for his appearance, but for his dogged approach, the way he kept plodding forward, chewing up wit-nesses in *little* bites. A workingman's lawyer, never spectacular, never slash-ing and dancing away like the more flamboyant courtroom wolves that the public sees on television. He'd just take the blows like a bulldog does, with a blink, a shake of the jowls, and the resolve to lumber on, stubby tail wagging, until the opponent was gripped by unyielding jaws.

Giannini went through the fires he had to defend, and only the Col-lege Hills calamity had real media appeal. Giannini talked about the Tele-trac and the prosecution's claims that John Orr was where he was not. And the defense lawyer tried to discredit claims that the incendiary device was a signature of the arsonist, but was rather a common device, so common that it was described in arson-investigation manuals. He described how feeble the witness identifications were, and then he got to the novel, something in which the media did have a real interest.

He said, "You're going to hear that John Orr wrote a book. And that the book is the prosecution's road map for this prosecution. There's no question that John Orr had access to fire information that is contained in the book. He's a fire investigator. He was present at some of these fires. The Ole's fire, for example, is described in the book. The fact that the incidents are in there does not mean that he set the fires. What it means is that he had *access* to the information.

"We live in L.A. Everyone's got a script or a book they're trying to sell. When you're putting together a manuscript, you try to put together the most exciting events that you can. The Ole's fire was clearly an excit-ing event."

And then it was time for this lawyer also to confront the Fire Monster, but he did it obliquely. He said, "I think the evidence will show that John Orr was a highly respected investigator. His opinion was valued by his colleagues. The evidence will show that he has been brought to justice for those fires that he's been responsible for. And that *this* final prosecution we don't believe will be proved to your satisfaction."

The first witness for the prosecution was Billy Deal, looking frail and older than his sixty-six years. Mike Cabral asked a few questions to establish that he had been at Ole's at 8:00 P.M. on October 10, 1984, and then he asked why Billy Deal had been there.

"We went there to buy some home-improvement materials," the witness said. "I was remodeling my home."

"Now, you said *we*," the prosecutor noted. "Who is *we*?"

"My wife and I and my grandson," the witness answered bleakly.

"Now, Mr. Deal, what was your wife's name?"

"Her name was Ada," the witness answered. "Ada Deal."

"Did she have a nickname she went by?" asked Cabral.

"Well, I called her Mommy," the witness answered.

And though fourteen years had passed since that terrible night at Ole's Home Center in South Pasadena, it came flooding back and the witness sobbed as he answered the questions of Mike Cabral. And so did many observers in the courtroom, especially when Cabral asked the witness how long he had stayed in the parking lot of Ole's Home Center on that night.

The witness answered simply, "Twenty-two hours."

Cabral's next question was, "Now, after splitting up with your wife in Ole's on that night, did you ever see her or Matthew again?"

"Not until I identified the bodies," the witness said.

John Orr's novel was addressed indirectly when Cabral asked his last question, "Now, prior to entering Ole's on that night, had you had a discussion with your wife and Matthew about what you were going to do *after* leaving?"

"Yes," said the witness. "As we were turning into the parking lot Matthew saw the Baskin-Robbins. And he wanted some goodies. And we told him we'd get him an ice cream after we got out."

"I have no further questions," Cabral said.

The defense lawyer knew he'd have to be very sensitive indeed with witnesses such as this one.

"Mr. Deal," Rucker said, "I understand it's difficult for you."

"Oh, yes," said Billy Deal.

"Any time you want to take a break, just let me know," Rucker said.

"I'd rather get it over with," the witness said.

Rucker got right to the ice cream testimony. It was dangerous for the
jury to think that John Orr might have put the discussion of chocolate
mint ice cream in his novel because he was at Ole's and had *heard* the
child begging his grandparents for an ice cream.

So Rucker said, "The only time that you discussed ice cream with your
grandson was when you were in the car driving into the parking lot?"

"To the best of my knowledge, yes," the witness said.

"You never discussed it in the store?"

"I can't recall," the witness replied.

"At any time you were out there in the parking lot, were you talking
with people, family, friends?"

"My daughter came over much later," said the witness. "I don't know
when it was."

"Were you talking to her, telling her what happened?"

"Yes, sir."

"Did you tell her you planning to buy an *ice cream* for him and things
like that?"

"I haven't the faintest idea," said the witness.

"Thank you very much, Mr. Deal," Ed Rucker said.

The jury at the moment must have been very puzzled by all the ice
cream fixation from lawyers on both sides.

Former Ole's employees were called, and it was astonishing how vivid the
memories were after fourteen years. Jim Obdam told his terrifying story
of trying to lead Ada Deal and her grandson Matthew in utter darkness.
And of the dense black smoke, and of praying, and managing to get outside where the flesh fell from his burned wrist onto the ground.

And Anthony Colantuano told of seeing his fellow employees Jimmy
Cetina and Carolyn Krause earlier that evening, but never seeing them
again. He made the jury understand how unbelievably fast a heavily fueled
fire can move when he said that one minute he saw nothing and then the
next minute, "I saw fire, flames and *everything* coming toward me!"

The jury heard from a provocative witness, the wife of a police sergeant, who testified that when John Orr got arrested she'd seen his photo
in the newspaper, and she'd recalled having seen him in Ole's the evening
before the disaster.

Rucker's questions were effective, but the witness was adamant, some might say too adamant for an event so far in the past.

He asked, "So it's been fourteen years since you've seen the man with your own eyes?"

"Yes," she answered. "It's been fourteen years since I saw him in the store."

"And you're one hundred percent sure that this is the same man?"

"Yes, sir, I am," she said.

She testified that she'd been on crutches at the time, that the man had almost walked into her, and she'd noticed he was wearing a basket-weave belt like police officers wear on duty.

Rucker asked, "Was the man wearing glasses?"

And she gave an extraordinary reply. "He was not wearing glasses at the time. He had sunglasses in the left front pocket of his shirt, and they had black wire frames."

Sometimes a witness's memory can be *too* good, so Rucker asked when was the next time that she'd had occasion to remember his face, and she said, "I saw his picture on television several years ago when apparently he'd been arrested for some other fires."

The witness then testified that after realizing where she'd seen the face before, she'd wanted to tell the South Pasadena police about it, but her husband had told her not to do it. She explained that she did not have a good rapport with "a certain captain."

"And had you made reports of your ability to identify people prior to that incident?" Rucker asked.

"Yes, sir," she answered.

"And had these prior reports resulted in you not being on such good terms with the captain?"

"Correct," she answered.

"How many *other* individuals have you reported that you were able to identify as someone you'd seen and later learned had committed crimes?"

"There have been two or three other large cases in South Pasadena where I have been able to tell the department that I'd seen individuals either committing a crime a week or two before they actually committed a larger crime."

"And is this based on seeing their photographs in the newspapers?" Rucker asked.

"One was. Two of them were not."

Further testimony revealed that the first time the witness officially had spoken with anyone about seeing John Orr was when her police sergeant husband got called to testify to Mike Cabral's grand jury and his wife had accompanied him there.

Of course, many media observers were thinking that her memory had been jogged by television or newspaper reports, but the witness said that the only television coverage she'd ever seen on John Orr was on the night of his arrest.

Then Rucker asked, "Had you read anything in the newspaper?"

"We do not receive the newspaper," the witness answered. "Our dog eats anything that comes near our yard."

The fire chief of South Pasadena, William Eisele, was called. Fourteen years earlier he'd been the fire captain who arrived a few minutes after the alarm was given. Eisele told of the event, about how he'd tried to enter and attack the fire. He told of seeing John Orr shortly after his arrival, and how the defendant had asked if he could shoot some photos. He gave important testimony about not seeing much smoke when he'd arrived, but his testimony would be attacked on cross-examination. He told of trying to ventilate the roof, and of having to bring his man down due to the danger of the roof collapsing. And he described a second fire that had occurred at about the time of the Ole's fire, a short distance away at Von's Market.

After the noon recess Ed Rucker reminded the fire chief that at his grand-jury testimony he'd indicated that they hit the "seat of the fire," meaning the ceiling, this being a defense attempt to prove that the fire took place above the ceiling in the attic space.

And then to explain his client's quick arrival at the blaze, Rucker asked, "Mr. Orr showed up at the fire and you saw him there, is that right?"

"That's true."

"And was it normal for arson investigators from adjoining jurisdictions to show up at fires?"

"That's true," the witness said.

"You didn't find it abnormal for an arson investigator to take photographs of a fire?"

"No."

"And without some fire-fighting equipment with him, you wouldn't have sent him into contact with that fire?"

"No no no no," the fire chief said. "He was an investigator."

"And during the course of the evening, several investigators from the adjoining jurisdictions showed up, did they not?"

"We had investigators all the way up to the state and federal level that showed up at the scene. We had everyone there."

"It was your opinion at the time that the point of origin was in the attic space?"

"It appeared to be the southwest corner attic space. This is just what it appeared," the witness answered.

"And you felt it was a low smoldering fire that occurred over a period of time in the attic?"

"Those were the findings of the investigators," Eisele replied. "I used the information gathered from the investigators."

"And it was *your* personal opinion at that time, that the fire, after smoldering in the attic area, broke down through some point in the ceiling?"

"That would be my opinion," said the fire chief.

Mike Cabral later said of the witness's troublesome testimony, "I was just trying to get *through* it."

So far, Cabral's case was not going well, and the Fire Monster was silent.

During the second day of trial an investigator for Von's Grocery Company testified about a fire that took place at Von's, a few minutes from Ole's, at about 8:00 P.M. on the night that Ole's burned. He said that the morning after the calamity, he'd had occasion to speak with John Orr. The witness testified that the defendant told him that the Von's fire had been intentionally set by a smoldering cigarette.

Rucker tried to portray the Von's fire as another accident, or perhaps a diversionary fire set by juveniles who wanted to shoplift. But on redirect,

Mike Cabral asked, "Did the defendant explain something to you concerning potato chips?"

The witness nodded. "About the volatility of the chips. The oils in the chip, and why the fire was so big in such a small area."

"Had you ever heard before of a fire in a potato-chip rack?"

"No."

"What about since?"

"No."

Ed Rucker had no questions on recross. The jury was going to learn about Pillow Pyro fires and potato-chip fires, so this witness had not been helpful to the defense.

The importance of potato-chip testimony was nailed down by the next witness, Dennis Foote, of the Los Angeles Fire Department, who'd been phoned by the defendant on the morning after the Ole's blaze. The witness testified that for four years prior to the Ole's fire, he'd been putting together information about a fire series in and around the city of Los Angeles that had taken place in retail commercial businesses during afternoon and early evening hours. He said that he'd investigated a fire at a store like Ole's, called Builder's Emporium, and that the fire had begun in the polyfoam section much like other fires he'd been tracking.

This was deceivingly dangerous testimony for the defense because the jury would eventually be hearing that the defendant had pled guilty to an arson at the same Builder's Emporium store, and that an identical incendiary device had been used.

The next witness was called to provide more information about diversionary fires on the night of the Ole's disaster. Scott McClure, a Pasadena fire investigator, said that a fire alarm came in at 6:45 P.M. on the night in question for a fire that had occurred at Albertson's Market. McClure had determined that the fire was incendiary in nature, and that it had broken out in the potato-chip racks. The witness said he'd called dispatch, asking for John Orr's location.

He said, "With the experience that he had, I always relied on his word as being the Gospel. I admired his work. So anything he said, I felt comfortable with."

This was another potentially dangerous witness for the defense, so when it was Rucker's turn, he began by establishing a time line that he hoped would prove that John Orr could hardly have set three fires in such a short period of time. He asked McClure to estimate how long John Orr had been at Albertson's and the witness said about fifteen or twenty minutes.

There was a great deal of talk about incendiary devices, and which was more common than another, but one could not help but take away from the day's proceedings that having *three* fires in retail businesses so close to one another in time and distance, whether incendiary or accidental, had *never* happened before in the experience of any of the local fire investigators.

On the last day of the week, the first witness called, whom the defense had no wish to cross-examine, was Karen Berry, née Karen Krause, the sister-in-law of Ole's victim Carolyn Krause. She told of the night of the fire, and that she'd been a community-service officer for the Glendale Police Department.

"What if anything did the defendant later say to you concerning the fire?" Cabral asked.

The witness answered, "In discussing the investigation he was somewhat disappointed and upset because it was not being investigated as an arson."

"And did he say anything else concerning that?"

"Yes, he said there had been a number of other such fires in home-improvement companies, specifically the Builder's Emporium in North Hollywood, where a fire had been started in a polypropylene mattress which was subsequently extinguished by the sprinklers. He said there was a possibility that the Ole's fire may have been set the same way."

"Did the defendant say anything else to you concerning the nature of the cause of that fire?" the prosecutor asked.

"Yes. In the previous fire that he mentioned in North Hollywood, he said that a time-delayed device had been set in the polypropylene mattress."

"And did he tell you anything concerning the autopsies of the individuals who died in the Ole's Home Center fire?"

"Yes. He expressed disappointment because there were no investigators present at the autopsy for any of the victims. He felt the materials that may have been given off by such things, such as polypropylene mattresses or other flammable items, may have left particles of some material in the victim's lungs or in their tracheas. Or there may have been some gases present that might have otherwise been absorbed in the body that could've been discovered during the autopsy."

There were many good reasons for Rucker not wanting to cross-examine this witness, and it was not just because of the defendant's distress that the Ole's fire had been called an accident. It was the dreaded name of Builder's Emporium.

For the next several hours the jury was going to hear from the first of the experts who were going to offer opinions as to whether the Ole's fire was or was not correctly called an accidental fire. The first of these was Wayne Martin, a retired fire-protection engineer and civil engineer, who had served for twenty-two years with the Los Angeles Fire Department.

The witness testified that he'd been contacted in 1993 by the D.A.'s Arson Task Force to review all the reports available from the Ole's fire. He quickly got to the point by saying that he did not agree with Sergeant Jack Palmer that the disaster had probably been caused by an electrical fire in the attic.

He said that if it had been an attic fire reaching temperatures of one thousand degrees or more, he would expect the flashover to take place in the attic first. He explained that the venting of the roof by firefighters is done to allow the smoke and gases to escape, so that the firemen can see open flame and sometimes the fire's source, in order to more effectively extinguish it.

The defense quickly launched an attack on Martin's credentials. The witness said that he'd never served with the Arson Investigative Section, and had never testified as an arson expert in a court of law. He made it clear that he'd only been called upon to give an opinion as to whether or not the Ole's fire was consistent with an attic fire.

Ed Rucker did a thorough job with questions about what the witness did *not* know about the Ole's fires, about neighbors of Ole's who did smell or see some smoke that must have vented from the roof. The defense attorney demonstrated a thorough understanding of what materials were used in the roof composition, and he asked hypothetical questions about ceiling tiles and wind directions, designed to cast doubt on the witness's opinion about the fire's point of origin. Rucker tried to get an admission that if some ceiling tiles were missing, an ember could have dropped through, igniting a second fire on the retail floor of the building.

The entire testimony of the witness could be summed up in one question and one answer, both of which came after hours of repetitive and technical questions and answers. It boiled down to this: Did the fire start up and drop down? Or down and climb up? Which is more likely?

When court resumed on Monday of the second week, John Orr's friend and colleague Jim Allen, formerly of the state Fire Marshal's Office, was called. One of the first answers he gave that was helpful to John Orr was that he couldn't say if the fire had started in the attic or on the floor of the building.

But what was *not* helpful to the defense, and what any layperson could readily understand, was that this man whom Allen called a social friend as well as a colleague had never mentioned to him that there were two potato-chip fires that evening. And further, that John Orr had been at one of those and was the official investigator at the other. That was an extraordinary thing for his friend to have kept from Allen when they were at the Ole's investigation the next morning.

Cabral asked, "Would knowledge of those two fires have had some impact on *your* investigation?"

Allen answered, "Yes. I would've spent more time with the sheriff's lieutenant who ordered us out, by trying to convince him that there had been *other* fires, therefore we really needed to thoroughly investigate *this* one."

Mike Cabral called another L.A. Fire Department employee, James Daneker, who had earned a doctorate in pharmacy prior to joining the fire service. Captain Daneker had more than twenty-five years service with the LAFD, and was to testify only to fire dynamics. Daneker's job had been to use the radio recordings of the fire department to try to establish at what point during the Ole's fire some of the things described by witnesses had occurred. He said that if there had been a genuine attic fire, flames would've come out the roof before coming out the doors, because fire obeys the laws of physics and chemistry.

As before, when it was Ed Rucker's turn, he went directly at the qualifications of the witness, pointing out that Captain Daneker's educational background was in pharmacy, not fire dynamics. Daneker countered that he was currently in command of Fire Station Number 39 in Van Nuys, and that he'd qualified in court as an expert on fire cause and origin on many occasions. Like other witnesses, the fire captain stressed that he was not there to say that the Ole's fire was an arson, or anything else about the cause, but merely to say that in his opinion the origin had *not* been in the attic.

Again, Ed Rucker conducted a lengthy cross-examination about the witness's knowledge of the building materials that went into the construction of Ole's roof and ceiling, but the witness kept giving direct, simple answers to very complex technical questions. And no matter how long the questioning went on, or how the questions were framed, the witness kept returning to the laws of physics. He might as well have had Isaac Newton sitting on his lap.

After hours of questioning, Rucker pointed out that Sergeant Jack Palmer of the L.A. Sheriff's Department, and many other arson investigators at the scene, had called the fire an accident, and asked if those reports would have at least been useful to the witness in forming his own opinion.

But the fire captain replied, "Not necessarily, because those were all investigations after the fact. And what's important to me in deciding whether or not Ole's was an attic fire was the dynamics while the fire was still going on."

Like the trained pharmacist he was, the fire captain relied on the properties of matter, and that was that. His time on the stand could have ended in twenty minutes, and the jury could have accepted it or not. But it ground on from both lawyers until the witness had to repeat his opinion in every possible way without exiting the English language.

The dogged prosecutor finally arrived back full circle, and mercifully concluded with, "And fire is always going to be trying to rise?"

The witness said, "Yes. That's one of the rules of physics, the transfer of heat."

The prosecution's next witness was Frank Randall Holmes, an electrical contractor and electrician with about thirty-seven years of experience. It was his and his father's company that had done the electrical work for Ole's a few years before the night of fire.

When Ed Rucker took over he established that most of the physical overseeing of the actual work had been done not by the witness but by his foreman. And he also elicited a statement by the witness that the business had gone bankrupt. The reason became clear when Rucker asked the witness if he'd settled the huge lawsuit with the plaintiffs, hinting at culpability.

The witness was asked about track lighting, and the lighting fixtures in the display canopy, and he admitted that there were some breakers in the store that were not holding their capacity and had tripped from time to time, requiring service calls. His people had spoken to the store employees about taking more care with their light displays, so that too many fixtures were not put up.

On redirect, Cabral asked a question that got a nod from most non-lawyers in the courtroom: "Mr. Holmes, if you know, did *everyone* who had anything to do with any of the remodeling or construction at this Ole's Home Center get sued?"

The witness replied, "I believe everyone did, yes."

"No matter what they did at the site?"

"I believe so."

Cabral asked the witness to repeat that the main service for Ole's had been a sixteen-hundred-amp service, twice what the store had been using, and had been extremely adequate.

All of the television media, composed of people with the attention span of sand fleas, had fled halfway through the testimony. In fact, most of the gallery, except for the die-hard rail birds, had also hauled ass. Thus far, the trial was so technical that even the Fire Monster might have keeled over from fatigue.

17

REDACTIONS

The time had come to expect another law-enforcement witness to fall on his sword. Jack L. Palmer was called to the stand. The witness testified that he'd been a sergeant on the Los Angeles County Sheriff's Department assigned to the Arson/Explosives Detail, with twenty-five years of service at the time of the Ole's investigation, and he'd retired three years later. John Orr said that Jack Palmer looked like every other retiree from the sheriff's department that he'd ever met, a beefy, mustachioed old cop, but this one had little of the customary swagger, not on this day.

Jack Palmer listed his qualifications, among them that he'd investigated five thousand fires in his career, and then Cabral took him directly to October 11 at 10:30 in the morning.

Cabral placed the diagram of Ole's on the board for the witness to study, and asked him to make marks with a laser pen. Palmer testified that in 1984 he'd drawn his conclusions about how the fire had vented by looking at heat patterns on the exterior walls where the ceiling had caved in. He talked about the steel girders having twisted due to that intense heat, and that he'd thought the hot spot was in the south end of the structure.

After considerable questioning, Cabral asked, "Did you ever determine from talking with employees where the polyfoam was stored?"

The witness answered, "No one ever told me there was any polyfoam *anywhere.*"

"And would that have been significant?" Cabral asked.

"Yes," the witness answered, "it certainly would have. Because polyfoam, once it gets in an open flame, goes like wildfire."

Cabral asked, "Now, Sergeant Palmer, how long did you spend at the location before you made your determination?"

"My first determination, I was probably there about an hour, hour and a half."

"And what determination did you reach?"

"That I was unable to eliminate electrical shorting in the attic area."

"And that was because the attic area was gone?"

"Yes. What was very very very hard in reading a fire like this is because you have so much of a fuel load in there. So we had secondary fires. When you get overhead burning, materials fall down and start another fire. So you have numerous hot spots depending upon what your fuel load is."

The witness testified that he'd interviewed the first-in fire captain, William Eisele, and "a couple of employees," including James Obdam, who had barely gotten out alive.

And then the prosecutor mentioned the names of other employees whom Jack Palmer had *not* interviewed, and Cabral repeated what Anthony Colantuano had seen, the fire boiling from the racks toward the center of the store. And how the fire had exploded out the door behind the fleeing employee.

Jack Palmer said, "I never heard any statements like that."

"Okay, would it be significant to your conclusions?" Cabral asked.

"Sure it would," the witness said. "I had a high fire. We dug that area out completely and we could not find evidence of a low fire in there."

"By low fire, what do you mean?" Cabral asked. "If the fire started two to three feet off the floor, you wouldn't necessarily have been looking for that?"

"No," Palmer answered. "Unless I had a pattern of fire-sets like that."

Then Cabral took the tack that everyone was waiting for. "You *were* aware on that night that there were two *other* fires in the area, and they were both arson fires. Is that correct?"

"Yes, they advised me of those," the witness admitted. "Those fires they told me were in stores, grocery stores. And were set in potato-chip racks, open flame to potato-chip bags. I mean, I don't . . . I considered the information, but as an investigator, I know what evidence I need. I know when I testify I have to be sure in my mind that I have eliminated all accidental sources."

The Bulldog kept chewing away at the witness's pride, little bites at a time: "Now, if there had been additional information that in fact there was a *history* of fires involving potato-chip racks, and polyfoam, and a particular device, would *that* have affected your opinion and your evaluation of this fire scene?"

"Yes, had I known there was polyfoam in that area," the witness said, partially agreeing.

"And during the course of your time there, were there a lot of investigators there?"

"Yes, there were."

"If any of those investigators were familiar with this pattern that was occurring, would you have expected them to talk to you about it?"

"I certainly would."

Cabral was speaking of the defendant when he asked, "And did anyone talk to you about any pattern of fires or anything like that concerning the two other fires?"

"They did not."

Again referring to the defendant, the prosecutor asked, "And did anyone tell you that they had any information that led them to believe that this was an arson fire started in the polyfoam, using a specific device?"

"No, sir, they didn't."

"And would you expect an arson investigator to explain that information to you?"

"Yes, I would."

"I have no further questions," Cabral said.

Ed Rucker asked questions to point out that Palmer had had five other members of the LASD arson unit with him at Ole's that morning, as well as numerous other arson investigators. And that *nobody* had expressed vocal disagreement with Palmer.

Rucker made the witness repeat that what he'd seen at the site led him to believe that it was a high fire that had burned *down* and started a secondary fire on the floor, and that Jim Obdam had told Palmer that a couple of days before the fire the lights had gone off.

Rucker asked, "And has it been your experience that electrical shorts can result in ignition of material?"

"It certainly can," the witness said.

Rucker asked, "Did the fact that there were other fuel loads on the floor where the secondary fire fell down . . . that's not going to change what you saw as those fire indicators, is it? Those burn patterns up above the ceiling level?"

"If I had a set fire with a petroleum product, it would cause a rapid fire. There would've been the same result."

"And you can't draw a distinction on what you saw between the two interpretations of what happened? Both seem reasonable?"

"Both are reasonable."

"Has anything you've learned since then brought you to change your conclusion?"

"Not anything that I've learned since then, no." Then he hedged, "I understand, you know, the facts of the case. But I . . . if you want to give me a hypothetical, I would say, if I knew a fire was set in that foam, then that is my rapid fire. That is my source. But when I read the fire fourteen years ago, I did not eliminate the electrical."

When Cabral got his witness on redirect, he had to take him on. He said, "Were you aware that Investigator Jim Allen felt that he was kept out of the scene for some period of time by the lieutenant from the homicide division?"

"A couple of the other team members had said, you know, that he was complaining about that," the witness replied.

And one more time the balkanization of American law enforcement was demonstrated. Palmer had never been told by anybody from the other agencies about the potato-chip file, not by anyone, including the defendant. Nobody had talked about market fires as possibly being diversionary arsons. Nor was Palmer ever told anything about the prior polyfoam fires, nor that Builder's Emporium in North Hollywood had experienced such a fire. Everyone kept everything to himself. And nobody had seemed willing to dispute the Lean Green Machine.

When the witness left the stand, observers would have to say that he hadn't significantly helped either side. The case was not going to be

decided by Sergeant Jack Palmer's testimony. He had refused to fall on his
sword for the D.A. In fact, all he'd been willing to accept was a paper cut.

The next witness, Marc Lewis, a former lumber salesman for Ole's, testified to the stunning speed and agility of the fire, leaping across display racks.

Then the lucky young man said, "As I was leaving, I heard the fire
door starting to go down. I saw a guy come out this other door, and then
flames came flying out after him!"

On cross-examination, Ed Rucker worked at finding out from where
the fire had emanated, and the witness said he'd seen it coming from a
rack of welcome mats, both woven and plastic, not from the polyfoam
racks, possibly indicating a secondary fire.

Then Mike Cabral called one of his task-force members, Rich
Edwards, who testified that he'd been with LASD for twenty-six years,
but when the Ole's fire had occurred, he was a new kid on the block as
far as arson investigation was concerned. He said that he was the only
investigator who'd been present on the scene in 1984 and had also had
the opportunity to examine all of the later task-force information.

"And based on all of this information," Cabral asked, "do you have an
opinion as to the cause and origin of this fire?"

"The fire was incendiary, or arson," Edwards said. "And the fire
started in highly combustible merchandise that was stored adjacent to the
southeast corner of the aisles."

When Ed Rucker got the witness, he made sure that the jury understood that Edwards's opinion was based on information he'd gathered
since the task force was formed in 1992, eight years *after* the Ole's fire.
But Edwards was the first sheriff's department investigator to testify that
he'd heard Investigator Jim Allen complaining that he wasn't being given
enough time at Ole's to conduct his investigation.

Edwards gave an astonishing statistic: since the task force was formed,
they'd secured reports on twenty thousand fires to see if they fit the M.O.
And moments later, much to the surprise of everyone, Cabral rested his
Ole's case insofar as prosecution witnesses being called to testify.

Eleven days after the start of trial, Sandra Flannery took over her part of
the prosecution of John Orr, and began calling witnesses to the College
Hills fire. Her first witness was a retired U.S. Air Force major.

She asked, "On June twenty-seventh, 1990, did you have an occasion to drive into the city of Glendale?"

The witness testified that he was driving on Verdugo Road near Glendale College at about 3:30 P.M. when he saw that the hillside was in flames. He'd decided to stop his car to alert people in a nearby apartment building that they were in danger. When he'd slowed to stop he'd seen a man outside the building talking to a woman.

In response to the prosecutor, the witness said he'd seen a pickup truck parked nearby, and that after the man stopped talking to the tenant, "He stopped and looked, and he just momentarily stared at me with a kind of a shocked look."

The witness then had decided that the tenants had been alerted by the man, so he'd driven to the nearest gas station to make a 911 call.

Sandra Flannery asked, "At some later date, did you have an occasion to see any photographs of that man you saw?"

"One evening on the news there was a flash of an individual who was supposedly involved in an arson case, and all of a sudden I just told my wife, I said, 'That was him. The gentleman we saw at the Glendale fire.' "

Flannery asked, "What was it that caused you to recognize the man in the photograph as the man you saw on the landing by the fire?"

The witness answered, "When I see something that is very unusual and it happens to go in my memory bank, I don't realize it. Later on when I recognize something, it just pops out. It ties back and I say, that's him."

The witness testified that at the grand jury he'd been shown a photo six-pak, and chose the photo of John Orr. But of course, that was after the face had been fixed by TV coverage. Then he identified the defendant seated in court, allowing for the fact that the defendant had aged and gained weight.

"I am a retired air force pilot," the witness explained. "And in the training of air force pilots you make momentary or split-second memories of items that you see. And that was carried throughout my air force career. At times I would be behind the Iron Curtain, and I would be required to identify an individual or look at an individual. And then when I would be returning, I would have to identify who they were or try to tie them back to some kind of a photograph."

When the witness was handed over, Peter Giannini asked several questions to establish where the witness had been in relation to the fire and the apartment building, and more important, that he'd seen no other cars on the street except for the pickup truck. It was helpful to the defense because John Orr drove a white Chevrolet Blazer.

When Giannini got to questions about the witness's extraordinary memory, the witness said, "I was both qualified in photographic intelligence, and learned how to recognize various things in hundredths of a second. I should tell you I have a photographic mind, so something that is important automatically clicks."

Glendale fire captain Greg Jones took the stand and testified that he'd seen the defendant uphill from them when they'd arrived, and he'd found it "a bit strange" because he couldn't understand how John Orr had got his car there without passing the fire engine, implying that he must have been at the area of origin before anyone else had arrived.

The witness told how he'd asked the defendant to take a hose to a house that was threatened, but that John Orr "was agitated and didn't seem in control of what he was doing." He related how the defendant had just tossed "a salvage cover" over a couch and left the scene, while firefighters were fighting a blaze that was threatening the house itself.

Moses Gomez, of the state Fire Marshal's Office, told of his peculiar and aimless drive around the fire scene that night with the defendant in his white Blazer, and of John Orr showing him a cigarette-lighter incendiary device that he'd stored in a vial. He described a strange press conference where the defendant told the media everything about the device, thereby destroying its confidential value to investigators if an actual suspect was found.

Giannini's cross-examination sought to show that John Orr's behavior during the press conference when he'd told about the incendiary device was not detrimental to a later investigation, and that he'd been asked by his boss to make a statement to the press.

The witness testified that two months after the fire, at a round-table meeting of arson investigators, John Orr had informed the group that he was no longer sure of the cause of the College Hills fire because subsequently he'd found additional disposable lighters in the area.

The questioning intensified after the witness expressed an opinion that the College Hills fire was incendiary in nature.

Giannini said, "I'm confused. Are you calling this an arson now?"

"If I'm allowed to explain," the witness said.

"Well, no. Just answer my question. Are you calling it an arson?"

"Yes, I am."

"So that's different than what you said before?"

"Yes."

"You're changing your opinion as you're sitting here talking?"

"I'm changing my opinion based on the questions that are posed to me to explain how I did things on that particular afternoon."

"Well, let me ask you, did you eliminate all possible accidental causes?"

"Based upon where I was, no."

"It *might* have been an accidental fire, isn't that right?"

"That's correct."

"So how can you call it an arson?"

The witness tried to say that his opinion on this day in court was based on information he'd later received that he thought was credible.

The judge interjected, "And in your brief reviewing of the scene, you didn't see anything to contradict that. Is *that* what you're saying?"

"That's correct," the witness said, probably grateful that the judge was testifying *for* him.

"All right," Judge Perry said. "Because you didn't investigate as thoroughly as you would've had it been your responsibility to do the investigation?"

"That's correct, Your Honor," the witness said.

"I think we've covered it," said Judge Perry.

John Orr reported later that he saw the judge as a witness for the prosecution.

One of John Orr's associates was his former partner Don Yeager, who had retired after twenty-seven years with the Glendale Fire Department. When Yeager was called to the stand he testified that when he'd arrived the day after the fire he'd found his partner at the command post appearing "tired and haggard."

Yeager recalled that when he'd suggested canvassing the neighborhood for possible-suspect leads, the defendant had told him that he'd turned that job over to the police department, which Yeager had found very strange. And after Yeager had taken it upon himself to do some canvassing, he'd learned that the police had not done anything, the suggestion being that John Orr had just stonewalled the whole thing.

All of the testimony was directed toward the hypothesis that the defendant had done almost nothing to investigate the greatest fire disaster that his city had ever experienced, and didn't seem to want his partner working on it either.

When Giannini took the witness, his questions were designed to show that John Orr's duties might have been extensive, if not apparent to Yeager.

Suddenly, the judge interrupted Giannini, but this time his questions helped the defense elicit the testimony it needed.

"Let's try to get through this," the judge said. "Mr. Giannini was talking about Mr. Orr getting statistics together, information on how the homes burned, basically trying to defend the fire department or at least putting information together that the fire department could use in talking to the public. The point is, he *was* involved with statistics he was gathering in relation to the College Hills fire?"

"Oh, yes, absolutely," the witness agreed.

"You wanted more *investigative* effort put in the investigation on the *cause* of the fire?"

"Yes, yes," the witness agreed.

"And you became frustrated and you went to the supervisor, is that correct?"

"Yes."

"All right," said the judge, "but you're not saying that Mr. Orr was not *working* on College Hills?"

"No, absolutely not," Yeager said.

Giannini said, "Thank you, Your Honor, I couldn't have done it better."

Judge Perry seemed to feel, along with many observers, that the lawyers and witnesses were in desperate need of a good editor. Regardless, the defendant still saw him as Judge Roy Bean, with a law book in one hand and a rope in the other.

Then came the reference to something that had been mentioned in opening argument, a "DR number." It was the number assigned to a crime, by which the reports could be tracked for all time. The prosecution wished to show that in such a major disaster, one that the defendant had initially called an arson, there had never been a crime number requested or assigned, as one would do with something as ordinary as juveniles setting a trash can on fire.

At this point, late on a Friday afternoon, the judge seemed frustrated with the lawyers on both sides for not having asked fundamental questions in a straightforward manner.

Judge Perry said, "I will just *ask* it. Would you have expected a DR number to have been pulled for the College Hills fire?"

The witness replied, "Absolutely."

"All right, let's wrap it up," said Judge Perry.

And then he wished everyone a pleasant weekend, reminding them to allow plenty of time for their Monday morning commute. And everyone got out of there and careened into the nightmare of Friday afternoon traffic in Los Angeles, where frustrated people routinely stare at one another through tinted glass and contemplate acts of violence.

On Monday of the trial's third week, John Orr's immediate boss, Assistant Fire Chief Christopher Gray, was called to explain how, because of the media blitz and public criticism, all personnel of the Glendale Fire Department had been ordered by the fire chief to account for their activities on the day of the fire. In describing his activities on that day, the defendant had written, "I was performing a reinspection at the end of Whiting Woods Road when the first alarm was called. I drove to the area and arrived as the final first-alarm units were arriving."

When asked by Flannery, Chief Gray said that Whiting Woods Road was about two miles from the College Hills fire, and that a subsequent search for documentation of John Orr's reinspection activities was negative. In fact, he could not find documentation of a first inspection prior to the alleged reinspection.

A fascinating question and answer had to do with the fact that after the College Hills disaster, the budget cuts that the fire department had been facing were never implemented.

On cross-examination, Giannini had Gray explain the media madhouse that had surrounded the command post that day. The chief estimated that there were about sixty people milling around with cameras, boom mikes, and tape machines. As to whether he'd instructed John Orr to speak to the media, Chief Gray couldn't say, but agreed that it could've happened.

The chief testified that it wasn't until a year after the fire that he'd learned from a story in the *Glendale News-Press* that his arson sleuth had changed his mind about the disposable lighter as having been the open-flame incendiary device that had started the massive fire, deciding instead that it may've been started by a time-delayed incendiary device.

The next person called by the prosecution was Constance Schipper, who'd been manager of the paint and plumbing department of Builder's Emporium in North Hollywood. She testified that on the afternoon of December 14, 1990, six months after the College Hills fire and one year before the arrest of John Orr, she'd become aware of a small fire in a shopping cart full of throw pillows.

The employees extinguished the fire, and in the white residue on the floor she'd noticed a small object that turned out to be a cigarette butt and paper matches wrapped by a rubber band. She also testified that eighteen months after that, she'd been shown a photo spread and had recognized photo number five as having been a person who frequented the store.

Giannini asked some perfunctory questions, and the judge informed the jury that this was one of those "uncharged acts" they'd been told about at the start of trial. They were to learn later that this one resulted in a guilty plea.

A Tulare police officer was called and talked about the fire at the Family Bargain Center on January 16, 1987, and that an identical incendiary device had been found, including a piece of unburned notebook paper.

The judge said to the jury, "Let me remind you, this evidence, if believed, may not be considered by you to prove that the defendant is a person of bad character, or that he has a disposition to commit crimes. It may be considered by you only for the limited purpose of determining if it tends to show modus operandi."

So all of the nonlawyers were supposed to believe that because the defendant had pled guilty to the Builder's Emporium arson, it would not necessarily mean that he had a disposition to set incendiary devices in retail stores. Nor should the jury think of him as a man of bad character. The Fire Monster might've keeled over laughing at *that* one.

And then the witness was called whom many had dubbed "the ball game" as far as the prosecution of John Orr was concerned: Marvin G. Casey of Bakersfield. The fifty-seven-year-old retired firefighter testified to his twenty-eight years of service with the Bakersfield Fire Department, and his current business experience as a fire investigator, and then he told about the CraftMart arson and of finding the incendiary device including the yellow note paper.

One couldn't help but be reminded that had Casey received proper fingerprint analysis, John Orr would have been arrested and convicted in 1989. There would not have been a College Hills disaster, or an L.A. fire series, or a novel. And the Ole's fire would've remained an "accident." Many task-force members believed that nobody regretted the fingerprint screw-up more than did the defendant, John Leonard Orr, who doubtlessly would have been paroled in 2002.

On Tuesday, May 19, Steven Harvey Patterson was back in the John Orr case, having enjoyed his first month of retirement from the Burbank Fire Department, and respite from his obsession with the murder of Mary Susan Duggan. Patterson told the jury about the events surrounding the Warner Brothers Studios fire. And the jury heard of all the curious business about Patterson standing out there with a flashlight, and after a while calling John Orr again only to learn that he was already at the *Waltons* set and hadn't needed directions at all.

By far, the most damaging prosecution witness in the Warner Brothers case was John Egger, the studio's director of security, who testified that he had been there while the fire was raging, when only the Warner Brothers fire engine was at the scene.

"As the fire was burning, did anyone approach and identify himself to you as an investigator?" the prosecutor asked.

The witness said that a man had walked through the gate and that the man was John Orr, adding, "I didn't know him personally, but I'd been introduced to him and seen him at a few law-enforcement events."

Peter Giannini did not confront the witness. He asked a few questions about the gate having been open, and ascertained that a security guard had been there, and that was it. If the witness was correct, John Orr had been at the scene twenty to thirty minutes after the fire call had been placed, and three hours before he'd met with Patterson and needed directions.

Witnesses were called from the "uncharged" fires in Bakersfield, Lawndale, and Redondo Beach who'd identified John Orr as having been a customer in their stores.

It was very difficult to discredit all the testimony without drawing too much attention to the arsons with which he'd not been charged, but at least Giannini managed to get across that many of the people who'd identified John Orr in the six-pak photo lineups had seen his face in the newspaper or on television *before* having seen the lineup. The strong indication was that they'd been influenced by pictures of a man whom the police had already arrested.

There was damaging testimony to the defense from Rich Edwards, who was recalled to testify about the Kennington fire, and about photos that John Orr had shot of the house before the fire, and photos of the structure while the house was burning. Rich Edwards testified that the photos had been mounted on a board in John Orr's office, possibly a before-and-after lesson as to what can happen if you don't pay attention to brush-abatement warnings.

Mike Cabral came back to ask questions about the San Augustine fire from Battalion Chief Gary Seidel of the L.A. Fire Department, who recalled having seen John Orr driving on the 210 Freeway shortly before the chief spotted a column of smoke from a brush fire.

Giannini did his best to minimize the importance of the sighting, but still, the jury had been made aware that once again, where there was fire, there was the defendant, alone.

Some of the most interesting conversation which the jury never heard took place at the bench when the lawyers and the judge squabbled over which passages from John Orr's novel should be redacted. With Mike Cabral, Sandra Flannery, Ed Rucker, and Peter Giannini standing there, each with a manuscript, dialogue took place that might have perked up the jury who'd suffered through such technical and legalistic argument up to then.

It was quite a scene, really: The wiry judge peering out through those metal-rimmed spectacles. Peter Giannini looking Armani prosperous, with the mane of dark hair and basso profundo dominating. Ed Rucker looming, like a graying NBA player debating with normal-sized referees. Sandra Flannery prim, slim, speaking in low-key whispers. And of course, hairless Mike Cabral busting the seams of his size 50, with a body no miracle fabric could contain, except maybe the Shroud of Turin. And *all* of them unsmiling and serious and lawyerly.

At one point, Judge Perry said, "Now, the next section is at page sixteen. What will be excised is as follows: 'Judging by the size of your dick right now, I'd say it was a pretty good fire.' I don't think that adds anything to the case. So that will come out."

Nobody argued to save the dick.

He later said, "At page twenty-seven, four lines up from the bottom: 'He watched her large breasts hanging loose under her T-shirt.' That is gratuitous, unnecessary, and in my view should be excised or redacted."

And later, " 'Nice shirt, he said as she passed. Fuck you! She spat at him, as he walked to a nearby car.' That will be stricken."

And still later, "I think it's appropriate to excise these two sentences. 'Her loose T-shirt fell away from her waist as she bent, showing one of her firm breasts from below. His body tingled as he wandered to the rear of the store.' My view is that it would be viewed as prejudicial. It would invite the jury to consider that the author had some type of sexual fixation."

And then there was debate about excising *all* references to Trish's breasts, for fear of the jury thinking that the author liked hefty hooters.

Peter Giannini said, "There's a line in there after 'nice tits.' "

The judge said, "Everything comes out starting with 'nice tits' to 'she never wears a bra either.' Those seven lines are going to be excised. I am going to allow some limited reference to masturbation while the fire is going, but it is past tense, unrelated to any fire I believe that is charged in the case. And I'm going to sustain the objection on page sixty-four to the following: 'He remembered his binoculars and focused on the teenage girl as she fled. Aaron fondled his cock then. And he found himself unzipping his pants now as he relived the excitement he felt.' I'll hear your argument, but I don't think that one is necessary for the people's case."

Sandra Flannery wanted the wanking: "Your Honor, as the court knows, the defendant had some binoculars in his briefcase. Also in his briefcase were the components of the device that he used to start fires. I believe that this passage ties the binoculars to the setting of fires. And it also indicated that one of the benefits he derived from setting fires was that at a later opportunity, he could relive the fires in his mind and have the sexual excitement that the fire provided."

The judge said to her, "Well, that's a good argument. I think that the first sentence is not particularly objectionable. But what is objectionable is that 'he fondled his cock, and then unzipping his pants and reliving the excitement.' "

The last and best deletion took place near the end of the session, when the judge said, "And then on page three-fifty-nine, I agree with the defense about the line, 'With an obscene acronym across the front of it.' That comes out."

The excised acronym was for "Tactical Watershed Attack Team."

18

UNCHARGED ACTS

The prosecutors called most of the witnesses from the Pillow Pyro Task Force whose testimony had helped to convict John Orr in Fresno. Now they were testifying to "uncharged acts," as though somehow, ordinary inhabitants of planet earth could hear all of that and not get a pretty good idea that the man seated before them, more likely than not, had some character flaws.

Glen Lucero came back to talk about the incendiary device recovered from Stats Floral in Redondo Beach, which seemed like a lifetime ago. Peter Giannini made good attempts with each witness, pointing out discrepancies such as that the fireman who'd found that incendiary device had said it contained six to eight matches, but Lucero had found only three, marking the "signature" of the Pillow Pyro arsonist. But it was all cumulative, mistakes and all, those crushing "uncharged" crimes that were being dumped on the table.

A former employee of Ole's sister store in Pasadena testified about an attempted arson that her store had experienced three months after the disaster in South Pasadena. She told of finding an incendiary device consisting of a cigarette and matches held together by a rubber band. The jury was to be reminded that in John Orr's novel, his fictional arsonist tries to torch a store after the stupid cops fail to give him "credit" for the calamity he's wreaked at Cal's in South Pasadena.

When Mike Matassa testified, it was to an abbreviated version of all that the Pillow Pyro Task Force had done during its existence, including the arrest of John Orr. But what most hurt the defense were the questions by Cabral concerning the guilty pleas.

Matassa's job was to sit there like a ventriloquist's dummy and say, "Yes."

Cabral asked, "Special Agent Matassa, on March twenty-fourth, 1993, were you in the state district courthouse for the Central District of California, number one?"

"Yes," said the witness.

And then Cabral asked a series of questions to establish what had been going on in the courtroom that day, questions dealing with John Orr's having given affirmative answers to understanding the charges, and to his plea on the arson counts from Atascadero.

Finally Cabral said, "And was he asked how he pled to the December fourteenth, 1990, Builder's Emporium fire in Los Angeles County?"

"Yes," said the witness.

"And how did he plead?"

"Guilty."

"And did the court say: 'On December fourteenth, 1990, sometime before one P.M., did you enter the Builder's Emporium, located at six-six-oh-one Laurel Canyon Boulevard, North Hollywood, California? Did you then place a lit incendiary device in pillows located inside of the Builder's Emporium with the intention of starting a fire that would damage property in the store?' What was his response to that?"

"Yes."

"I have no further questions," said Mike Cabral.

And all of the lawyers could spend days and weeks, and call their hundred witnesses, and argue and harangue, but when it got right down to it, any layman could see that prior convictions and uncharged acts could cripple a defense, but guilty pleas could inflict fatal injuries. Hearing of guilty pleas, the jury loses its ability to rationalize away prior convictions which *may* have been based upon inadequate representation, or law-enforcement malfeasance, or erroneous testimony.

When the jury hears the words of acknowledgment that were uttered by a person accused of violent serial crime, it's less a crippling blow than a beheading. That Friday afternoon, sixteen days after the start of John Orr's murder trial, the Fire Monster was heard to *roar*.

On Tuesday, May 26, one of the jurors approached the bailiff and ratted out Juror Number Ten for doing a crossword puzzle during the taking of testimony. The judge and the lawyers had a long conversation before the jurors were seated, and they finally decided that the matter could be settled by a general warning from the bench.

When the jury got seated, the judge got all atwitter. He said, "My goodness, Number Two! Are you okay? I want to state for the record that Number Two is wearing a large bandage over his left eye. My goodness! Memorial Day was not good to you, apparently?"

"No," said Juror Number Two.

"Golly!" the judge said. "Well, I certainly appreciate your being here. Can you tell us what happened?"

Juror Number Two said, "My two-year-old . . . there was a book we were reading, and he turned the page, and the tip of it went right up in the top of my eye. So I went to urgent care and they said I need to keep the patch on it for at least forty-eight hours. I told my fellow jurors I didn't want to, you know, take a day off or anything."

The judge then told a story that "amused" him, about long civil cases when the bailiff would go through jurors' notebooks after trial. He said they'd found that some of the jurors "had basically been engaged in what might be called doodling . . . And so, I guess my point is, it is inappropriate to be drawing pictures, or maybe *working on crossword puzzles,* or playing games, or anything like that."

Nonlawyers could wonder why the judge didn't ban hand puppets, since he was talking to them as if their education had peaked at traffic school.

When Mike Matassa got turned over to Peter Giannini for cross-examination, the defense lawyer did the best job yet of attempting to chip away at the long list of charged and uncharged fires to which the jury had been exposed. For example, he tried to point out that the L.A. fire series sometimes had suspect descriptions that did not resemble John Orr.

Moreover, he made the witness repeat statements by his boss during the interrogation of John Orr, whereby Cornelison offered a carrot by saying, "We're *not* going to charge you with the College Hills fire," suggesting that the feds figured there wasn't much of a case, and yet here he sat in a state trial for those very same crimes.

Giannini attacked the importance of the incendiary materials found in John Orr's briefcase, extracting testimony that John Orr had explained that the materials were for use in his training class. And the attorney for the first time elicited admissions that the task force had sent questionnaires to people who'd taken training classes from John Orr, verifying that he had indeed conducted training with similar devices, if not the exact device.

Another tidbit that Giannini brought out was that a month after John Orr's arrest, another search of his office led to the discovery of a piece of paper with the notation "3:30 Stevenson School," which might help with a time-and-place alibi for the Warner Brothers Studios fire, if the jury could be persuaded that the undated note carried enough weight.

Giannini's approach was to intimate that John Orr had already been convicted of, or pled guilty to, all of the arsons he'd ever committed. And that this state case was an example of the authorities attempting to clear up everything on the books, including the Ole's fire of 1984, by ganging up on an exposed and vulnerable defendant.

The lawyer made Mike Matassa concentrate on the differences between things portrayed in the manuscript and in this case, rather than on the similarities. The judge agreed to let Peter Giannini effectively take the witness through many passages in John Orr's novel wherein the author had portrayed fires that did not resemble anything that the task force had investigated, indicating that John Orr's novel was not some sort of diary, as the prosecution claimed.

When Mike Cabral got Matassa on redirect, he had the witness clarify for the jury why his task force had never investigated or interrogated the defendant regarding College Hills and other brush fires, explaining that they were not federal crimes. And Matassa related that the statute of limitations had expired on Ole's insofar as being a prosecutable arson in federal court, where there was not even a federal murder law, so all of that had to be dumped onto Mike Cabral and his task force.

After Mike Matassa was excused forever from the prosecution of John Orr, a surprising development in the College Hills case was announced during recess by Sandra Flannery. The College Hills apartment dweller who'd seen a man near the fire's area of origin, a man who'd warned people in the apartment building to get out, was back from the Midwest. And she was ready for the very first time to state that the man she'd seen was the defendant.

This stunning revelation had come about during a phone call from Sandra Flannery, wherein the witness said that she'd never seen a news photo of the defendant even by the time she'd testified before a grand jury, but after that, she'd happened to see his picture in the newspaper and "her hair stood on end" because she'd realized that they'd caught the suspect.

The judge made the obvious comment out of the jury's presence: "The thing that occurs to me is that this is kind of a two-edged sword for the people. I mean, the defendant interviewed her. He was *in* her bathroom. Why in the *world* didn't she say at that point, 'This is the guy I saw over there at the fire scene?' I'm not sure, were I prosecuting this case, I would want to get into it. Eight years later he has a lot less hair. He's wearing glasses. You expect her to make an identification?"

When the witness took the stand, Sandra Flannery asked, "On June twenty-seventh, 1990, at approximately three-thirty P.M., did anything happen outside your apartment?"

"Yes," the witness said. "I looked out my bathroom window and I noticed a car parked on the side of the road facing north. And I saw a man get out and walk towards the hill and sort of lean over towards the hill. And I thought, well, maybe he lost something. After I got into the living room I heard a male voice knock on the door of the apartment below me, and he said, 'Your hill's on fire!' And I saw a ball of fire coming toward me and one joining it, and all coming towards the building!"

As to her failure to recognize the defendant when he had actually entered her apartment that day, Sandra Flannery asked the witness, "Do you remember if anyone was with Officer Masucci when he was there in your apartment?"

"That I can't recall," the witness said. "I just can't recall it."

"At some time after you testified in the grand jury, did you see something in the newspaper?"

"I recall there was a picture that they had of him. About the person that had committed the fires."

"When you saw the photograph, what was your initial reaction?"

"I was kind of in shock. It kind of threw me in a bit of shock. Because I thought, Oh, my God, that's him!"

"And did you tell anyone that you'd seen in the newspaper a photograph of the man that you saw outside the window?"

"Unfortunately, I didn't. I thought, well, at least they know who did it."

"And, by some chance, do you see the man in the courtroom today?"

"It's just so vague," she said. "I can't recall. It's been so long."

Exhausted observers would say, that's it? For this they brought a witness from the Midwest? All of the argument to let the witness testify to her latter-day epiphany was for that?

The best legal tactic for the defense might have been just to say, "No questions." But in this case, less was *never* more. Peter Giannini asked scores of questions, *hundreds* of questions of a witness whose muddled testimony had just spoken volumes *for* the defense.

It got down to, "What kind of pets did you have?"

"Kitties."

"I'm sorry?"

"Kitties. Cats."

"Cats?"

"A couple cats. Mommy and daughter."

When all was said and done, there were only two questions that laymen would've wanted answered, and not by the witness, but by the lawyers in that courtroom: *Why* would the prosecution have called this witness? *Why* would the defense have cross-examined this witness?

The College Hills arson count was far from a prosecutorial slam dunk, dependent as it was on the testimony of this witness and the air force major. The prosecution had never needed the Fire Monster more, to say to the jury: *What does it matter? Any of it? He's already pled guilty to serial arson!*

On Friday of the fourth week, ATF agent Jerry Taylor was called once again to testify that the incendiary device used in so many of the charged and uncharged fires was a "signature device," and that altogether, it established the M.O. of a serial arsonist.

And the people rested.

The first defense witness called was Jack Vanderlaan, a retired firefighter and arson investigator, formerly of the Los Angeles Fire Department, now a private investigator who'd been hired in 1984 by the insurance carrier for W. R. Grace Company, the parent company of Ole's.

In 1984 he'd come to the opinion that the fire had originated in the attic space, agreeing with the L.A. Sheriff's Department. Unlike the fire experts for the prosecution, this investigator said that he was not surprised that no one had smelled a smoldering attic fire.

When Cabral got the witness, he determined at once that Vanderlaan had gotten to Ole's after the heavy equipment had arrived, and that he'd never entered the building. Nor had he spoken to any of the employees, nor to fire captain William Eisele. He didn't have a recollection of when firefighters had chopped through the roof, and had never seen building plans. He admitted that his conclusion was based in part on that of Sergeant Jack Palmer.

After hundreds of questions, it boiled down to the next question: "Now, if the employees testified that they'd observed a small fire in the third or fourth aisle from the eastern fire wall, and that they'd watched the fire burn quite rapidly across to the west, and quite rapidly across to the northwest, would that be consistent with an attic fire?"

"It could be, if there was drop-down," said the witness.

There it was. No matter which side the expert was on, it all came down to one basic question that everyone could understand: Was it more likely that the fire had dropped down, or burned straight up?

The prosecutor gave the witness more questions based upon what Ole's employees had said, and he got concessions, and the witness admitted that he, like Sergeant Jack Palmer, had not known about the polyfoam.

The most damage to the witness was done, once again, by potato chips: "Now, were you aware that there were a couple of *other* fires on that night in the vicinity of Ole's fire?" Cabral asked.

"Other than the fact they were in supermarkets, no."

"So you weren't aware that there was a *pattern* of fires associated with someone using a device to ignite potato chips?"

"I don't recall anything being said about a device."

"And having three fires in the same vicinity on the same day in commercial businesses open for business is rare?"

"Yes."

"In fact, it is extremely rare?"

"Yes."

"And would you agree that that is a good indicator that you *might* have an arsonist setting fires?"

"It would certainly be an indicator," the witness said.

Another defense witness was a former cashier from Ole's who testified that the ceiling in the housewares department used to leak when it rained, implying that smoldering embers could've dropped down from an attic fire and ignited store merchandise. She said that they'd had to replace thirty to fifty ceiling tiles after one downpour.

There were conflicts. Six years earlier she'd told Rich Edwards that the tiles had been replaced prior to the big fire, but now she was saying that she'd been busy on the day that Edwards had interviewed her, and only later had remembered that they had *not* been replaced.

Another defense witness testified that she'd seen "rowdy" juveniles hanging around Albertson's Market on the day of the arson attempt. And that although she didn't recall what they'd said exactly, it could've been something like: "Burn, baby, burn!"

At last, a defense witness arrived whom Mike Cabral admitted that he'd feared. The man had a *twenty-three*-page curriculum vitae. Cabral had never seen one like it. The witness was a mechanical engineer, licensed in eighteen states. He had a background in chemistry and mathematics, and was a member of honor societies both in general engineering and mechanical engineering. He'd designed projects in other states and foreign countries, written peer-review technical papers, and been published twenty-five times or more.

Some of his articles dealt with fire growth and behavior, as well as with smoke and its control. An example of his esoteric knowledge could be gleaned by one of his articles delivered to the Society of the Plastic Institute, at its Thirteenth Combustibility Symposium.

And the witness had once delivered a paper on "Scale Modeling of Multistory Atria Fire Scenarios for Determining the Effectiveness of Mechanical Smoke Control Systems." It had been given in London and translated into multiple languages.

The witness just about wore out the court reporter, who, like everyone else in the courtroom, understood nothing except that he'd taught for a number of years at U.C.L.A. on "Fire Safe Building Design" and "Smoke Measurement and Control." He'd been retained several times as an expert involving civil litigation, and had authored various sections for building codes throughout America.

The portly prosecutor had been sweating right through his suit coat after getting the résumé of this witness. And no doubt he'd prayed to Our Lady of Fatima or whoever it is that Portuguese kids pray to when they're in big trouble. Until he took a gander at the witness and at the jury gawking at the witness.

"Do you know what ZZ Top looks like?" Cabral commented later, when asked his impression of the distinguished engineer.

The guy had a belt-touching gray beard you could hide Ally McBeal in and a gray ponytail just as long; he did look just like one of the Texas blues-rockers whose hits included "Arrested for Driving While Blind" and "Jesus Just Left Chicago."

After he'd finally gotten through the curriculum vitae, the witness was asked various questions in connection with the Ole's fire, and whether the fire's behavior was consistent with a fire that had started in the attic, to which the witness answered in the affirmative. The engineer then said he'd been supplied with drawings representing what the building had looked like before it was Ole's Home Center, other architectural and construction drawings, and arson reports from various experts, as well as many photographs.

The witness said, "In summary, all of the information that was provided to me would tend to support their original finding."

Over objections and arguments, Rucker got to ask the witness some questions about lights flickering and breakers having been tripped, and finally, the judge cut off further questions about electrical failure as being beyond the witness's expertise. But it soon became apparent that almost nothing was beyond *this* witness's expertise.

During recess, the judge had a discussion with Juror Number Ten, the crossword puzzler, about a doctor's appointment. The judge was stunned when the juror said she could *not* move her appointment to suit the court, and in fact, she'd been instructed "to go through my attorney," if necessary, to get to the appointment on the only day that the doctor could fit her in.

The judge said in astonishment, "You say you are going through your *attorney?*"

The American jury system had come to this: A juror was threatening the judge with legal action if she could not be excused for a doctor's appointment. Yet if asked, every one of the strange fish in that litigation tank would proclaim with indignation: "Of course our jury system works!"

When it got to polyurethane foam, the engineer enlightened the jury on the different types and subcategories of foam, both rigid and flexible, and that he'd done studies on foam in regard to fire inhibitors built into it. But he couldn't say much about the foam products at Ole's without more data.

He looked at a photo of polyfoam and said, "I am not certain just looking at this picture which it is. It looks like it could be polystyrene as opposed to polyurethane."

And of course, he was the *only* one who had any idea what polystyrene was. He said that, in order to give an opinion about each type's ignition characteristics, he'd have to know "the *geometry* of how it's stored." So, Euclid had joined Isaac Newton in the witness box.

Then Rucker asked the witness a long series of questions about smoke detectors, and the witness talked about draft stops and suspended ceilings.

When Rucker asked if there was an attic fire above a suspended ceiling, would people down below smell it, the witness answered, "You would if it were set up as a plenum."

Nobody knew what a plenum was, and Rucker didn't ask.

Then the witness became the first to say that draft stops in the attic could actually exacerbate fire by containing it to a smaller area, thus allowing it to heat up and "accumulate excess pyrolysis aids" which could result in backdraft or flashover.

Neither the court reporter nor anyone else knew how the hell to spell "pyrolysis" and Rucker wasn't about to ask that either.

Then the witness got a hypothetical from Ed Rucker, one that he'd asked others: "Are those facts inconsistent with a fire on the floor, or a fire in the attic?"

The witness said, "Inconsistent with a fire on the floor."

"Okay, thank you, sir," said Rucker.

The judge said, "All right, cross-examination."

"The people would have no questions, Your Honor," said Mike Cabral, with a little grin.

Ed Rucker later said that his expert witness hadn't been particularly helpful. It could be that during the testimony the defense lawyer had spotted twelve people doing crossword puzzles.

Peter Giannini called Chief Gray once again, this time as a defense witness. Giannini showed Gray a two-page report concerning brush clearances made four months after the College Hills fire, indicating that the defendant had been doing work relating to the blaze.

Flannery countered by taking a totally different tack, soliciting testimony from Gray that John Orr had a badge with a removable police banner, which had prompted a fire department inventory of all badges to see if others were being improperly used.

A Warner Brothers Studios firefighter testified that he'd been called out to the *Waltons* set, and that he'd seen the electrical panel "arcing" when they'd put water on the structure. That witness helped the defense, and the next witness, a fire inspector for Warner Brothers Studios, helped even more. The inspector corroborated that there had been arcing of wires when the firefighters were applying water to the blaze.

Joe Lopez, John Orr's last partner, again came to court as a defense witness, testifying to having been at training sessions where John had used a cigarette, matchbook, matches, and rubber bands to set a delay device for training purposes. He said that on one occasion he'd even kept the cigarettes and matches in case they might be used again, which helped with the defense position that the items in John Orr's bag had not been suspicious.

After verifying that his partner *had* found three lighters at College Hills, Lopez was shown a video seized from John Orr's office. It displayed bad brush clearance, including shots of the Kennington house before and after it had burned, all designed to demonstrate to the jury that the sinister could be made simple.

When it was Cabral's turn, he went at Joe Lopez in regard to the badge with the removable police banner that John Orr had possessed. He asked, "You *were* aware that it was illegal to represent yourself as a police officer when you're not?"

"Yes, I am aware of that, yes," the witness said.

When Cabral asked about the Builder's Emporium fire on December 14, 1990, he said, "You later learned that John Orr pled guilty to setting that fire, is that correct?"

Joe Lopez answered, "I don't recall *which* charges he pled guilty to."

The supposition was that Joe Lopez still believed John Orr was guilty of nothing, and that the guilty plea had been a bad legal tactic, just as his mentor had so long maintained it was.

When asked if John had informed his partner that he'd found a tracking device on his car while in San Luis Obispo, the witness said, "I don't recall, no. I don't *believe* he did."

Toward the end of his cross-examination, Cabral asked, "You said that the location on Verdugo Road had fires almost every year?"

"Yeah, there were numerous fires in that general area, on the hillside."

"Have you had a fire on that hillside since the College Hills fire?"

The witness said, "It would be hard to have a fire anymore since our brush-clearance program is so aggressive."

Cabral wouldn't settle for that: "So is that, no, you *haven't* had any?"

"Not that I am aware of, in that area," said the witness.

At a later time Joe Lopez said that the year he'd worked with John Orr had been the most productive, educational, best year of his career. The year after John Orr's arrest had been the *worst*. His mentor had complained in his chronicles about not liking a partner hanging on to his leg, but he'd enjoyed unwavering loyalty from this one.

The defense saved for last the woman who'd also remained loyal and constant since John Orr's arrest six and a half years earlier. Chris had even taken a part-time, unpaid job with Peter Giannini, in order to assist with work on behalf of John Orr. She was a small woman with a chestnut bob, and like his fourth wife, Wanda, wore little makeup and was businesslike, articulate, and very presentable.

Giannini established that she had a ten-year-old daughter who'd attended Robert Louis Stevenson elementary school in Burbank. He asked if there had been something scheduled at the school on the day of the Warner Brothers Studios fire. Chris answered that there had been a parent-teacher meeting which she could not attend, and that John had attended in her place.

She testified that John was there when she'd gotten home, and that they'd ordered a pizza, but he got paged before the pizza arrived, and had to go to Warner Brothers Studios.

Sandra Flannery later maintained that she and Mike Cabral had had no game plan for her to deal with Chris in a way that might inflame married female jurors, yet the first words out of the prosecutor's mouth were, "Good morning. When did you begin your *relationship* with John Orr?"

"Objection, irrelevant," said Peter Giannini.

The judge overruled Giannini, and Chris said, "I met John sometime during 1989."

Sandra Flannery then said, "And at some point in time during your *relationship,* did you become aware of the fact that he was writing a novel?"

"He had mentioned it, yes," Chris said.

"In fact, were you aware of a character in the novel named Chris?"

"Yes."

"And you understood Chris to be, in essence, *you.* Is that correct?"

"He had told me later on that it was lightly based on his knowledge of me, yes."

"And on the *relationship* you had with him?"

Sandra Flannery emphasized the word *relationship* so much that she got the witness doing it. "I had not read the novel, and we did not get into the extent of the *relationship* with the character in the book."

"And during this time, how often would you say you saw John Orr?"

"Regularly."

"How many times a week?"

"It would depend on both of our schedules, but I would say on an average of at least twice a week."

"Three or *four* times a week, would *that* sound right?"

"Could be, yes."

"Are you presently John Orr's girlfriend?"

"I am a *friend,*" the witness replied. "Prior to his arrest. And I've remained a friend."

"Prior to his arrest you were his *girlfriend*?"

"Yes," Chris admitted.

"And you are presently working on the defense team?"

"Yes, I mean . . . I have *volunteered* my time to help."

"And you've been here every day during the trial?"

"Almost every day."

"And you've sat through the testimony every day that you've . . ."

"Yes yes yes," said the witness, cutting off the prosecutor.

"At some point in time did you help John Orr in giving an arson investigator's conference or instruction class of some type?"

"He asked me to assist as a role player."

"And did you play the role of an arsonist's *wife?*"

"Yes."

"And is it correct that the week before John Orr got arrested, he was planning to leave his wife for you?"

"I don't have knowledge of that."

"Did you ever make that statement to an investigator who worked for ATF?"

"I might have. I don't remember it, though."

After the witness was excused, a teacher from the Stevenson school testified that John Orr had come to the parent-teacher meeting at around 3:30 to 3:40 P.M. for a half-hour conference on the day in question, looking well dressed, composed, professional, and, in answer to a question from Giannini, "not smelling of smoke."

Sandra Flannery's cross-examination of Chris about the "relationship" was effective lawyering because it insinuated that John Orr was a serial philanderer in addition to being a serial arsonist, and to some jurors, that might be nearly as bad. And as to Sandra Flannery's disingenuous claim that the prosecution would never resort to exposing the defendant's womanizing, or to insinuate that Chris was a little home wrecker who'd inspired the hot scenes in John Orr's novel, one might respond to Sandra Flannery as Verdugo Dispatch had done when the lead-footed arson sleuth had tried to assure them he wasn't engaging in high-speed pursuits, but was only *following fast*: "Yeah. Riiiiiiiight!"

That afternoon the defense rested. Rebuttal was to begin the next day.

19

THE MANUSCRIPT

The people's rebuttal case began on Wednesday, June 3, four weeks after the trial had begun. Sandra Flannery called employees of Warner Brothers to testify that the trees around the *Waltons* set were not dry and deciduous, but evergreen for shooting purposes, and that the set was muddy, not parched. And she brought in the electrical foreman for lots of testimony about sparking, arcing, voltage dips, AC cable, DC cable, and amp loads, as if the jury hadn't had enough of that in this trial. *None* of the testimony sparked, not even a little bit.

And then a witness was called who hurt the defense's attic-fire hypothesis at Ole's Home Center. His name was Patrick Snyder and he had done work for the electrical contractor when Ole's Home Center was remodeled in 1981 and 1982. He'd personally inspected all of the electrical conduit in the attic, and he said that the attic was so well vented that the vents let in enough natural light that workers could see up there. And most important, he said there was no electrical material where Ed Rucker had suggested an electrical fire had erupted.

When it was Ed Rucker's turn at cross-examination, his first question was, "Mr. Snyder, you were an *apprentice* electrician at that time?"

"Yes, sir," the witness said.

But this witness was somebody who'd actually done the physical work in that attic, and on cross-examination he even remembered the plan for smoke detectors, and that everything in the attic was up to code and protected inside of conduit, with no high-voltage wires whatsoever outside of that protective conduit, and *nothing* where Ed Rucker had suggested it was.

Rucker later said that in every trial there seems to be one witness who unexpectedly inflicts more harm on a lawyer's case that all the others that the lawyer prepares for so diligently. And this was the one, an apprentice electrician who knew from firsthand experience how well vented the attic was, which suggested that an attic fire would have billowed smoke and heat out from the roof.

"One little working guy really hurt us," Ed Rucker later said.

The people finally rested their case, and the judge gave the jury a thirty-minute break, asking that they return in a half hour for jury instructions.

After the jury had filed out, Peter Giannini said to the judge, "Mr. Orr says he doesn't want to be here for the jury instructions and he'd just as soon go back, if that's okay with the court."

The judge said he'd have to take a waiver on that, and he informed the defendant of his right to remain and hear arguments about jury instructions, but John Orr said to the judge, whom he distrusted for being a former prosecutor, "It's getting old here. I'd like to use the time to relax."

So even the defendant, on trial for his very life, couldn't bear any more of the wandering convoluted verbosity that passes for discourse in the courtrooms of the most litigious nation on the planet. It seemed that the law and everybody in it needed several semesters of Remedial English 101, but you'd still have to hold the lawyers' family members hostage to make them stop beginning questions with, "At some point in time . . ."

Since the case of the *People v. John Orr* was based entirely on circumstantial evidence, the boilerplate jury instruction on that issue might seem important. The judge read the following to jurors: "Circumstantial evidence is evidence that, if found to be true, proves a fact from which an inference of the existence of another fact may be drawn. An inference is a deduction of fact that may logically and reasonably be drawn from another fact or group of facts, established by the evidence."

Probably about 5 percent of nonlawyers and 10 percent of lawyers actually understand that instruction, which is recited daily in the courtrooms of our land. So that makes it just about perfect for all of the strange fish that lazily glide, blowing gas bubbles that pop ineffectually on the surface of the litigation tanks in which they live and breed.

The next instruction, concerning felony murder by arson, was a repeat from eons earlier in the trial. This one was exceedingly understandable and exceedingly preposterous: "In considering count one through four, evidence has been introduced for the purpose of showing that the defendant committed crimes other than those for which he is on trial. This evidence, if believed, may *not* be considered by you to prove that the defendant is a person of bad character, or that he has a disposition to commit crimes."

To which a juror could only say, "Am I a silly goose! How could I *ever* think that a person is bad when all he's done, according to you, is try to burn down California from Fresno to Los Angeles?"

The judge explained that there would first be a closing argument by the people, followed by one from the defense, and a rebuttal by the people because they have the burden of proof. And then, at long last, Mike Cabral stood up.

After greeting and thanking the jury for enduring testimony from a hundred witnesses, he set out to explain just what it had all been about. And this was the kind of arena where a bulldog can enter a ring and outpoint Pomeranians and poodles. The downtown jury was looking at someone like them. He'd never tried to be a wordsmith. In fact, he'd sometimes tangle tenses and scramble syntax and drop pronouns like George Bush the elder and the younger, but unlike the other fellows from Yale, Cabral was clearly a blue-collar guy who couldn't look preppy if you dressed him in the cap and gown of Jesus College, Oxford.

He'd never talked down to the jury because he seemed to be down there *with* them. Like maybe a car mechanic who'd toughed it out at night school. Not for him, soaring oratory. He did it by doing what bulldogs do: plodding forward relentlessly. Everybody who'd watched him work offered similar descriptive language: he was a relentless, dogged lawyer.

John Orr, not an admirer of lawyers in general, had one observation to make about this prosecutor's work ethic that he hadn't made about any other attorney: "Cabral *never* made a mistake."

"Now, all the experts that you heard," Cabral began, "and there was a handful of them, agree that fire generally burns up and out. The fire triangle requires three sides: oxygen, heat, and you still don't get a fire without fuel on the third side. If you take out one of the sides, your fire goes out. It's actually very simple to understand."

That was his message, and he kept going back to it throughout his argument. Then he talked about experts agreeing that a fire will take the path of least resistance, burning up, mushrooming along a ceiling, seeking air. He talked about the various uncharged crimes, all of those where incendiary devices were used.

And after bombarding them with so many of those M.O. crimes, he might've been in danger of losing them to crossword puzzles, but he changed the pace and spoke of a witness who'd described the arson suspect as "kind of chubby."

"Now you know," Cabral said, "when people use words such as *chubby* and *average build,* it's obviously subjective. One man's chubby is another man's slim. There's no way of quantifying those types of terms. Some people might even say *I'm* chubby, but I don't happen to think so."

And of course, those jurors from the inner city—folks who'd never heard of arugula with tomato aspic, or chicory and beet root salad, and didn't know that from West Hollywood to Malibu it was a misdemeanor to eat a French fry, folks who porked out on chimichangas, burritos, and Fat Burgers—had to love it. He was *one* of them, saying that all the confusing technical crap they'd been listening to for weeks was really simple after all!

Cabral discussed Marv Casey's fire and the Bakersfield witness Laverne Andress, who'd discovered the incendiary device, and that allowed Cabral to loop back to the Ole's fire by way of making a comparison: "Now, remember what Chief Eisele said. When he got to the fire, what did he see coming out the southwest door, but a blue flame. Well, Laverne Andress tells us what that blue flame was. It was the polyfoam burning.

"And there was one other thing that Chief Eisele said: he said that the fire was hissing. And what did Laverne Andress hear? She heard a hissing sound. And that erupted into blue flame clear up into the ceiling. A hissing sound. Both fires. Blue flame. The people submit: polyfoam. *Both* fires."

The jury could not fail to make his connection. Bakersfield. Fingerprint. Polyfoam. Hissing. CraftMart. Ole's. Attic irrelevant.

He discussed the fire that had occurred months after the Ole's calamity, at Ole's sister store. He talked about the manuscript and how it depicted an actual event like that, implying that the novel was a diary.

He went through all of it: the tracking device, and how, when John Orr had found it, he didn't confront anyone about it. Once again, he tied the defendant into the Los Angeles fire series by reminding the jury that John Orr had pled guilty to that Builder's Emporium fire.

Then Mike Cabral picked up *Points of Origin* and said, "I want to read one chapter of the book."

He began: " 'The hardware business prospered in the small community of South Pasadena. . . . Madeline Paulson went there at least twice a week to shop. . . . Tonight she was baby-sitting with her three-year-old grandson, Matthew. He wasn't sleepy so she took him to the Baskin-Robbins ice cream store next to Cal's. While standing in the parking lot sharing a chocolate mint cone, she decided to entertain Matthew by walking through Cal's. . . . In less than six minutes, both Madeline and Matthew would be dead.' "

The courtroom was very quiet indeed when Cabral got to the encounter with the arsonist: " 'As she rounded the corner, she almost ran into a man walking with his hands in his pockets. Both were startled as she saw that they wouldn't collide. She heard his breath suck in, and he mumbled his apologies as he continued on. She recovered quickly too, and walked toward the back of the store.

" 'Minutes later, she heard a shrill whistling noise. . . . She then heard excited talking and the word, "Fire!" She started toward the sound, realizing now it was a smoke detector. She saw a slight haze at the ceiling level. Her heart raced, and as she rounded the corner, she saw that the smoke was now swirling around the ceiling like a whirlwind.

" 'The fire, originating in polyurethane cushions, raced to the ceiling, and within forty-five seconds, one-thousand-degree temperatures were being pushed toward the annex door opening. . . . The annex opening was protected by a metal-clad door, designed to close when a lightweight metal link melted from fire and allowed the door to roll down its track, closing and preventing fire spread into the main store. The design was for fires happening after hours when no one was inside, not for hours when the store was occupied. It was a fatal design.

" 'Madeline held Matthew close to her, and stopped briefly to look down the aisle where she saw the fire boiling out of the displays fifty feet away. She stared at the fire, not yet feeling the heat, fascinated, yet terrified. . . . The fire burned through a light fixture and shorted out all the lights in the annex . . . leaving Madeline, Matthew, one other man, and three employees in complete darkness.

" 'Quickly, the tremendous heat breached the attic above the fire and found a ready source of oxygen. The smoke, just above head level when the lights went out, now crashed down on the heads of Madeline and Matthew. Instinctively, they dropped to the floor as they heard the black man's voice. She screamed back at him and within seconds he was at their side. Still in total darkness, the toxic smoke attacking their lungs, the three crawled. . . . The smoke, choking and thick, was stealing their oxygen quickly and causing disorientation.

" 'He held Madeline's hand as Matthew clung to her neck. She heard Matthew's sobs as well as her own. She now felt the heat and saw flames in front of them. She screamed at the employee as he squeezed her hand tightly, continuing down the aisle toward the fire. . . . He suddenly realized he was going the wrong way, turned back and they reversed their direction. . . . She felt herself losing her grip on Matthew and his grip loosened from her neck, and slipped down her body as they crawled.

" 'Unable to go any further, she felt the employee's hand drop hers. He continued on. The last thing she heard was a tremendous roar as the fire burned through the roof and vented to the outside. The smoke momentarily lifted, but was then replaced by solid fire as the contents of the annex exploded into flames. Their last breaths were of eight-hundred-degree heat that sealed their throats closed.

" 'When Madeline's body was found, she was on her back with Matthew clinging to her ankles. The employee leading them was found face down five feet in front of Madeline, just twenty feet short of an open fire escape door. One other employee had managed to escape and collapsed outside. Ironically, the other dead employee and customer were also found within ten feet of Madeline.

" 'There was never a follow-up investigation. The fire was ineptly termed accidental. Aaron was so furious that he set a nearly identical fire in Hollywood, at another hardware store. The investigating agency termed the fire arson, but no correlation was made to the Cal's fire. Aaron wanted the Cal's fire to be called arson. He loved the inadvertent attention he derived from the newspaper coverage, and hated it when he wasn't properly recognized.' "

Cabral was not yet ready to read the final lines, which described how the arsonist felt about the people he'd killed. When he put down the manuscript there were jurors staring at John Orr, and the courtroom was very very still.

The prosecutor said, "The people submit to you that chapter six of this book is the Ole's fire. It describes the Ole's fire in detail, even down to the ice cream store."

Like most lawyers, Cabral couldn't leave a word unsaid, and he then sent jurors slumbering with a lot of talk about the technical testimony they'd heard. However, what was possibly the most remarkable thing about this prosecutor was his uncanny recall of what those hundred witnesses had said during the month of testimony. Seldom did he misstate the evidence, as often happens in long closing arguments after a complicated trial. Jurors could've hoped that he'd kept things more chronological, but nothing was missing. He just didn't forget *anything,* and that made for a tedious but always amazing performance.

Cabral had begun talking at 9:30 A.M., and other than during the lunch break, was still at it when court adjourned at 4:00 that afternoon.

The next morning the crossword puzzler was late, but after she arrived, Cabral resumed his closing argument by launching his assault on all of the investigators who had called the fire an accident. Probably his most scathing criticism was reserved for Sergeant Jack Palmer of the L.A. County Sheriff's Department.

"He spent about an hour, hour and a half, before making his determination," Cabral said. "The people submit to you that was inappropriate. He had four dead citizens. He doesn't talk to Mr. Obdam until the next day, after he's already made his decision. He's already reached the conclusion before he even talked to a single witness who could tell him what happened inside that building. And the people submit that that is a fatal flaw, and that flows to every conclusion of every investigator who didn't go inside that building and dig it out. Because they all say only one thing: I relied on Sergeant Palmer.

"He just said, a high fire here. Okay. Can't eliminate electrical in the attic. Let's go home. Let's pack up our stuff and let's go. We're done. We've been here an hour and a half. Potential homicide off our hands. We've done all we need to do. We don't need to talk to any witnesses. But oh, tomorrow, I'll go talk to the one who was the last person out of the fire to see what they think."

Cabral related once again, from memory, the testimony of the defendant's friend, Jim Allen of the Fire Marshal's Office, about how he and John Orr were not satisfied with the finding of accidental fire. What was significant was that Jim Allen had never been told by his friend John Orr that he'd been at the scene of all three fires on that night.

And then Cabral disparaged the opinions of defense experts. Cabral kept pointing out that virtually none of the experts had talked to any of the witnesses the jury had heard. It was effective to let jurors know that they'd heard testimony from the lips of survivors that expert witnesses had never heard before they'd arrived at the attic-fire conclusion.

And finally, at noon, when a lunch break was imminent, Mike Cabral said, "The people submit that the evidence is clear, the evidence is incontrovertible, that on October tenth, 1984, the defendant, John Leonard Orr, entered Ole's Home Center shortly before eight P.M. That he walked into that location, down to the aisle where the polyfoam is stored, placed a device consisting of the cigarette, three matches, a rubber band, and a piece of yellow lined paper into that polyfoam. And after he exited that store, that device ignited a fire which, within minutes, spread throughout the bottom of the area, caused the flashover, and took the lives of Jimmy Cetina, Matthew Troidl, Ada Deal, and Carolyn Krause. And I ask you to return a verdict as to guilty on those four counts. Thank you."

After lunch that day, Sandra Flannery summarized the other counts of arson that she maintained were linked by modus operandi.

She said, "As to those counts, when compared one to another, the evidence also shows patterns and similarities which emerged, that dispute any type of explanation by which the defense could try to explain away these similarities. These patterns, these similarities, are like common threads of facts and circumstances that seem to reappear through these counts. They are the mark of a human hand, because we humans, whether we like it or not, are creatures of habit, are we not?"

She first discussed the Kennington fire, and that John Orr had arrived before the first engine and had begun videotaping while the fire was still burning, when there was not a fire engine in sight. She discussed that on a portion of the tape the house was not on fire, denoting that he'd taken that video at another time, as a before-and-after lesson.

She discussed the Warner Brothers fire, and that a security guard had testified that the defendant was also at that fire while it was burning, and that upon being called by Steve Patterson, the defendant had pretended not to know how to get there.

She next talked about the Hilldale and San Augustine fires and she gave a compelling Teletrac argument: "Well, we know that the defendant was at the location very early on. We know that he showed up at the San Augustine fire within one to two minutes, even though the dispatch to the San Augustine fire gave the wrong location. And yet, John Orr, once again, in his remarkable timing, is *there*."

Then Sandra Flannery turned to her big case, the College Hills disaster. She talked about how the defendant had been seen by other firefighters near the area of origin in the early stages of the fire, once again emphasizing his "remarkable timing." And she discussed her witnesses, the air force major and the apartment-house resident who'd lived in the epicenter of the disaster, both of whom had identified John Orr after the news coverage of his arrest.

Sandra Flannery gave a try at sanitizing the testimony of the woman in the apartment building who'd identified John Orr just prior to this trial, but had never done so before, even though he was *in* her bathroom. But at last she was forced to say, "The value of that experience is up to you to weigh and decide."

Sandra Flannery concluded her argument at 4:00 P.M. by implying that John Orr had dumped his partner Don Yeager out of the arson unit because he didn't want a lot of investigation into Glendale's fire of the century. Then she spoke the truest words that the jury had heard thus far: "Although we've gone on *endlessly* . . ."

After that apology, she said, "I'm going to ask you, in evaluating this evidence, to understand that these patterns that emerge . . . these things that consistently come up make one thing clear, it's impossible for all of these things to arbitrarily coincide in time and space with innocent explanations. All of these things as they converge create a clear pattern of circumstantial evidence which has only one reasonable interpretation: that John Orr set these fires.

"And that's why I'm asking you to return a verdict of guilty as to these remaining counts, five through twenty-five. And I'm asking you to find him also guilty of the special allegations on these counts. And I thank you very much for listening to me today."

On Wednesday, June 10, five weeks into trial, Ed Rucker was first up for the defense's closing argument, and he gave the jury a dose of truth when he said, "Unfortunately, in this particular case, you've been put under a terrible burden. There's a great obstacle, and I think it's only right we talk about it. Let's be straight with each other, okay? You've heard evidence that John Orr pled guilty to setting fires. Come on, that's *got* to affect you. We're rational people, but we're emotional people. And an emotion can sometimes blow away, in the wind of anger, our ability to be rational and our ability to do what we know is right.

"You may dislike John Orr. You may *despise* John Orr. You may think he's done some terrible things. You may think, 'Doggone it, he set fires *before*. Why am I sitting here struggling over this evidence? Why not convict him of this one too? What difference does it make? He's not one of us. He stepped outside of us.'

"You've taken an oath as a juror. And your service, I know, has become to many people a burden. It's become sort of a subject of jokes. But we as a community, as a nation, hand over to you the most immense power that one person can have over another. You've got his life in your hands. You're going to make important decisions in your life that affect you, affect your family, affect your loved ones. But how many times are you going to make a decision that affects another man's *life*? In a sense, this doesn't have anything to do with John Orr. In a sense this has to do with the integrity of our system. Are you going to decide the Ole's case on the facts and the law, as judges?

"The central question that you have to decide in the Ole's case is the one everybody's been telling you about: Did the fire start up in the attic, probably from an electrical cause, and smolder up there for a while because it didn't have enough oxygen? And at some point during that phase, find a way to drop down some burning part onto the merchandise floor of Ole's?"

Rucker then sketched the prosecution scenario for the Ole's blaze, and talked about how people arrive at conclusions based upon circumstantial evidence.

"Here's the point," Rucker said. "A finding of guilt as to any crime may not be based on circumstantial evidence unless the proved circumstances are *one,* consistent with the theory that the defendant is guilty of the crime, and *two,* cannot be reconciled with any other rational conclusion.

"An interpretation that points toward John Orr's setting the fire—and an interpretation that this was an attic fire that dropped down—we've got *two* reasonable interpretations. What do you do? You *must* adopt the interpretation that points to the defendant's innocence, and reject that interpretation that points to his guilt. That's the law. That's what this is all about: whether you're going to be able to get over your anger at John Orr, and follow the law, and decide if a reasonable interpretation of the facts points to an attic fire."

Rucker reminded the jury that Sergeant Jack Palmer and other law-enforcement arson investigators had all called Ole's an accidental fire, and he said something interesting. "When Sergeant Jack Palmer says it's arson, it's *arson.* When he says it's not, it's *not.*

"How many men sit in jail cells right now, prison cells, on the testimony of these men? Now, none of these men in their entire professional careers was ever asked to reexamine one of these opinions. These are not rookies. These are not unqualified men. No prosecutor has *ever* come to them and said: 'You know what? I think you made a mistake.' *Never.* In fact, Deputy Rich Edwards worked under him, and could not name a single fire where he ever thought Sergeant Jack Palmer had made a mistake, not once. There were fifteen to twenty trained, experienced arson investigators there. Nobody disagreed."

Then Rucker began to examine the case, point by point, much as Cabral had done, but from his side of the courtroom. He talked about burn patterns, and shredded insulation, and charring, and twisted beams. And then he confronted the heart of the prosecutor's thesis: the polyfoam.

"Mr. Cabral is probably the most able prosecutor you're going to get in a courtroom, on this kind of case. Do you think after talking to Jack Palmer as many times as they have, if the facts would've changed his opinion, they would have asked him that? They didn't. They asked him very cleverly: 'Do you think that polyfoam on the floor is significant?' Well, yeah. But they *didn't* ask him: 'Does that change your opinion?'

"I asked him: 'Did anything you've learned during all of this change your opinion?' What did he answer? *'No.'* "

During recess, in response to an objection by Cabral, the judge admonished Rucker about a reference to the fact that the jury was hearing a death-penalty case, making a life-and-death decision. The defense lawyer agreed that he wouldn't do that again.

After lunch it was back to ceiling leaks and even polyfoam, and a rehash of the testimony by Ole's employees, but the defense interpretation was that the polyfoam had been ignited by a drop-down fire.

Rucker was very effective when he got to the fires that the prosecution had called diversionary. He read to the jury the testimony of Pasadena arson investigator McClure, who had radioed for John Orr to assist him with his investigation at Albertson's Market. If the opinion of Sergeant Palmer and others that Ole's must be an accident was the heart of the defense case, the alibi time line was the lungs. Rucker indicated to the jury that it would have been impossible for John Orr to have set three fires and still have been where witnesses put him during crucial moments.

"We know that at seven-forty-five P.M. McClure pages Orr," Rucker told the jury. "At seven-forty-seven, they page Orr from Verdugo Dispatch. It's on the tape. McClure said that Orr was there with him for about fifteen or twenty minutes. The first call to the fire department for Ole's was at eight-oh-six. And we know that at eight-twenty-two Orr is calling dispatch. It's on the tape: 'I'm in South Pasadena. Here's the number at the gas station.'

"Let's say it takes fifteen minutes to drive from Ole's to Albertson's. If he's setting a device at Ole's, he drives to Albertson's and let's say he meets with McClure for fifteen minutes, not twenty. And then he's got to drive back to be near Ole's at eight-twenty-two at the gas station where he leaves the phone number.

"So, if as the prosecution tells you that he sets the device shortly before eight and drives to Albertson's in fifteen minutes, and stays there for fifteen minutes, and drives back to South Pasadena, there's no way he's getting back there at eight-twenty-two. Can't do it. The only way it works is if he's near McClure in Pasadena on the night of the World Series. It could be he's in a bar having a drink, watching the game. He's near Pasadena. But here's the point: if he's near McClure in Pasadena at seven-forty-five, he's *not* setting any device at Ole's at eight, or even at seven-forty-five.

"And if you throw in there that the prosecution wants him also to have set a fire at Von's, down the street from Ole's, when's he going to do *both* of those? Get to Pasadena? Get back? It's *not* going to happen."

It was a very good alibi scenario that Ed Rucker had presented, and Cabral knew that he'd have to deal with it on rebuttal.

From that, Ed Rucker went to the manuscript of *Points of Origin,* and probably infuriated his client more than anything that had ever been said by lawyers on either side. Rucker said: "Now, the manuscript John Orr wrote, what's that do for us? One, it gives you an example of some real *bad* writing, I'll tell you that. But does it allow you to draw a conclusion that John Orr set the Ole's fire? The fact that something is fiction that's based on fact is just that, *fiction*. Every police officer who writes novels, every firefighter who writes novels, writes about what they know. They write about *real* fire, *real* crimes, changing the facts as best they can."

He pointed out that the scene John Orr wrote wherein the doomed child wants an ice cream from Baskin-Robbins was logical and coincidental, because there was a Baskin-Robbins store there by Ole's. And that it certainly *didn't* mean that he'd overheard the child talking while he was in the store setting an incendiary device.

Rucker discussed the witness who was the cop's wife, who remembered the defendant seven years *after* the Ole's fire when she'd seen his face on the news, and later testified that she'd seen him in the store on the night before the fire.

Rucker said, "Do you remember a person you walked by at a supermarket last *week*? How about the person that walked by you a *month* ago? A *year* ago? *Two* years ago?"

He reminded the jury that she had been with her husband at the grand jury where he was to testify to an entirely different aspect of the case, when she'd suddenly "volunteered" to tell the grand jury of having seen John Orr those many years ago, on the night before the fire.

Rucker said, "Why did the prosecutor use her, if he has a case that's beyond a reasonable doubt that this is an arson? Why would a prosecutor of his abilities, and he is *good,* put on a witness like *that*? He wouldn't need a witness like *that,* would he? But he did. And I think that tells you something.

"All right, this is it," Ed Rucker said. "I hate to stop talking. When I stop talking, that's *it*. Because I can't talk to you again, and the prosecution gets another argument, and I can't reply to it.

"But I am just going to tell you this: that mischaracterizing the facts doesn't change the facts. Telling you the ceiling line is here or the fire moved there doesn't establish that as a fact. It has got to be *proved*."

At this point in his closing it became more clear why he and Giannini had allowed a former deputy city attorney prosecutor and a retired deputy sheriff to sit on the jury. Rucker was depending on the law being carefully explained to these people, not just from the bench but in the jury room.

"You decide this case on the facts, and you follow the law," he said. "Because you don't want the oath you took to mean nothing. I am asking you, not for John Orr, I am asking you for the integrity of this system.

"The way you decide on those *other* fires, you decide. But on *this* one, on the *Ole's* fire, I am asking you to come back with a not-guilty verdict, because that is what the facts are, and that is what the law is. Thank you."

At 4:00 P.M. that day, Ed Rucker had distanced himself and his case from Peter Giannini and *his* case in very direct and forceful language. Ed Rucker hated the death penalty and would have accepted Cabral's tentative plea bargain in order to guarantee against it. He told his associates that he had to stop defending capital murder because he could no longer bear the responsibility and the toll that death-penalty cases had taken on him.

In effect, Ed Rucker had given the jury permission to convict the defendant on the other arsons, but not on this one. He couldn't let them *kill* John Orr.

20

DEATH HOUSE

The June gloom of Southern California had set in, but at least the forecast of possible showers had proven inaccurate on Thursday, June 11.

Peter Giannini got his chance at closing arguments that morning, quickly reminding the jury that John Orr had learned in San Luis Obispo that he was a suspect after finding the tracking device on his car. He said, "You heard a lot of argument from the prosecutors that he was trying to avoid detection. Well, he probably *was*. So keep that in mind when you're looking at *these* fires. There were no fires from that point until he was arrested, no fires similar to any of the ones that they'd been investigating. Now, that's a sign that he'd *stopped*."

Giannini was saying in effect that his client was a serial arsonist who'd been scared straight, a daring defense to say the least.

"So, in order for him to be guilty of the fires that happened after that, you would either have to believe that he'd changed his method or changed the type of fire. Why would somebody do that if they know they're being tracked? I don't think anybody will argue that John Orr was *stupid*."

This jury had heard innovation from both defense lawyers. Rucker had told them he didn't care much if they convicted John Orr of Giannini's fires so long as they acquitted him of the Ole's blaze. Giannini was saying that John Orr may have done all of the Pillow Pyro fires, but wasn't dumb enough to have done the oddball fires that had occurred just before his arrest. Neither of his attorneys was saying what John Orr said to everyone: That he had never set *any* fire, not one, not *ever*. And that he wanted to testify, but had been strongly cautioned against it. And that his guilty plea had been a legal ploy that supposedly would have allowed him to walk free by the year 2002, at the age of fifty-three.

Giannini began attacking the Hilldale and San Augustine testimony, as well as the Teletrac, which had only shown him in the general area of some fires.

He continued with the *What is he, stupid?* theme when he mentioned photos and videotapes that the task force had seized, saying, "After he *knew* that he was suspected of starting fires, he's going to put these pictures of fires up on the wall? Announcing that he had before-and-after pictures of a fire that, according to them, he'd started? Does *that* make sense to you?"

He tried to refute witnesses, and testimony, and warned against suppositions based on little evidence. And then he went to the College Hills fire, briefly depicting the prosecution's case as being based on the testimony of the air force major and the woman in whose bathroom John Orr had stood, unrecognized, a short time after she'd allegedly seen him at the fire's point of origin.

It was probably Peter Giannini's best defense work. He portrayed the air force major as "a man that claims he has some kind of special memory powers that the rest of us *don't* have." He pointed out that the major had said that there were no cars on the street in College Hills, and that it had been an unusually quiet day, yet the firefighter witnesses said that traffic was so heavy they had to approach on the wrong side of the road.

"The man with the photographic memory," Giannini said, "had memory *failure*."

Once again, Giannini returned to the *What is he, stupid?* defense, saying, "If John Orr had actually been there setting that fire, there is *no* way he'd have gone up into that apartment with Gomez and Masucci."

When he got to the Warner Brothers fire, he was equally dismissive, if not contemptuous, of Burbank arson investigator Steve Patterson's contention that he thought it had been an incendiary fire based on accelerants. Giannini said, "This is an open TV set. It's like an unframed house in the back. I guess it means that John Orr had somehow gotten through one of those security-guard gates with, what? A gallon of gas? And spread it all the way along the back of the set?"

About the alleged pretense that the defendant hadn't known his way to Warner Brothers Studios, Giannini said, "John Orr didn't say, 'I don't know *how* to get to the lot.' He said, 'I don't know how to get to where the *fire* is.'" Giannini called it a "mix-up."

As to the security director who'd remembered Captain Orr having been at the fire in progress, Giannini said, "His recollection is that John Orr came while the fire was still burning. Well, nobody else remembers that. Nobody else testified to that. How do we know he's wrong? There was in fact a parent-teacher conference that was scheduled at three-thirty to three-forty, and it lasted thirty minutes to thirty-five minutes. It's also backed up by the Teletrac."

At one point he said, "He knew about fires. He was at a lot of fires. He was *supposed* to be at a lot of fires. So the fact that he's there, and he's the fire guy, means he was doing his job. That's *all* it means. We've learned from all the investigators who we've talked to that that's the only time you catch somebody, if you're going to catch them.

"This is not about fires other than the ones that he's charged with here. It's not about whether he was a good arson investigator. The common threads that Ms. Flannery told you about are essentially common to *all* arson investigators. So look at the facts, testimony, and the exhibits. Apply the law, and I think when you do, you'll find that none of these charges have been proved beyond a reasonable doubt. I think you'll find that the facts can reasonably be interpreted to point to innocence for each one of these particular fires. And when you find that, your job is done. You must find him not guilty. And I ask you to find him not guilty. Thank you."

After the noon recess, Sandra Flannery was first up with rebuttal. She apologized about the trial seeming to have gone on endlessly, and promised she wouldn't go on endlessly, and then she and Mike Cabral went on almost endlessly.

She started with the Hilldale and San Augustine fires, reiterating all of it, beginning with how John Orr had gotten there quickly. She theorized that the defendant had set one fire, set a delay device at the other, gone home and switched from his own car into the Teletracked city car, then had gone back to the fire scene where the tracking device picked him up.

It was a sort of bad-guy-in-his-own-car, good-guy-in-the-arson-car theory, which mirrored what Sandra Flannery and Mike Cabral privately thought about John Leonard Orr. They believed that he had been the man at the College Hills apartment house who had tried to warn the occupants to get out. They believed it was the good half of John Orr who'd spoken to the press after the College Hills calamity when he said he thought the arsonist "hadn't meant" to touch off such a major disaster. They saw him as *both* firefighters in *Points of Origin,* two people in one skin, constantly at war with each other.

After going point by point through the testimony, she then addressed the psychological premise in Peter Giannini's defense. She said, "Does the fact that John Orr was under investigation prior to the time of setting these remaining fires suggest that he dared not set these fires? There's a significant change in the type of fires. You no longer see the fires set in open retail establishments during business hours with a time-delay device."

When she got to the Warner Brothers fire, it was to bring up more Teletrac argument that he'd been close to Warner Brothers. But there were too many Evil Twin timing problems, with him in two places at once, so she did little to remind the jury that the Warner Brothers director of security testified that he'd seen John Orr enter while the fire was burning. Task-force members admitted that when all was said and done the Teletrac testimony was about as explosive as a mouse fart.

College Hills was her major arson, so she devoted most of her rebuttal to it. In fact, she got a bit sardonic for the first time, and said, "In reference to John Orr's weed-abatement program, he talked about transient arsonists that go from town to town setting brush fires everywhere. I guess the transients must've gotten word of John Orr's weed-abatement program and stopped setting fires, because a photograph taken not long ago shows plenty of brush at the College Hills area. It's always nice to have transients to blame things on."

She made an attempt to explain the eyewitness who hadn't recognized John Orr when he'd stood in her apartment, saying that the defendant had been in the bathroom doorway, so the witness hadn't really gotten a good look. After defending the air force major with the photographic mind, she then introduced a new ingredient to the stew being served. She said that in one of John Orr's weed-abatement memos to Chief Gray a year before the College Hills fire, he'd considered starting a small business in the field of fire-insurance survey.

It was the first insinuation to the jury that there could even have been a sinister profit motive connected with the brush fires, an insinuation that the defense would get no chance to refute.

When Mike Cabral got up that afternoon, he promised to keep it brief, but this jury had heard *that* one before. He went after each of the defense witnesses who'd seemed contradictory, and made a clever point about the testimony of the Ole's employee who'd said that the leaking ceiling had left a huge hole, something that the defense had used in saying there'd been a gap where a smoldering attic fire could've dropped down.

Cabral turned it around and said, "It is inconsistent with a slow smoldering attic fire if it, in fact, existed, and was as big as she said. We don't have, and all the experts agree on this point, we don't have a slow, smoldering fire that's oxygen starved, because we've got a huge hole in the roof where the fire would've pulled oxygen out."

He was saying that a big ceiling hole hurts the defense theory more than the prosecution's. With a big breathing area, an attic fire would not have smoldered slowly, but would've raged swiftly.

Alluding to the defense contention that it was not a really rapid fire, he said, "All that polyfoam is hissing, burning, that deep blue flame and the blue-greenish flame that Captain Eisele talked about. Look what Mr. Obdam says, five to ten minutes he had to get out of the building. Well, I don't know. Five minutes? I'm sitting in this place and somebody tells me I've got five minutes to get out before that whole place is engulfed in flames and I'm dead. That's a rapid fire. We got a sixteen-thousand-square-foot building. They don't even know where they're at. The people submit to you the evidence shows that those people were dropped to the ground long before ten minutes ever came."

When he came to ceiling tiles showing more fire damage on the attic side and confusing the investigator at the scene, he said that after the firefighters had vented the roof, the attic side of the fire burned freely where they couldn't get water on it. He said that paint on the beams did not

burn equally as it would have if a fire had charged the whole attic, and
that some beams burned and some didn't because the fire had risen up
from down below. Moreover, he said, the burning on the attic side of the
ceiling tiles could've been caused after the roof collapsed and formed a
lean-to space where the fire kept burning the top side of the tiles until
the firefighters could put it out.

Cabral was stopped by the clock at 4:00 P.M. on Thursday, but was
back at them the next morning, again trying to dismantle the testimony
of defense experts by pointing out that a lot of their testimony had been
based on two-dimensional photographs, making it impossible to tell anything about the depth of char. And no juror, nor anyone else with a
smidgin of common sense, could fail to conclude that the entire business
of fire investigation was enormously subjective, more of an art than a science, especially if one looked at photos of the pile of rubble that had
faced investigators out there on the morning after Ole's had been ravaged
by an inferno.

In a way, Mike Cabral made that point himself when he said, "So
what does that leave us? Do we want to eliminate all of these experts?
The people submit we probably can, and *still* decide the *how*. They've
given you a great deal of information about how fire progresses, and on
top of that you have a great deal of information about how *this* fire progressed. On top of that, you have the defendant's statements telling you
what happened."

Well, that perked up the dozing jurors. Defendant's statements? John
Orr had sat there for weeks and never uttered a peep.

"He told Karen Berry what happened," Cabral said. "He told Jim
Fitzpatrick what happened. That's all you need. That's all you need: the
fire-scene background and the testimony of the defendant establishes
what happened and establishes it beyond a reasonable doubt."

So after goosing the jurors with a cattle prod, he'd gone back to
smacking them with a pig bladder. He'd only been referring to those
post-Ole's opinions back in 1984 that John Orr had offered to various
people.

He resumed the technical dissertation and repeated what they'd heard
from the lips of witnesses who'd been in Ole's on the night of the fire.
The prosecutor reminded the jury that Albertson's Market in Pasadena
was seven miles from Ole's, and that Von's Market was only a few blocks

from Ole's. Then he told them that the experts had testified that the incendiary device would allow a fifteen- to twenty-minute delay. Then he gave them his time line, after the Von's device was set.

"So he's at Ole's," Cabral said. "He places his device in the location. He calls Verdugo. He's told he's dispatched to Albertson's. He drives for ten minutes. That gets him to Albertson's at seven-fifty-seven. He's there ten minutes. That would be eight-oh-seven. He gets back to Ole's, eight-seventeen. So we've got five minutes there that he can play with."

Rich Edwards had driven the route at various times, careful to observe the speed limit, and allowing time to enter Ole's and set a delay device. It was a *very* close time line, Edwards had concluded.

Cabral then decided to try to square the time at Albertson's Market with the fifteen or twenty minutes that Investigator McClure had recalled somewhat hazily, and he ended with, "Plenty of time, ladies and gentlemen. Plenty of time."

The prosecutor was suggesting that the defendant could have set a device at Von's at 7:40, and in his Mario Andretti mode, raced several blocks to Ole's to set another at 7:50, then sped several miles to Albertson's for a look-see, racing back to Ole's by 8:22 P.M. where he'd called Verdugo Dispatch from a public phone booth.

Plenty of time? No. Possible? Maybe. If the investigation at Albertson's had lasted five minutes rather than fifteen or twenty.

Proof that the courtroom was nodding off showed itself by the fact that nobody even laughed when Mike Cabral was trying to flip to his advantage some testimony from the Ole's defense witness named Beatrice, who'd testified to the hole in the ceiling where ceiling tiles had never been replaced.

Cabral said, "And it's the opening that gives the opportunity for the smell of smoke. The aerosols, not the fire itself. What would you expect to smell, in reference to Beatrice's hole?"

Toward the end, Mike Cabral got to the novel *Points of Origin*, particularly to the ice cream incident, implying that John Orr was not as creative as his lawyer implied, that perhaps he'd *heard* the little boy in the store begging his grandmother for ice cream.

"No other investigator said there was an arson," Cabral said, pointing his finger. "Only one. That man right *there*. The only person who said this was an arson, and then wrote a book about it. Only one person, who then, several years later, *admitted* taking a cigarette, three matches, wrapping them in a rubber band, putting them in a piece of paper, and setting fires to stores. In polyfoam. Only one person, the defendant.

"And I submit to you, ladies and gentlemen of the jury, that the evidence in this case is overwhelming, that the defendant, on October tenth, 1984, entered that store, set it on fire in the polyfoam, and caused the death of those four people. And I ask you to return a verdict of guilty."

So, on Friday, June 12, 1998, the case against John Leonard Orr ended as it had begun, with a reminder that he'd pled guilty to the Builder's Emporium fire in North Hollywood. Observers could only wonder how it would have ended if John Orr had gone to trial in federal court in Los Angeles and been convicted, just as he had in Fresno, but had *not* pled guilty. Would the dynamic of this murder trial have changed?

Once again, John Orr waived his right to be present for the read-back and jury questions, preferring to return to a nine-by-nine-foot cage at the county jail rather than to remain in the tank where strange fish swim.

The jury in the case of the *People v. John Orr* would deliberate for a full two weeks, and during the first week there were some things going on in the courtroom. One of the alternate jurors wrote a note asking if he could be excused for a conference out of state if deliberations were not over by June 16.

Ed Rucker, who'd noticed that particular alternate juror during trial, asked, "Was he asleep when he wrote that? Or is this one of the few times he was awake?"

The judge said, "I did watch him. And every time I thought it was time to kind of shake him, he would stir and move his eyes, so I do not think he was sleeping."

By Friday, June 26, Cabral made a motion asking that redacted portions of the manuscript be allowed back into the case if the defendant was found guilty and the trial proceeded to the penalty phase.

Rucker objected strongly, saying, "They're extremely inflammatory. They're very, very damaging. And we cannot say with any certainty that these are the feelings and emotions of the defendant. It is not a direct admission. It's not a confession, but the people will characterize it as such.

"Having created a *fictional* character, ascribed emotions to this character . . . to then assume that these are the emotions or the reactions of the defendant, given the highly prejudicial nature of those statements and the very callous nature of those statements, I would hope the court would exercise some caution here."

At 11:00 A.M. that day, after exactly two weeks of deliberations, the jury sent a note to the judge, saying, "We have reached a verdict on all but one count. We do not believe further deliberation would be of any value. What would the court want us to do at this point?"

After noon recess, the jury came back to the courtroom they'd left two weeks earlier, and handed the verdicts to the bailiff who handed them to the clerk.

Judge Perry said to a media-packed courtroom: "All right. The clerk will now read the verdicts."

The clerk read: "We, the jury in the above-entitled case, find the defendant, John Leonard Orr, guilty of the crime of first-degree murder, in violation of penal code section one-eight-seven-A, a felony, as charged in count one of the indictment. This twenty-sixth day of June, 1998. Juror Number Five, foreperson."

So it went through counts two, three, and four, including the special-circumstances allegation of multiple murder. And then through all of the rest, all through the College Hills counts, clear through count twenty-five, all except for count six.

It all had to be read, and then the question was asked, "Ladies and gentlemen of the jury, are these your verdicts, so say you one, so say you all?"

Collectively, they answered yes, and then individually, all twelve had to answer in the affirmative.

When it was over, Judge Perry said, "Let me address the foreperson regarding count six. Is it your view that this jury is hopelessly deadlocked on this count?"

The foreperson said, "Yes, it is."

"Do the people require any additional inquiry?"

"No, Your Honor," said Cabral.

"Are you moving to dismiss count six?" the judge asked.

"Yes, Your Honor," said Cabral. "We would."

"All right," said the judge. "That count will be dismissed."

And John Orr was acquitted of setting the Warner Brothers Studios fire.

Before dismissing the jury, the judge said, "All right, ladies and gentlemen, in light of these verdicts, there will be a penalty phase. And we would start that penalty phase on Tuesday morning at eight-thirty. I want to tell you that I believe there will be a considerable amount of publicity this weekend regarding your verdict. And I want to warn you again that you must be cautious, that you avoid any outside influences from family, friends, or loved ones, regarding the verdicts, and particularly not watch any television, news broadcasts, or read anything in the newspaper about this verdict. Thank you very much."

After the jury was dismissed, there were some matters to be taken up that were highly disturbing to Ed Rucker, who said to the judge, "There are certain issues that come to mind that the court should litigate, and I don't think Mr. Orr should somehow be put at a disadvantage because we haven't raised them earlier."

"Go ahead," said the judge.

"I believe the people intend to offer evidence of four additional fires that were not litigated during the trial."

"Well, let's ask Mr. Cabral," said the judge.

"People's Department Stores, Mort's Department Store, Bell's Cottage, and Howie's Market," said Cabral.

It became very clear to Ed Rucker that Mike Cabral, who had once suggested an off-the-record plea bargain and said he wasn't particularly interested in putting John Orr to death, was now preparing the syringe with more uncharged fires.

Rucker later said, "When I asked Cabral why he was doing this, he indicated that he'd had some sort of revelation over the weekend and thought now it was his duty to go all the way to the death house with John Orr."

Peter Giannini thought that the victims' families and renewed media interest had influenced Cabral's decision.

Mike Cabral was well aware that Ed Rucker was furious with him, especially when the towering defense lawyer turned to him and said, "Well, let's get to the *killing*."

———

As though the jury hadn't heard about enough fires while they were deciding whether to let John Orr live or die, Cabral wanted them to know that there were other unlitigated fires that had been set in retail stores. And Mike Cabral now routinely referenced John Orr's novel as if it were a diary:

"They are not merely property crimes set to burn a structure down," he said to the judge, "but the purpose of the defendant in setting these fires, *as noted in his manuscript*, is to cause havoc to the individuals inside the location."

The judge agreed, saying, "I do think that given the fact that the fires in the other establishments were open retail establishments where people were likely to be there, that that is sufficient to bring them within section one-ninety-point-three."

Rucker tried to keep the prosecutor from piling on at this critical juncture, and said, "I am not going to quarrel with the court's ruling, but I believe the people will offer evidence that these are time-delayed fires. As such it would be our position that it would be difficult to assume that the acts were directed at a person when it was unknown who would be in the store, or whether *anyone* would be in the store at the time they were ignited."

Judge Perry replied, "Well, I think you start with the crime of arson itself. And arson is categorized in some sections of the penal code as a crime of violence, isn't it?"

"A serious felony," said Cabral.

"It *is* a serious felony," the judge agreed. "And I just think that under the circumstance where the defendant is alleged to have set fires, albeit with a time-delayed device in an open retail establishment, I think that is enough."

"All right," Rucker said. "Just so that the record is clear, we would object on constitutional grounds that this would be a violation of due process for allowing unlimited or nonrestricted evidence that the people intend to offer."

When the jury was brought into the courtroom, Judge Perry read the lengthy instructions regarding murder in the first degree, with special circumstances alleged which had been found true, namely that there had been multiple fatalities in the Ole's fire.

"In the guilt phase of this trial," he said, "you were instructed that you could not consider sympathy or sentiment. You were also instructed that penalty or punishment was not to be discussed or considered. Those instructions no longer apply. You may now consider sympathy, and you must consider the consequences of your verdict. It is up to the jury to decide whether the defendant shall be sentenced to life imprisonment without the possibility of parole, or death."

Sandra Flannery was up first, and she said to the jury, "At the end of this case, we will maintain that the aggravating factors are so substantial in relationship to any mitigating factors, that the penalty of death is warranted, and that it is the only morally appropriate punishment in this case. Having set a fire that killed four people, John Orr continued setting fires, endangering the lives of more people. Under the guise of being the protector of good, John Orr was, in fact, the perpetrator of evil. At the end of this, we will zealously urge you to impose the penalty of death as the only morally appropriate sentence in this case. Thank you."

When Ed Rucker stood, he said, "Well, I hoped we wouldn't be here. But we've reached a point where we're now going to embark together on a very difficult journey that's going to affect all of us. And you have to decide whether it's appropriate, it's just, it's something your conscience can live with, that John Orr should spend every single day of the rest of his life in a cell until he dies in that cell. Or whether he's taken, strapped in a chair, and given lethal gas to kill him.

"Now, to assist you, we would hope to present to you, that like all of us, all human beings, there are parts to him. He is not a one-dimensional monster. He is not just a man who has set fires. He's a man who's lived a life, perhaps not an exemplary life, but a life. And we'll present to you some family members to talk to you about his boyhood, his joining the air force and the fire department.

"I'm confident that you can make the right decision here if you're guided by the goals of punishment, which would be to protect society and to punish John Orr. And at the conclusion, I'm going to ask you to spare this man's life. I'm going to argue to you from my heart that living the rest of his life in a cell is punishment that protects society from him forever. And it's one you should all be satisfied with."

And then Mike Cabral began to call the family members of the Ole's victims, and it was heartrending. Luis Cetina, older brother of Jimmy, told about how he'd wanted to play catch with Jimmy on that last day, but when Jimmy didn't, Luis had said, "I'm not gonna play catch with you anymore."

Little memories produced big guilt. And he told about all the promise that the gifted young athlete had had, and how Jimmy was so loved that the church could not hold all of the mourners. He told of the Volkswagen that his family had bought but never driven because they could not afford insurance. He told them that the first time the car was ever driven was behind the hearse that carried Jimmy Cetina's body to the cemetery.

After the jury had filed out, Ed Rucker had something to say to the court: "I would object to the manner and content of the testimony elicited from Mr. Cetina for victim impact. The testimony is elicited in a narrative fashion that allows a witness to speak at some length. We're at a very distinct disadvantage in this type of proceeding, in that to object is going to result in resentment from the jurors. Consequently, I would ask for the court's assistance to try and focus victim-impact testimony. I understand the difficulty of all this, but nonetheless, we have to have some order in a process even as bizarre as deciding whether someone is going to die or not."

Judge Perry said, "I felt that Mr. Cetina's testimony was generally responsive to the questions that were posed to him, and I felt that he was expressing in his terms what the loss of his brother had meant to him and to the family. And I felt that that was appropriate. Mr. Rucker, you know, I have great admiration for you and your opinion on such things. We're here for them to describe what the impact has been to them, and I'll allow it. But your concerns are on the record, and I will try to be mindful of them."

On Wednesday, July 1, the prosecution was allowed to introduce an uncharged count, the arson at People's Department Store. Mike Cabral called a witness, and Peter Giannini cross-examined, and the jurors sat gaping, because they'd gone through this for weeks. They'd already convicted the defendant. It had to have been the most profound feeling of déjà vu that they'd ever experienced.

One of the more macabre moments took place when Peter Giannini was cross-examining an arson investigator. The courtroom was darkened so that the investigator could comment on a scene being shown on the overhead projector.

Giannini couldn't find the play button on the video machine, and said, "Okay, let's see. It's so dark in here. Anybody got a match?"

It would have been perfect, and what this theater deserved, if John Orr had popped up and said, "Yeah, I've got *three!*"

21

SURVIVORS

There were several witnesses from College Hills in court to tell the jury how the fire had destroyed everything they'd owned, and how it had such a profound effect on their lives. And Cabral introduced evidence from the Howie's Market potato-chip fire of February 4, 1985, and had an expert say that it had been set with an incendiary device like the others. He called investigators Carl Costanzo from the Burbank Police Department and Steve Patterson from the Burbank Fire Department to testify about the Mort's Surplus fire, one of those that John Orr had videotaped. Steve Patterson testified that he'd not known that John Orr had arrived at the same time as the first engines.

And through all of this overkill, Peter Giannini asked few questions or sometimes none, because what was the point? The defendant had already been convicted of arson in two trials, and he'd pled guilty at another one. How many *more* arson counts were needed?

The three-year statute of limitations on arson had barred the district attorney's office from charging John Orr with some of the retail-store fires and brush fires that the task force believed the defendant had committed. However, Section 1101 (b) of the Evidence Code allowed the introduction of "uncharged crimes" if they could be demonstrated by a preponderance of evidence to be a likely M.O. crime committed by the defendant. In the penalty phase of a capital murder trial, *any* criminal activity that demonstrated the defendant's propensity for force or violence could be introduced and argued.

To nonlawyers it simply meant that the jury had to endure *another* mini-trial, and had to hear *more* testimony and *more* argument about what a bad guy the defendant really was, after they'd already thought he was bad enough to convict him of capital murder. It became a trial *after* a trial, with the statute of limitations tossed out the window.

At the end of it all, one realized that nonlawyers, using mere words, could never adequately render a portrait of the world inside the litigation tanks of America. It would take a painting by Salvador Dalí.

The prosecution called the owner of Bell's Cottage, a gift and home-accessories store in Burbank, to testify about a Dumpster fire that had broken out by the rear door of her business. When she'd discovered the blaze, she tried to call 911 but her phone was dead, and when she'd hurried around to the back of the building, the structure was in flames, and so was her car.

A man and two women had been standing nearby watching the fire. The man said he was a deputy sheriff, and asked about a house adjacent to her business. When she'd told him that an invalid lived in the house, the man leaped over the fence and ran to the door to warn the occupant.

In a few minutes, all of the fire watchers had left the scene, including the would-be rescuer. Five months later, Detective Costanzo of the Burbank P.D. showed the store owner a six-pak photo spread and she'd identified John Orr as being the "deputy sheriff."

Giannini asked as many questions as he should have asked. Then Sandra Flannery asked the witness if the "deputy sheriff" was in the courtroom, and the witness pointed to John Orr.

This was another of the fires in which Mike Cabral and Sandra Flannery believed that John Orr had been showing the two faces of the firefighters in his novel. Bad Aaron Stiles had set the Bell's Cottage fire, and good Phil Langtree had had a sudden attack of remorse and came to the rescue by leaping over a fence to warn an invalid. Even though, by flashing a badge and speaking to the arson victim, he'd exposed himself to the peril of being identified.

The prosecution team believed that he'd done the same thing in the

College Hills fire, by setting the blaze and then by trying to warn the nearest apartment dwellers, when he got spotted by the air force major and the woman in the building. It was an interesting theory, but could not be reconciled with their assertions that John Leonard Orr was a "classic sociopath," to use the preferred law-enforcement term.

One could find arguments for a diagnosis of psychopathy with this defendant, starting with admitted impulsiveness, a need for excitement, a manipulation of partnerships. His multiple marriages suggested shallow emotions and an inability to love and empathize. There was a certain grandiosity and egocentricity which could be documented.

But if he was the classic sociopath they believed him to be, then it was unlikely that he would be setting fires *and* trying to warn potential victims, at grave risk of being discovered. His responses would be more like those of his fictional arsonist, Aaron Stiles. Since the true psychopath is without a proper superego, he is guilt-free and remorseless, with little ability to turn off his symptoms. This left one to wonder if John Orr really *was* the man who'd shouted warnings at College Hills and at Bell's Cottage. The prosecutors couldn't have it both ways, not if logic was to guide this exercise. And the prosecution also spiced its arguments with words such as *evil,* which indicate a moral judgment rather than a clinical diagnosis.

Task-force members often used other words like *complex* and *contradictory* when describing John Orr. And they talked of a "dual personality," whatever that may have meant to them. In the one arson he'd been acquitted of committing—the Warner Brothers Studios fire—the prosecution believed that he'd sped to the fire, set it, and sped back to the school for a parent-teacher meeting, like the good surrogate father that he was. None of them had alluded to the irony that Robert Louis Stevenson Elementary School was named for the man who'd given the world *The Strange Case of Dr. Jekyll and Mr. Hyde.*

After yet another uncharged count of arson was argued, the prosecution called the father of Matthew William Troidl. When the accountant was asked how old his son had been on the day of his death, Matthew Troidl answered, "He was two years, eight months, and twenty-seven days old." Then he added, "He'd be sixteen and a half now. And I'm sure he would've tried to beat the July first deadline to try to get his driver's license. He'd like the girls, and he'd be athletic and good in school. We'd be talking about college now, and where he wanted to go, what he wanted to do."

Sandra Flannery asked, "In the past few years, in the past few *weeks,* how has this loss affected you?"

The witness replied, "About four years ago, we got a call from the deputy DA asking us about the fire and what we knew about it. And we'd always been told it was an accidental electrical fire. But they were looking into charging John Orr with this. And I started coming into court. And I came to almost every pretrial hearing for the last three years.

"I wanted everyone to know that my son was *important,* and that he was a human being. And he was *somebody.* Mr. Cabral read the three pages out of the manuscript and I was stunned to learn that he'd used my son's name in his book."

"Thank you," Sandra Flannery said. "I have no further questions."

The mother of Carolyn Krause was called to testify, and she looked at a photo of her daughter, a good-looking, fair-haired California girl with her baby strapped in a carrying pouch. Carolyn Krause's mother related a very sad tale of how her only daughter's death had affected her life and that of her grandchildren. She told of the widower remarrying a young woman who'd been a friend of Carolyn's, and how, as a grandmother, she'd eventually had had to go to court to get grandparent visitation rights. Carolyn's daughter was no longer living with her father and stepmother, and Carolyn's mother had not seen her grandson for ten years.

It was a tragic portrayal of how premature violent death tends to shatter things, all sorts of things.

By far, the most ravaging testimony was offered by Kimberly Deal Troidl, daughter of Ada Deal, mother of Matthew William Troidl.

Cabral began by asking the schoolteacher, "Do you remember October tenth, 1984?"

"Yes," the witness replied.

"And why is that?"

"It was the night I lost my son and my mother," she said.

And then the witness began a wrenching narrative, telling how they'd heard news of the fire and had driven to Ole's, where they'd found her father, Billy Deal. And how he'd looked at her and said, "I did everything I could!" and started crying.

She told of how she'd looked at flames that seemed hundreds of feet high, and told herself: "I have to go *in* there because there is nowhere that my baby could go that I will not follow him. And I started walking. I wasn't afraid. My baby was in there and I had to be in there *with* him. And all of a sudden a voice popped in my head, and it wasn't *my* voice, and it said, 'What about Bethany?'

"And I stopped walking. My mother wouldn't be there to take care of her. Bethany had lost her little brother. If she lost me on top of it, it would destroy her. So I had to stop. And I had to turn around. And that was one of the hardest things I've ever done. I couldn't leave her. And I have always told her that the only reason I'm alive today is because of her. I would not have stayed for anybody else.

"As time has gone on we have our son David, who's twelve now. And he had to grow up without knowing who his brother was. And I keep pictures up in the house, and we tell stories about him. My family does the same thing with my mom. We have to try to keep them alive.

"For myself, I frequently feel like the way a cat looks if you hold it by the scruff of its neck in midair, with arms and legs, everything going everywhere, and it is trying to get some kind of perch, but it can't. Because when I lost my mom I lost the person who had held my hands when I learned to walk. I lost the person who put the veil on my head when I got married. My *mom,* you know? The one person that I probably would've turned to, who could understand a mother's loss of a child, was my mom. But she wasn't there to comfort me.

"And in losing my child . . . I carried him for nine months. And I watched what I ate. I wouldn't even sit too close to the TV or go near the microwave because I didn't want anything to happen to him. I baby-proofed my house. Nobody outside my parents baby-sat him.

"And he had this game that he liked to play. And I sometimes wonder how much children know that we don't know, because he would lay in his father's arms, and he would lay really limp and close his eyes, and then he would open them and say, 'Mommy, if I died, would you save me?' And I would get so upset when he did that. And I would grab him up out of his father's arms, and I would smother him with kisses and hold him really close and say, 'Yes, Mommy will always save you.'

"And I have lived with that guilt and the shame of it every single day because I know . . . I'm a mom . . . I *know* how he was afraid of dying in that horrible place. I know he thought Mommy would come and save him because that's what mommies do. And I never came!"

When she paused to gather herself, Mike Cabral, a man with three children of his own—who'd kept a photo of Matthew William on his desk as inspiration during all the years that he'd worked on this case—asked a question to which he knew the answer: "Mrs. Troidl, has this affected you when people ask how many children you have?"

"I have two answers," she said. "If I'm someplace where I'm not going to see these people again, like on a plane or something, I tell them I have three children. And I tell them that Matthew William is two and a half. And I tell them all the stories I can tell them, making it sound like they just happened. But if it is somebody I know that I'm going to be around again, people that I work with, I tell them I have two children. And then I'm ashamed again, because I feel like he's lost so much, how can I deny him the fact of his *existence*?

"But then if I tell people about him, then they want to know about how he died. And I have to talk about it. And it was a horrible way to die. It was a horrible way for my *mom* to die. And I can't talk about it. I *can't*."

"I have no further questions, Your Honor," Mike Cabral said.

Following noon recess, the younger of John Orr's attractive daughters was called to the stand. After she was sworn, Peter Giannini said to her, "Lori, tell us who you are and why you're here."

The witness gamely answered, "I'm the daughter of my dad, John Orr. And I'm here to save his life today."

"How old are you?"

"I'm twenty-four."

"What kind of work do you do?"

"I'm in human resources for foundation health."

"And are you married?"

"Yes."

"Do you have any children?"

"Yes, I do."

"When you were young, your mom and dad were divorced, is that right?"

"Yes."

And then she told the court how John Orr had been a good father even though he hadn't lived with them, and was always a good guy, in her mind. Since his arrest she'd talked to him on the phone and written letters. She showed the court a photo of her son and said of the photo, "That's on his birthday when he got his fire truck."

"Does he know your dad?" Giannini asked.

"He knows *of* him. He knows pictures of him. He knows him on the phone. He calls him Grandpa John. He just knows that he lives far away right now, and that he can talk to him on the phone, but he can't go to his house."

She told the court that John Orr had been there for the big events in her life, and she said, "He was always a hero to me. We'd see him on TV. He saved someone's life. He saved a dog. He saved a bunch of different people. And we'd go to school, you know, and say, 'That's my dad. He's a fireman.' We were so proud of him."

"How did you react," Giannini asked, "when he got arrested? What was your response?"

"I cried. I mean, I was shocked. I didn't know what to . . . what to make of it."

"How do you think you'll be affected if your dad is executed?"

"Badly. I mean, not only for myself. But I'll have to explain to my son some day why his grandfather was killed. And I don't want to have to do that. My son didn't do anything wrong. And I didn't do anything wrong. And I just . . . I want what I can have of my dad. I don't want that to end. I mean, that's what I've been used to the last seven years. And I've still stayed in touch with him. And I still get things from him, as a father. You know, I still *need* him."

"Nothing further," Peter Giannini said.

And though it was customary for the adversary to say "No questions" at such a time, the prosecution chose to ask a few.

"At some point in time," Sandra Flannery asked, "when you got older and looked for an apartment, did your father advise you to only live in an apartment building that had fire sprinklers?"

"Not sprinklers," she said, "but alarms. And to make sure that they were always working."

"And how did you react when you learned that your father had pled guilty to setting three fires?"

And the daughter of a man who had never admitted to setting any fires, other than during his tactical plea bargain, said, "Well, my dad had discussed that prior with my sister and I, and told us why he felt he had to do that. And so I was, you know, prepared for it, and for his reasons for doing that."

The defense lawyers thought that the question to John Orr's shaken daughter was gratuitous and insensitive, and they were right.

The next witness, John Orr's father, took the stand and informed the court that he was hard of hearing and would be eighty-four years old in December. He sketched his family's early life together, what John Orr had referred to as Ozzie-and-Harriet time. He talked of picnics and birthday parties, and said that his youngest son had been an excellent student and an obedient boy.

He told of John Orr enlisting in the air force, and serving honorably, and how after his son had had children of his own, he'd bring them to see their grandfather.

Ed Rucker said, "You understand that your son has been convicted of these murders that he was charged with?"

"Yes, I understand," the witness said.

"Do you still care about your son?"

"I love my son," the witness said, and started crying. "I love my son."

"What affect would it have on you if he got executed?" the lawyer asked.

"It could be very bad," the old man said. "I live alone. He calls me about every week. I talk with him, and I write to him. I send him pictures, and I send him magazines. I do whatever I can do. I send him money. I don't want to lose him."

"Thank you, sir," said Ed Rucker. And this time Sandra Flannery wisely said, "No questions."

John Orr's first wife took the stand and told the jury that her marriage to the defendant had lasted for six years, and that he'd always met his financial obligations after their divorce. And that he'd been a good father.

Rucker asked, "What do you think the effect on your daughters would be if John was executed?"

"Oh, I hate to even think . . . Carrie will be totally and absolutely devastated. Lori will have a very difficult time trying to explain to her son what happened to his grandfather. I . . . I don't know exactly."

"You understand that, given his convictions, he's going to be sentenced to prison for the rest of his life, unless the jury decides that he should be executed. You understand that?"

"Yes, I do," she said. "But at least we can have contact with him. Talk to him. Write to him. Include him in what's happening with the family. I mean, he . . . he would still be *around* to have contact with."

Sandra Flannery always got the job of confronting the female witnesses, and she did it again. "A few months after he started his job with the Glendale Fire Department, was there an event that precipitated your divorce?"

"He decided that he wanted to leave and have a divorce," said the witness.

"And how did you learn that?"

"He packed and left."

"And you came home one day and he was just gone?"

"Um-hmm," the witness said. "With no notice. He left a note and phoned me a day or two later."

"And is it correct to say he left you with no money?"

"Well, yeah, I . . . I guess. I had no job. I mean, I had the two girls, but he did send me money and take care of my rent and so forth, as soon as he contacted me a couple days later."

"And were you nonetheless forced to go on welfare?"

"A few months after that, yes. I didn't want to leave my young children at home and get a job right away. And it gave me time to think about . . . figure out what I needed to do. So, yes."

"And as your daughters were growing up, who attended the parent-teacher conferences?"

"I pretty much did that on my own," said the witness. "I'm not sure if John attended any or not. He may have attended a few. I don't even know if my second husband attended any or not. I pretty much did those on my own."

"Shortly after John Orr left you, did he remarry?"

"I would say that it was about a year after."

"And do you know who he remarried?"

"I know her name."

"And by any chance do you know what part of Los Angeles she lived in?"

"Absolutely not," the witness said.

Sandra Flannery took the witness through John Orr's last two marriages, so the jury would know of his inconstancy, and then asked the same question about her husband's advising his daughters to live in an apartment with fire sprinklers. The reason that the prosecutor had mentioned sprinklers on two occasions was to remind the jury that other people's children had not had the benefit of sprinkler protection, that the part of Ole's that burned did not have a sprinkler system, and that perhaps the fire setter had been well aware of that.

It was an obscure reference, the talk about sprinklers, but these warrior prosecutors would never let a bullet go unspent. They just had to keep firing until their barrels melted down, and then they'd draw bayonets for the coup de grâce.

When Ed Rucker called John Orr's mother to the stand, the judge said to the elderly woman, "You can pull the microphone up and speak loudly into it."

But she declined, saying, "I got a big booming voice anyway."

Ed Rucker had her introduce family photographs, and asked her to describe the scenes depicted in them. She told the court how, as a boy, her son John had taken a younger mentally handicapped boy under his wing and shown him every kindness. She told how hard he'd worked while in high school, making extra money and helping his older brothers with loans.

Like the others, she said that if her son was sentenced to prison for life, she'd visit him and write to him. "Whatever I have to do to be with him," she said.

The last defense witness was John Orr's daughter Carrie, who told the court that she was twenty-seven years old and married.

Giannini asked her, "How did you react when your dad was arrested?"

"It was a huge shock that came out of nowhere," she said. "I don't know, just complete shock. I mean, I wanted to know what was going on. What happened. Where did this *come* from?"

"How do you think it would affect you if they decided to give him the death penalty?"

"It would be horrible!" the witness said. "I mean, I'd lose my dad. I don't know . . . I don't know how . . . I mean, even though I hardly see him now because of the situation, I would *never* be able to see him again!"

"So is there anything else you'd like to say to this jury?" Giannini asked. "Anything at all?"

And the distressed young woman said a wiser thing that day than lawyers in that courtroom had said for many days: "I don't know really *what* to say. I don't *know.*"

22

THE DEBATE

With the courtroom now full of lawyer-spectators wanting to hear the death debate, exhausted jurors met on Monday, July 6, to listen to arguments about whether John Orr should be sentenced to life without parole or suffer execution. But not before they got to hear another defense witness, Ronald Markman, M.D., whose book Mike Cabral had studied on a houseboat vacation when everyone else had been having a good time. The psychiatrist specialized in forensic psychiatry, and by his own estimation had evaluated two to three thousand people in homicide cases. In response to Peter Giannini's questions, he testified that he'd seen John Orr on three occasions and had formulated a working psychiatric diagnosis.

"And what is that diagnosis?" Giannini asked.

"Well, there is an access to diagnosis of an obsessive-compulsive personality disorder," the witness said. "And assuming that the behaviors for which he's charged are correct, a diagnosis of pyromania."

Giannini asked, "About obsessive compulsive personality disorder, in Mr. Orr's case, how does that manifest itself?"

"He's a very meticulous guy," the witness said, "who has very very controlled, constructed views of issues. He's very, very demanding of others and of himself. He's interested in crossing every *t* and dotting every *i*."

After discussing psychiatric terms and citing examples of the disorder, he continued, "Obsessing is a thinking process. It's a thought focus. Compulsive behavior is a component of obsession, but they're psychiatrically different. As you think and obsess about something, you elevate or increase your anxiety level. And people can only tolerate an optimal level of anxiety, if I can use that term."

"Then what happens?"

"Then they either have to do something or they deteriorate."

"Tell us a little bit about pyromania," Giannini suggested.

"It is one of the diagnostic categories in the statistics manual," said the witness. "Pyromania is the underlying requirement or need to set fires."

Dr. Markman said that male fire setters outnumber females overwhelmingly, and that some studies have put it at nine to one. He said that there are three categories of pyros, the first being the crazies who have to save the world, the second being those with a need for revenge or profit, and the third being those who set fires in order to dissipate internal anxiety.

"Is there an evil intent in the setting of fires for those in the third category?" Giannini asked.

"No," the witness said. "There's no consciousness or willingness to either injure people or destroy property. The goal is to have the fire. The fire is the goal. Unfortunately, fire consumes."

"So that leads to the obvious question," Giannini said. "Is Mr. Orr, for example, able to *control* his fire-starting compulsion?"

"Well, Mr. Orr is not psychotic," said Dr. Markman. "If he had anxiety that was intolerable, and he had the need to act to dissipate the anxiety, and that need was based on setting a fire, if a policeman were right there, he wouldn't set a fire. However, ultimately he *would* have to set a fire."

"Did you find any indications of early childhood symptoms of pyromania?" asked Giannini.

"He did talk of match playing. We see that in children, overwhelmingly in boys. Much of it has to do with unresolved parental conflicts."

The witness said that the conflict usually involves father identification when boys are no longer competing for their mother's affections. In case of childhood fire setting, people don't seem to get concerned because the fires are usually set in garbage cans. He finished by saying that the controlled environment of a jail relieves the fire setter of his anxiety.

When Cabral cross-examined, he elicited an opinion that pyromania affects less than 1 percent of the population, and was told that the defendant had only admitted to childhood match playing, not to childhood fire setting.

"Who gave you information about him setting some fires after he was tracked?" Cabral asked.

"Well, Mr. Orr's position on all three visits was that he did not set *any* of these fires. So the information came in discussions with Mr. Giannini and Mr. Rucker."

"And Mr. Orr says even the fire where they found his fingerprint, he *didn't* set?" Cabral asked.

"That's correct."

"Even the fires he pled guilty to? He maintains he's innocent?"

"He said that that was done as a result of a plea bargain. He felt that he was somewhat undercut in terms of the plea bargain that was given."

"Have there been a lot of studies on the course of treatment for pyromaniacs?"

"Not really," the witness said, "because of the limitation in the treatment population and the longevity required to treat. These are long-standing problems and have to be dealt with over years."

"We really don't know whether or not it's treatable at all?"

"It is treatable. Can you cure someone of it? You could probably get to the point where he can control the impulse, and maybe convert that symptom into something else that would be more socially tolerable."

"Did you review anything else?"

"Oh, yes. I reviewed his novel. And I did have his report from the city of Los Angeles with regard to his psychological testing when he'd applied to get on the police force."

"And he talked to you about that? His rejection by the LAPD?"

"That to me was a *significant* event in his life."

"He's still disturbed by that even today?"

"He denies it, but I believe he is."

On redirect, Giannini asked, "Given the history and diagnosis of pyromania, and the reasons for it being the release of anxiety, what would admitting to having set fires mean in terms of his psychological balance?"

"Oh, my, it would be devastating! It would destroy the orderliness of his life. It would demonstrate to him that he's been a failure all of his life."

While the jury was out, the lawyers and the judge haggled over yet more prosecution witnesses that Cabral wished to call, women John Orr had dated between or during marriages.

One of them, who'd worked for the city of Glendale, was called for the purpose of demonstrating that the defendant's propensity for fire setting was not restricted to the compulsive variety described by the psychiatrist. With certain legal parameters specified, the judge said he might allow her testimony, but wanted to hear what she had to say, so she was called while the jury was out of the courtroom.

She testified that her relationship with John Orr had begun one month before the Ole's fire, and at the time she'd owned a Chevrolet Camaro.

Cabral asked her, "What did you tell the defendant about your car?"

"Just that it was a pain," she said. "That it was overpriced, and I wished I'd never bought it."

"And in response to that did he say anything to you?"

"We were discussing how vehicle fires can be conceived as an accident, that if I didn't want my car he could take care of it. Just never to ask any questions."

"Did he explain how a fire could be set and not detected?"

"Yes, he did. Taking paper towels and putting them underneath the dashboard and setting them on fire. It would be determined to be an electrical problem."

"What happened after that?"

"Nothing. I never discussed it again. It was never an option in my mind."

Ed Rucker asked one question: "Did Mr. Orr ever say to you that he would *burn* your car?"

"No," she said.

Rucker then argued to the court that John Orr had not offered to commit an act of force or violence, that there were no steps taken to burn the car, and that this testimony was not proper rebuttal to anything that the defense had brought up.

The judge did not agree that the defendant had not made an offer to burn the car. Cabral argued that it *was* rebuttal to Dr. Markman's testimony regarding compulsive fire setting, saying that burning for profit was a whole different matter. The judge decided that her testimony would be allowed.

Then the judge wished to hear from another ex-girlfriend of John Orr, this one a former police officer, who took the stand with obvious discomfort.

When asked by Cabral, "Did you have a relationship with John Orr?" she answered, "I did."

"Do you see that person in court today?" Cabral asked.

"It's been twenty years," she answered, looking at the defense table. "I think that's John right over there."

The witness testified that she'd dated the defendant for about six months, and then Cabral asked, "Did you discuss with him events surrounding his application to the Los Angeles Police Department?"

She said, "I believe he mentioned that he had applied, and was not offered a job. But I don't really remember why."

"Did he explain to you anything about how he felt about that event?" Cabral asked.

"He seemed quite disappointed," she replied.

"Did he seem angry at being rejected?"

"It *has* been twenty years," she said.

"Did the defendant ever tell you during this relationship how he felt in relation to police officers?"

"I seem to recall that he felt like he was smarter than the average cop." Then she said, "And he probably *is*."

"Did he ever do anything that you considered to be playing games to get away with things?"

"Whenever we would meet on duty, he would like to kiss me while I was in uniform, which I was very uncomfortable with because we were not supposed to do it. But he would kiss me on duty. It didn't happen often, a very few times."

"Anything else like that?" Cabral asked.

And at last, the courtroom rail birds were going to get a chance to hear something titillating. About John Orr getting his mongoose milked by an honest-to-God cop. In full uniform. In a place where they could *both* get caught and fired. The risk! The *symbolism* of it all!

But what did the rail birds get—those poor old pensioners who wander the courts, clickety-clacking when they whisper because they can't afford Fixodent? What did they get?

"Are you referring to an incident in the basement of the firehouse?" she asked Cabral.

And of course, he was. But Mike Cabral faltered and said, "No, I'm not."

And the judge, knowing full well what had gone on in the firehouse basement, proved Cabral's trepidation was well grounded by saying, "We're *not*."

Cabral forged on halfheartedly: "Did you feel that the defendant had the attitude that he was going to do things to get away with it, and pull the wool over the eyes of the police department?"

"I seem to have the impression that he had that kind of attitude. John is a very bright man, and I believe he knew it."

"Did you form some conclusions about the defendant's behavior?"

"I think he has some sociopathic tendencies, but I am not an expert witness on sociopaths," she replied.

"Did you find him to be manipulative during your relationship?"

"Yes."

"And how would that show itself?"

She said, "It's been so long, Mr. Cabral. I really *can't* come up with any examples."

Gathering his courage for one last try, Cabral asked, "Other than the basement incident?"

"I am sorry?" she said, not quite hearing him.

"Other than the *basement* incident?" he repeated, louder.

"Yes," was all she said.

And Mike Cabral's yin and yang must have been fighting the impulse to yell: "Yes, girl, the basement incident. Spit it *out*. Why do you think we flew you here? The goddamn *basement* incident!"

But Cabral uttered a plaintive: "I have no further questions, Your Honor." And he gave up.

The judge was not impressed that this witness had demonstrated anything relevant regarding John Orr's alleged need to strike back at law enforcement, so he said, "I don't think you have made it, Mr. Cabral. I will sustain the objection by the defense. Thank you."

"I am free to leave?" the witness asked, relieved that she was not going to be made to tell the world what she'd told Cabral about "manually manipulating" him in the basement of that firehouse, about the weasel whacking from a real cop in a real uniform, wearing a real police shield, not a bogus badge like the one he'd carried as a Sears security officer.

As she was walking by the counsel table John Orr gave her a wave and mouthed: "Thank you." And she got outraged!

She waited outside the corridor for Cabral, and demanded to go back on the stand and tell everyone about the "incident in the basement." How *dare* he think she'd slanted her testimony for *him*!

"Too late," Cabral told her. Too late. Too freaking *late*.

Then the Glendale city employee was called, and told the jury the same story to which she'd testified out of their presence about the inferred offer to torch her car for insurance money.

Rucker didn't bother to cross-examine her, and the people at last rested. But then the four lawyers and the judge haggled over jury instructions, variations of those the jury had already heard. And they went on and on about mitigating factors, and aggravating factors, and they started citing cases, until even the most die-hard rail birds had flown to more promising feeding grounds in their never-ending search for stories more wretched than their own.

When the jury was brought out for the last time, they were read the jury instructions, and Judge Perry reminded them that there is no burden of proof in the penalty phase, and that this time the defense would have the last word.

Sandra Flannery was the first prosecution lawyer, and she said, "Well, I thought I would begin by wishing you a good morning, but I do have to say, to come to you on behalf of the people of the state of California and ask you to impose the penalty of death causes me hesitation to ever call this a good morning. But that is what I am here to do. And I do ask you to choose for John Orr the penalty of death."

She told them that they were the "conscience of the community," and that they were here "because of John Orr's choices."

"It was not an impulsive act," she said. "It was an act done with great deliberation. It was a *choice*. With each match that John Orr took out of that matchbook he made a *choice*. As he positioned those matches on that cigarette in just the right manner, at just the right position to create the amount of delay that he wanted and that he needed, he made a *choice*. He used his specialized knowledge of fire dynamics to set a fire in a place and in a manner that would send that fire racing against life itself. That was the *choice*.

"He could have set his device anywhere he wanted. But he chose to go onto the side where there were no ceiling sprinklers. He made that *choice*. You see, when it came to his own personal safety, and the safety of his family, John Orr was keenly aware of fire dangers and chose to prevent them. But when it came to the safety of the people at Ole's, John Orr was keenly aware of the fire dangers and chose to exploit them.

"He knew, based upon his specialized knowledge of fire dynamics, that by going to the housewares department and choosing to place his ignition device in the polyfoam, he would be setting a fire of inescapable proportion. John Orr would like you to believe that he was driven by some obsessive compulsion to set fires, and yet if that were the case, how did he restrain himself enough to make it to the polyfoam stack, which he knew would ignite as though it were petroleum itself?

"He alone knew how many minutes separated life from death. He was as much a killer as someone who shoots their victims face-to-face. Only how John Orr did it was with so much more terror and deception. Under the guise of being the protector of good, John Orr was in fact the perpetrator of evil.

"John Orr, through his job, was given power, but that power was not enough. He needed more power and he wanted more power, and he set his fires to gain that power. I guess you could say that knowledge is power. If that is the case, then isn't it also true that *secret* knowledge is *secret* power? He had secret knowledge and that gave him secret power over the lives of other people through setting the fires, watching their reactions, seeing who would *survive*.

"How long did his delay last? Ten minutes perhaps. When you deliberate in the jury room, take ten minutes to be alone with your thoughts. Ten minutes is a very long time to reflect upon what is the right thing to do. And yet in those ten minutes did John Orr make the choice to turn around?

"He could have gone back. He could have extinguished his device. But instead he chose to let his device burn and extinguish the *lives* of

Carolyn Krause, Jimmy Cetina, Ada Deal, and Matthew Troidl. Then, as the fire burned and ravaged the inside of that building, where was John Orr? He was outside taking photographs.

"The defense has suggested to you that there's some type of obsessive-compulsive behavior going on, driving John Orr to set these fires. A doctor came in and suggested that in three interviews he had gotten to know the *real* John Orr. But I suggest to you that each of you have gotten to know the *real* John Orr. John Orr's fires were moral decisions. He *chose* to set them. The mere inability to understand why someone can do something, and have an outlook on life that is so different from yours, doesn't transform that outlook into a mental illness.

"John Orr had an attitude about life. His attitude was that he wanted power, that he was superior to others, that he could create circumstances and situations that no one could figure out but him. He had secret knowledge that gave him secret power.

"To not require the ultimate penalty for the ultimate crime would be to diminish and devalue those lives that were taken. It would be an act of cruelty to the victims, under the mistaken belief that you are extending compassion to the defendant. If John Orr is permitted to live and replay the Ole's fire and its pleasure over and over and over again in his mind, then it will be as though he has killed Carolyn Krause, Jimmy Cetina, Ada Deal, and Matthew Troidl over and over again. Thank you."

It was easily Sandra Flannery's best work. Lawyer-spectators in the courtroom were impressed with her flashes of eloquence in a long trial that had seen so little of it.

"Ladies and gentlemen," Peter Giannini began, "John Orr will be punished in this case. As a society you will be protected from him. The only question is not *will* he get out of prison. The only question is *when*. Will he die, because *you* say he must die, by lethal injection? Or will he die when *God* decides that he dies, if he is sentenced to life without the possibility of parole? It is a long, slow, tedious kind of death. Is it worse than death? I don't think so. I think life is sacred. Every life is sacred. John's life is also sacred.

"Every one of you individually is being called upon to make one of the most difficult decisions of your life, and it is not a collective decision.

It is your decision individually. There is nobody else to turn to. If every single one of you doesn't agree that death is the appropriate punishment, it isn't.

"What did God do? What did he do when Cain killed Abel? He put a mark on his head, set him out to wander alone in the world. He banished him. He gave him life without the possibility of parole.

"The prosecutor said in her closing statement that the ultimate crime deserves the ultimate punishment. You have to ask yourself, is this the *ultimate* crime? There are thousands of homicides in the county of Los Angeles every year. Very few of those are death-penalty cases where you get to first-degree murder with special circumstances. Where you have to start talking about the possibility of a penalty phase. What does that mean in this case? The *only* special circumstance charged against John Orr in this case is that more than one person died in that fire. If everything else about this case was the same, everything else you had heard in this case was identical, but only *one* person died in that fire, we wouldn't be in this phase of the case. There'd be *no* penalty phase."

Despite the hyperbole about *thousands* of homicides, that argument by Peter Giannini probably represented his finest moment in the case, effectively exposing the quirkiness of the law: One arson murder, no capital crime. Two arson murders, capital crime.

"I think his history speaks for itself," Giannini said. "He's extremely sick. He's not normal. He lacks the kind of control the rest of us have. With John Orr it's always the same or similar conduct. Repeated conduct. It's a compulsion. The testimony of Dr. Markman is uncontradicted. The people could have put a psychiatrist up here to say there's nothing wrong with this guy. They chose not to do that. You have to ask yourself why. I think the reason is because he *does* suffer from a mental defect. He couldn't stop himself. He knew he was suspected. He knew he was being tracked."

So it was Peter Giannini himself who became the one to confront the premise of his earlier argument, that John Orr was too smart to have torched Warner Brothers, Kennington, and San Augustine, knowing that he was probably being tracked. Giannini had at last decided that compulsion trumps intelligence.

"When this trial is over, you're going to want to put it behind you. If you vote to kill him, it might not be that easy to do. You'll have to live with it for the rest of your lives. The challenge here is to punish him, to protect all of us, and to hold John Orr responsible for the rest of his life for what he did. And the challenge here, I think, is to do that without losing sight of our own human values, our higher values, and our ability to show mercy.

"It's never wrong, it's never weak, it's never a mistake to let somebody live. However you might feel about John, you've got to take pity on his father, his mother, his daughters, his four-year-old grandchild. These are innocent people too. They haven't done anything. If you kill him, you're going to destroy them. An eighty-three-year-old man is sitting back there. Let them live out their final years without the horror of John's execution ruining their lives every day. His grandson needs his grandfather to be alive. How do you say, 'My grandfather was executed at San Quentin'? If you do this, you're condemning him too.

"You can't bring back the people who died in that fire. God didn't give you that power. God only gave you the power to take life, not to give it back. All you do if you kill John is you create *another* funeral. Another innocent mother and father suffering the same anguish that we've seen. That's all. Another death, another funeral, another *grave*.

"There's been enough death here. There's been too much death, too much suffering. Don't make it worse. Don't make these other people suffer. They didn't do anything to deserve this. I'm asking you to show mercy to John, to his father, mother, daughters, and grandson. Give him life without the possibility of parole. Thank you."

When Mike Cabral had his moment, Rich Edwards from his arson task force was there, and Sandra Flannery, as usual, sat in the second chair. When Cabral got up, he said, "Ladies and gentlemen of the jury, I stand here before you with a heavy heart, because as a representative of the people of the state of California, I'm going to ask you to go back and deliberate. And at some point to come out of that room and look at me, Ms. Flannery, Deputy Edwards, Mr. Rucker, Mr. Giannini, and the defendant, John Orr, as well as the thirty-one million people in the state of California, and say that *that* man there deserves the death penalty for his crimes.

"A man who, twenty-some-odd years ago, undertook an oath to protect the people of the city of Glendale, to be a firefighter, to save lives.

And then his reign of terror came down upon the citizens of California. And when you come out that door after deliberating on this, you will have to tell us all that justice was served in this case. The people submit to you that the only morally justified punishment in this case is death.

"It is not an easy decision, but that is, in fact, the case about a man who is trained to protect and investigate and arrest the exact people that he has become. That's what we trained him to do, but he took that training, that special knowledge that we gave him, and turned it against us. He used it to take the lives of four innocent people, four innocent people who went to work that day or to shop that day."

Mike Cabral called on a righteous God and biblical passages to counter Peter Giannini's Cain and Abel allusion, just in case scriptures would carry the day. Then he confronted Giannini's characterization of the Ole's crimes.

"Now, Mr. Giannini says, well, Mr. Orr really has not crossed the line into the worst of the worst. He has taken the lives of four innocent citizens. How is that just your ordinary arson murder? The people submit that would be a gross miscarriage of justice and deny the victims their due day in court.

"Now, Mr. Giannini spoke to you, and right near the end of his argument he said the defendant is a man of compassion and empathy, saying look how he'd tried to help the man at Bell's Cottage. But I ask you to scour the evidence in this case for signs of a conscious empathy on the part of the defendant. Did he show any empathy for the victims of the Ole's fire? The evidence reflects he took pictures. Then what did he do to add insult upon Mr. Troidl's two-and-a-half-year-old son? He used his name in his manuscript. This is what the defendant has to say about those four people in the Ole's fire."

Cabral then picked up the manuscript and said, "Now, if you look at page ten you'll see that it ends with, 'Aaron had already killed five people in one of his fires.' But what does the rest of that paragraph say?"

He read aloud the paragraph that he'd been holding back for this moment: " 'He rationalized the deaths as he did everything. It wasn't his fault. People to him just acted stupidly. And their death had nothing to do with the fact that he set the fire. They just reacted too slowly. It was too bad about the baby, but, shit, it wasn't my fault.' "

Cabral diluted his message by overexplaining what they'd just heard. After that he turned to the manuscript and read more: " 'He loved the inadvertent attention he derived from the newspaper coverage, and hated it when he wasn't properly recognized. The deaths were blotted out of his mind. It wasn't his fault. Just stupid people acting as stupid people do.' "

He put down the manuscript, and again characterizing the novel as a memoir, said, "Now, I ask you, ladies and gentlemen of the jury, if you have heard any evidence that Carolyn Krause, Jimmy Cetina, Ada Deal, or Matthew Troidl did anything to be called stupid, because of the way they died? The only thing those individuals did was they had the misfortune of getting in the path of the defendant as he continued his reign of terror throughout the state of California.

"You heard Dr. Markman. He says the defendant is a sick man. Well, you heard the testimony of his former girlfriend concerning her car. Rather interesting, since the defendant supposedly set fires only under compulsion, trying to relieve the tension from his obsessing over something, we're not certain *what*.

"The people submit to you that his fire-setting pattern was all about power and control. He talks about that in that book, how he loves the *power* of watching these people come screaming out of the store. The *power* as it affects everybody's lives. And he requires the fire department to come in and bring all their units. He's in *control*.

"And then what does he do with that? Well, if he's got a video camera, he turns it into a video so everybody can see it. He's got his little secret. His little secret is that he knows he did it. He knows that *he* did it.

"Dr. Markman goes on to say it would be devastating to his life if the defendant had to actually admit that he had done these things. All he did was plead guilty, and then felt he was being undercut in doing it. Dr. Markman says it would be devastating to his life because it would be an admission that his life was a failure.

"Ladies and gentlemen of the jury, the people submit to you that his life *is* a failure. That's what the evidence in this case clearly establishes, that he is a complete failure in life."

Mike Cabral talked about punishment and retribution, saying that life in a prison cell was much better than what the defendant had given to his victims. And he asked them to remember the frail and devastated Billy Deal, the first prosecution witness in the case—and it must have seemed long ago to that jury. He talked of how Billy Deal had lost the wife with

whom he'd wished to grow old, and his grandson, and that now Billy
Deal could not grow old in peace.

"The defendant took that away from Mr. Deal," Mike Cabral said.
"But he asks you to give it to *him*. To allow *him* to have that. And the people say, once again, that the only moral, just penalty in this case is death."

For the remaining several minutes he kept repeating what the victims
and their families had lost, but each repetition seemed to diminish the
impact. In a sense, Mike Cabral's remarkable memory, which had allowed
him to cover every detail, might have worked against him here.

In the end, he chose not "conscience of the community," as Sandra
Flannery had done, but retribution and revenge: "Certainly the defendant's family is entitled to your sympathy. There's absolutely no doubt
about that. But the people submit to you that their sympathy is outweighed by the impact that this fire had on all the victims, including
Matthew Troidl, Ada Deal, Carolyn Krause, and Jimmy Cetina. Because
the defendant's grandson, unlike Matthew Troidl, will get to see his
grandfather again, to tell his grandfather about the happy events in his
life, to grow up with his family, spend time with his family. The very
things that the defendant has denied his victims.

"And twenty years from now, as Mr. Giannini referenced, John Orr's
grandson will be twenty-four years old, a young man. He may have a
family just like Carolyn Krause did. May actually be able to go and see his
grandfather and show him the family pictures. But Carolyn's children
won't have their mother there to show pictures to, and to gush over the
children that they have raised. Her children won't have their mother
there to prepare for all the rites of passage that we have in our teenage
years and into adulthood.

"The defendant asks you to give him that mercy. The people submit
that it is unjust to give him that mercy. The people submit to you that the
aggravating factors in this case, the circumstances of the crimes, the impact
that it's had on the victims and the defendant's secret knowledge, all
aggravate this case well beyond any of the mitigating evidence in this case.
And we ask you to return with a verdict of death. Thank you."

The victim's families, particularly Kim Troidl talking about her son and
mother, had shown this jury the face of consummate human agony. A

juror's mixed feelings about capital punishment, retribution, or the value
of human life might count for little upon recalling that woman's desola-
tion. Facts could be forgotten, the law ignored, in a rush to provide her
with a drop of solace. One could easily imagine a juror thinking: Put him
to death if that's what it takes. Kill him. Kill him twice. *Anything* to ease
that woman's everlasting torment.

Ed Rucker knew that, and his argument was unlike any of the others.
It was intensely personal, at times was as much about himself as it was
about the defendant. He said, "I'm the last lawyer who will speak to you
and we'll be through with the arguments today. This is a rather awesome
responsibility, speaking to people who we can't have a discussion with,
about whether we are going to take somebody's *life*. I sure don't feel
qualified to do it. I wish we had the ability to bring someone in here to
help you. To bring in a minister, priest, rabbi, somebody to speak to you
with some wisdom, with more humanity. I don't feel wise enough to do
that. But this is our system, and I am going to do the best I can to help
you with this.

"The last few days I haven't slept much. I was up in the middle of the
night walking around the house thinking what I could say. And I think the
best thing to say is what I think you might be concerned about, and what
you would think about before you'd reach a decision of this magnitude.

"This is a crime from South Pasadena. I lived in South Pasadena for
twenty years, raised my family there. My sons went to junior high school
and graduated from South Pasadena High School. Every Fourth of July
we go back to South Pasadena High School to watch the fireworks.

"I think I know some of the concerns I'd have if I were sitting in your
spot. And the first concern is, you don't want to make a mistake. Nobody
wants to make a mistake about something like this. And I know how
conscientious you were about your decision. That was very obvious. You
took your time. You looked at all the evidence. It was a thoughtful decision on your part, and you were convinced beyond a reasonable doubt
that John Orr set that fire at Ole's.

"I accept that. I accept it. But now is not the time for us *not* to talk
honestly with each other. I'm telling you honestly from the heart, with all
due respect, *all* due respect, that I just happen to disagree with your decision. I accept it, but I happen to disagree.

"The death penalty is an absolute punishment. There's no coming back from the death penalty. In order to impose an absolute punishment you've got to be absolutely certain, and His Honor is going to read you a jury instruction about that. It is appropriate for the jury to consider in mitigation any lingering doubt it may have concerning the defendant's guilt. Lingering doubt or residual doubt is defined as that state of mind between a reasonable doubt and beyond all possible doubt. So if you have any doubt at all that John Orr didn't set the Ole's fire, you can use that as evidence in mitigation. Because this is something that has happened under our system. Men have been convicted, men have been executed . . ."

Cabral stopped that with an objection, and the judge said, "Yes, *that* is objectionable. Disregard the last comments."

Rucker continued, "Well, two hundred years ago, Thomas Jefferson said that until the infallibility of man's judgment is proven, I will not favor the death penalty. And that's common sense. So how certain are you? How certain *can* you be? Remember, this is a case of circumstantial evidence. No witness came in here and said, I saw John Orr set that fire. No police officer came in here and said, I arrested John Orr and he *told* me he committed that arson. You didn't hear any witness say they saw John Orr driving away from the fire. No device was found at that fire."

With this approach Rucker was taking a road less traveled. Lawyers seldom refute the jury's findings in the penalty phase of a capital murder trial. It's too easy to anger a jury by implying that they've been wrong, but that is what he did for several minutes.

He said that because so much time had passed since 1984, perhaps all witnesses had not been found, and he began to directly argue again, saying that there *were* witnesses who'd seen smoke coming from the roof. He was still arguing for his attic fire, a very risky tactic at this point, after the jury had already decided that issue. But he persisted.

Rucker told them that during Cabral's final argument, he'd suddenly realized for the first time that the fire could have gone up over the south exit, through the acoustical tile and back through the attic area, accounting for all fire burns in that area. Rucker couldn't stop. He was *still* arguing his case. Possibly, Ed Rucker could get away with it because he was so desperate to save another man's life. He was imploring them with passion and humility to have mercy on his client. This giant of a lawyer was figuratively on his knees.

"It was heart wrenching," he said, "to listen to those parents talk of the loss of a child, loss of a mother, loss of a loved one. Unfortunately . . . unfortunately, we cannot change that. We just *can't*!

"Now, you could not be lenient to John Orr if you wanted to. No words can describe how horrific a punishment life without the possibility of parole *is*. One cannot describe the man-made hell of steel and cement that you are going to drop that man into. Everything that we use to define life and living is taken away. And they suggest to you that he would sit there and somehow *enjoy* thinking about fires? He is going to sit there and think what he has done to his life, and what he has done to other people, and what he has done to his family, and have no respite from that.

"You are never required to give the death penalty. You have to *choose* to give the death penalty. I would suggest to you that John Orr is not so reprehensible. He has not led such a despicable life. He is not so lacking in redeeming human qualities that he falls among the worst of the worst. We *can* protect ourselves from John Orr. We can lock him up forever. We do not need to *kill* him. And the things that he has done in his life must count for something. They *must*. They must count to set him aside from the worst of the worst."

After describing how John Orr's family loved him, and his service in the air force, and lifesaving as a firefighter, he again tried to separate his client from the worst of the worst. He said, "This was not an act based on evil. This was an act based on a mental defect. Anybody who sets fires time after time after time—and doesn't do other antisocial things such as robbing banks or raping women—what does that tell you? He's not normal. He's got a mental defect. That is something under the law that you can consider.

"I don't think, in the rush of the moment, in the heat of anger, in the very understandable sympathy for the victims of these fires, that we always think about the consequences of a decision to take somebody's life. I personally think we all pay a price if we do that. I don't understand the twisted logic that says somehow we'll show respect for human life by *taking* human life. I think, as a society, we erode our respect for life when we do that. I think that's the signal we send to our children. And I think all of us in this courtroom will have to lose a little bit of our humanity if we vote to take a life. I think you are going to have to deaden a little part of you to do that.

"You know, one of the ghoulish aspects of this process is that as his lawyer, I get invited to the execution. So I will be living with this for a while. We pay a price. And you will pay a price if you vote for this.

"In all the years I have practiced law I have never known a juror who regretted passing up the opportunity to give somebody the death penalty. One of the most uplifting moments of my life is when I was in college at Berkeley, I had the honor of being on a committee to welcome Dr. Martin Luther King. I got to shake his hand. And I remember when he was shot down by an assassin, his wife, Coretta King, said she would not join the voices of cynical people who felt that the killer of her husband deserved the death penalty. She said that's not what Martin would have wanted. It's not what *she* wanted.

"Now, it's hard to speak to you about mercy, but I do know that there is some benefit to all of us if we stretch out a hand in an act of mercy. And mercy is not given to somebody who's earned it. It's not given to somebody who you have sympathy for. An act of mercy is given for your benefit. *Your* benefit. It's what makes us human. It raises us above whoever we sit in judgment on.

"If one of you, one, decides that John Orr should not receive the death penalty, he doesn't. So what that means is, each of you has the power to give life or take life. Each of you. It is very tempting sometimes, particularly for a man, to think that taking life is the brave thing to do. The strong thing to do. I don't agree with that. I don't know how brave it is to say, I want somebody else to take this man down a hall and strap him in a chair. You don't give medals for those who serve on firing squads.

"If you believe the death penalty is not appropriate, I'm begging you to be strong in your resolve. This is not a time for weakness. Each of you have equal dignity. If you don't vote your heart, and if you don't vote your conscience, that means somebody else gets *two* votes. And that means sometime in the future you're going to look back and say you didn't fulfill your oath and your responsibility.

"I'm asking you to spare this man's life. I am not ashamed of it. I am going to *beg* you, for my sake, for his sake, for his family's sake, for all our sake. I am going to ask you to be strong. I am going to ask you to bring back a verdict of life without the possibility of parole."

After the judge read his lengthy jury instructions an adjournment was taken until the next morning. Observers could debate the different approaches taken by the four lawyers in the courtroom that day, but if passion was an important ingredient in such circumstances, it was clear which side got the edge. Rucker looked like a man who would've closed his argument with a Glock .45 and a chain saw, if it would've saved his client's life.

Peter Giannini reported that Ed Rucker had been brokenhearted when the guilty verdict for the Ole's fire had come in, and he certainly wouldn't be getting much sleep as he awaited *this* verdict. One way or the other, Ed Rucker said he was through with death-penalty cases.

On Tuesday, July 7, Juror Number Eight was unable to be in court due to a personal emergency and was excused. Alternate Number Four was seated, and deliberations were begun.

Late in the morning, on Wednesday, July 8, the jury handed a note to the bailiff that read: "Is there a legal definition for the term force or violence? And if there is, is the commission of an arson considered the use or threat of use, of force or violence as used in CALJIC 8.85, subsection b?"

That was enough to get the lawyers and the judge into a legal dispute for an hour or so, and in the afternoon the jury was brought into the courtroom.

"This is our answer," the judge said. "The terms force or violence have their ordinary meaning. An arson of property is not considered to be criminal activity involving the use of force or violence unless there is the threat of harm or injury to humans, or a danger to human life."

On Thursday, July 9, with all lawyers present, the judge said, "We've received a note from the jury approximately forty minutes ago. That note reads, 'The jury is deadlocked. We do not think further deliberations would be helpful.'"

The jury was brought out and seated, and the judge made the inquiry: "Juror Number Five, do you think any additional read-back of testimony or any further instruction on the law might assist this jury in breaking the deadlock?"

"No, I do not," said Juror Number Five, the foreperson.

The judge then asked the same question of every other juror and received the same answer from each of them.

The judge said to the foreperson: "Can you tell us in what direction the last vote was, and what the numbers were?"

"It was in the direction of the death penalty. Eight to four."

"All right," said Judge Perry. "I have declared a mistrial. We are going to release you. I want to tell you that it has been a long road that we started on April thirtieth. I want to express my sincere appreciation for the devotion you have shown in judging this case."

Judge Perry set the matter for sentencing and asked for a declaration by the district attorney if the prosecution intended to seek a retrial on the penalty phase. The judge lifted all gag orders, but advised Cabral to be careful in talking to the press if he was *considering* a retrial.

And it was over, finally *over,* until sentencing on September 10 at 8:30 A.M.

Mike Cabral had a barbecue at his home, and all of his DA's task-force members were invited. Everyone but Walt Scheuerell, who was living in retirement near Yosemite, made the long drive east to Moreno Valley. And everyone agreed that they had experienced their "career case."

All in all, it was a lighthearted celebration with lots of kudos to Mike Cabral for being the first prosecutor ever to rehabilitate a very old case of "accidental fire," at the same time successfully prosecuting a defendant for a capital crime. It would certainly be his career case.

One of the people at that barbecue was former Burbank arson investigator Steve Patterson, who brought a trophy to Cabral on behalf of the task force. And they presented it with beers and cheers and as much seriousness as they could muster. Steve Patterson seemed to be enjoying his retirement, and almost, but not quite, made it through the afternoon without mentioning Mary Susan Duggan, saying what a pity it was that he couldn't have persuaded others to heed his theory, to listen to his evidence, to act on his hunch.

And everybody within earshot would suddenly get hungry and sidle away for some more barbecue.

The sentencing of John Orr was supremely anticlimactic. He came into Judge Perry's courtroom wearing jail blues, looking a decade older than he'd looked when he'd been taken into the county jail system nearly four years earlier. Peter Giannini stood with him and was not even acknowledged by the angry defendant.

Judge Perry sentenced John Leonard Orr to four concurrent terms of life imprisonment without the possibility of parole, plus twenty-one years on the additional fires. All in all, it was not an unhappy day for the defendant, who would now get out of county lockup and into a federal penitentiary where he could start to live like a human being.

Of course, the District Attorney's Office informed the court that they would not be retrying the penalty phase, and it was truly finished, except for the inevitable appeal.

Eighteen months later, on March 15, 2000, the Court of Appeal of the State of California, Second Appellate District, decided an appeal from a judgment of the Superior Court of Los Angeles County in the case of the *People v. John Leonard Orr*. The judgment of Judge Robert J. Perry's court was affirmed with a slight modification of the consecutive sentences in the College Hills fire. The appellate court agreed that the defendant's aim had been to set a brush fire, and the burning of homes was incidental to his objective, so the consecutive terms imposed were deemed in error, and the sentence was modified. That meant that after serving his federal term and his state term for all of his natural life, he would only have to serve another twelve years instead of twenty-one.

23

THE QUEST

After his appeal was rejected, life for John Orr was still worth living. His was not the kind of personality that turns toward a wall and shrivels. Indeed, his life at "Club Fed," the U.S. Penitentiary at Lompoc, was surprisingly tolerable. He lived in a room, not a cage. He called it, wryly, his "mini-apartment." He was in the Honor Unit, so the door to his room was left open unless there was a general lockdown for some reason, and he could come and go to the common bathroom down the corridor. And there was another common room with a TV where programs were selected by vote of the inmates in the Honor Unit. He wished for a good steak once in a while, but reported that he was in the best shape of his life. He looked younger and certainly healthier than he'd looked during his murder trial.

John Orr became a prison librarian and taught creative writing to a small group of inmates. He'd managed to write a voluminous autobiography called *Baptismal Fire,* describing how he'd been betrayed by a system of sinister investigators, incompetent lawyers, dishonest prosecutors, and biased judges, who'd demanded that he produce impossible "lunch with the pope" alibis, and convicted him when he couldn't.

He proclaimed his innocence to anyone who would listen and kept a fellow inmate, a "jailhouse lawyer," busy drafting an appeal of his government conviction under the theory that if he could have the Fresno verdict reversed all else would fall, because all else had been based upon that first conviction.

That was the theory, and he thought he could prevail by citing the Timothy McVeigh Oklahoma bombing case in a claim that government evidence had been withheld at his trial. The prisoner had twenty-seven phone numbers on his list of telephone contacts, and was allowed one ten-minute call per day.

Visitors were surprised by the facility in that beautiful part of the Central Coast, Lompoc being the flower-seed capital of America. Upon driving up to the prison, one would encounter less dangerous inmates jogging beside the entry road, and the climate was so mild that those prisoners could be outdoors just about all year. Even in the more secure part of the penitentiary, where John Orr lived, the guards wore blazers, white shirts, and ties, with nobody looking like the bulls from old prison movies. The visiting room was large and airy, and had food and drink machines and lots of kids running around on visiting days.

The real problem for him was that federal prison guidelines might mean that he could be paroled out of the federal system and into the state system as of 2002. He hoped that even if his appeal failed, he could find a way to stay at Lompoc for at least twenty years. Federal time was better than state time *any*time. State prison was what Ed Rucker and Peter Giannini had described to the jury as a living hell.

John Orr had managed to secure a literary agent, and both of his books, *Points of Origin* and *Baptismal Fire,* were to be published on-line as E-books. He was excited about that, even though no profits from book sales could go to him. Court TV interviewed him and he thought they'd done a fair job, better than other interviews he'd given. But after seeing the final product, he hated it.

And something else had happened. John Herzfeld, the Hollywood producer/director/writer, whom the Pillow Pyro Task Force had tried to enlist in getting a copy of John Orr's manuscript, had gotten his movie project off the ground. He was finally shooting his version of *Points of Origin,* having purchased the movie rights years earlier. It would be shown on Home Box Office and starred Ray Liotta as John Orr. Though the prisoner feared the cinematic depiction, clearly, he was thrilled by all the attention he was getting.

"Hoo-ray for Hollywood!"

So said Steve Patterson, after he'd been referred to John Herzfeld by Mike Cabral. Herzfeld and an associate came to his home and invited Patterson to a lunch at the L.A. Police Academy with actor Ray Liotta to chat about the secret life of John Orr. Steve Patterson was ebullient because John Herzfeld was the first person in years to want to hear about Mary Duggan, and Patterson found it all coming back, *pouring* back, washing over him. He persuaded Herzfeld to accompany him to the place where Mary Duggan's body had been found, and Herzfeld came to share Patterson's suspicion that John Orr *had* murdered her. He promised Patterson that he would try to exert pressure on Mike Cabral and the District Attorney's Office.

Two days later, Steve Patterson got a call from Cabral, who said, "Thanks a lot, Mr. Bigmouth! I get you a nice afternoon out with movie people and this is the *thanks* I get?"

"I hope I didn't get you in trouble," Steve Patterson told him.

Cabral said, "No, it's okay." Then he added, "To tell you the truth, I'd forgotten about Mary Duggan."

After the promised phone call from Herzfeld, Mike Cabral wrote a letter to the Burbank Police Department asking what had became of the vaginal swabs from the Mary Susan Duggan murder investigation of 1986. He informed the police that the District Attorney's Office was interested in pursuing a DNA test to determine if the genetic signature of the killer could be obtained. Cabral was told that a DNA test could be ordered, but would take six months due to the workload at the sheriff's DNA lab.

Mike Cabral went back to his busy life as the DA's arson prosecutor, and pretty much forgot about it again, especially after others in his office said, "Orr's doing life. What more do you *want*?"

Cabral could have told them what he'd said to John Orr's jury: that murder victims must not be denied their day in court. Steve Patterson said that's what he wanted for Mary Duggan, who had not lost her entitlement to justice. And that it was not *about* John Orr, it was about Mary Duggan.

After the six months had passed, Mike Cabral was prodded until he checked on his DNA request and discovered that nothing had been done. The genetic material had been misplaced, so after several frustrating calls to the police detectives and the DNA lab, the Bulldog finally got aroused.

In July 2001, he called Detective Carl Costanzo, Steve Patterson's former partner on the Burbank arson unit, and told him that the DA wanted *action*. Then Cabral asked for the homicide book on Mary Susan Duggan, but was told by the detective, "I'll have to check with my lieutenant on that."

The Burbank police seemed very anxious about being embarrassed if it turned out that there *was* a DNA match, after all the ridicule that Steve Patterson had endured, after so much time had passed when nothing had been done.

Cabral replied, "No, you don't understand. *Tell* your lieutenant that the District Attorney's Office is picking up that homicide file *today*. And I'm taking it home over the weekend to read it."

Only a few people learned about a peculiar thing that had occurred when Steve Patterson had first talked to John Herzfeld about Mary Duggan. Patterson thought that he was finished with his obsessive quest. True, he still kept a copy of the crime file in a bedroom drawer, and he couldn't help thinking of Mary Duggan occasionally. His daughter Jill may have brought it back when she'd experienced life's benchmarks. There was that, but for the sake of his emotional health, he believed that he'd put Mary Duggan away in a safe place and had moved on with his life.

But while he was sitting in his home telling Herzfeld about the murdered girl, a peculiar thing happened: his throat swelled, his voice broke, his eyes filled with burning tears, and he was astonished! Where had *that* come from?

It became apparent that Mary Susan Duggan, a young woman who'd been murdered and abandoned—and forgotten by the law—had not lost her champion after all.

A group from the California Conference of Arson Investigators had an idea that summer. They thought that by this time, John Orr *must* have mellowed, and might be willing to do something for his former profession in order to set right all of the wrongs. They contacted him at

Lompoc and requested permission to visit and shoot a video designed to explore the mind of the serial arsonist.

Perhaps none of them were aware of the seminal work done on psychopathy by Hervey Cleckley, who wrote *The Mask of Sanity,* a book with a catchy but misleading title that could have been called, more accurately, *The Mask of Normalcy.* Cleckley and others have pointed out that the psychopathic serial offender wears a mask, and that no one, not even the psychopath himself, peeks behind it except on the rarest of occasions.

John Orr's response to his former colleagues was terse: "If you want to study a serial arsonist, why have you contacted *me?*"

As summer ended, Mike Cabral became one in a long list of professional prosecutors to fall victim to political maneuverings. The newly elected district attorney decided that prosecutors who had been in the same job for a long time should be transferred. Letters protesting Cabral's ouster were sent by ATF, LAFD, LASD, and many fire chiefs in the Los Angeles area, all to no avail.

His national reputation, for rewriting the ATF course *Arson for Prosecutors* and for his arson lecture series given to psychologists and psychiatrists, all was deemed extracurricular. Cabral was sent to the Pomona office to handle ordinary cases, but was reminded that Pomona was much closer to the new home he had bought because their fourth child needed special education that only the Temecula school district offered. The girl had been born with a broken chromosome, and had vision, hearing, and learning problems.

However, Mike Cabral was a renowned arson prosecutor. Arson prosecution had always been his passion, so his voice lacked conviction when he told everyone that the arbitrary transfer closer to home was "probably for the best."

On September 11, 2001, John Orr's circumscribed world was immediately touched by the shattering events. Fellow inmate Mohammad Salameh, convicted of the World Trade Center bombing of 1993, was whisked from the unit never to return. He would eventually be transferred to a federal facility where he and the other WTC bombers could be more easily protected from fellow inmates.

A court order was signed by a Los Angeles Superior Court judge in October 2001 to extract blood and saliva from John Leonard Orr at the U.S. Penitentiary in Lompoc for a DNA comparison, reason unspecified. At first, John Orr was worried.

"What're they trying to pin on me?" he said, half joking. "The Chicago Fire? Or maybe . . . a *murder*?"

But then he figured that it had to do with his recent request for a DNA test, claiming it could clear him if there were still traces of DNA material on the cigarette butts used in the incendiary devices.

Mike Cabral saw John's request as a grandstand play to bolster his appeal. Cabral said that John knew very well that the cigarette butt in his trial had been dipped in ninhydrin for fingerprint traces. But the ploy was okay with Cabral as long as John donated his blood and saliva.

Had John Orr known Cabral's true reason for the DNA test, he'd have said that it was proof that the Los Angeles District Attorney's Office would never rest until they strapped him on a table in San Quentin Prison and killed him.

As he awaited the results of the DNA testing, Steve Patterson said that if there *was* a match, this fifty-seven-year-old retired firefighter would climb to the top of a promontory and blow a trumpet, as Gunga Din had done in the old movie. But perhaps Steve Patterson had forgotten that Gunga Din got shot down during his moment of greatest glory.

On January 14, 2002, Mike Cabral received a phone call from the DNA laboratory of the L.A. County Sheriff's Department. The material from the vaginal swab taken from the body of Jane Doe Number 39 did not match the DNA from the blood sample of Lompoc inmate John Orr. The killer of Mary Susan Duggan was still at large.

After Cabral phoned Steve Patterson, after profound disappointment,

Steve Patterson said, "Well, Mary's DNA and her killer's are finally on file. Maybe now Mary's killer can get caught."

Nothing had changed for him. Hopeful and unyielding, he was ever her champion.

And there was absolutely no more to be done by the People of the State of California in the strange case of John Leonard Orr.

EPILOGUE

erhaps it was fitting that the two people who'd tried so hard to be heard, who'd endured bureaucratic indifference and ridicule and sometimes hostility, were classified as law-enforcement officers but were not from the police ranks.

Marvin G. Casey of Bakersfield, though his contribution would always be demeaned by some from the Pillow Pyro Task Force and the DA's Arson Task Force, *had* solved the mystery of the Central Valley and Central Coast fires of 1987 and 1989. If other law-enforcement officers had been as instinctive and diligent as he, John Orr would have been arrested back then. Whether or not John Orr would have been linked to the Ole's blaze is doubtful, for he probably would not have written *Points of Origin*, a work that contributed much to putting him in prison for life. So some might argue that when Marv Casey was let down by law enforcement, the Ole's victims got their day in court.

Others would argue that law-enforcement mistakes—the classification of the Ole's fire as an accident, the grievous error with the fingerprint, the failures with the tracking device, and the unsatisfying interrogation—had all been redeemed by law enforcement. By the diligence of Mike Matassa, Glen Lucero, and their task force, and by the tenacity of Walt Scheuerell, Rich Edwards, and their task force, one might say that their work atoned for all of the mistakes, and made the arrest and prosecution of John Leonard Orr a success unlike any other.

In the end, it seems ironic that the most passionate investigators were not career law-enforcement officers, but firefighters. Marv Casey of Bakersfield and Steve Patterson of Burbank were firemen who'd attended training sessions conducted by John Orr and had admired him tremendously. Both Casey and Patterson had brought something extra to the investigation: the zeal and drive to right the wrongs that one of their own had done. The cops from both task forces had never taken the investigation so *personally* as had the firefighters, for after all, a cop is very different.

A friend and colleague of John Orr, Jim Allen of the state Fire Marshal's Office, a man who'd served at one time as a deputy sheriff and knew both sides of the coin, said: "Firefighters are cooperative, obedient team players. They pull levers, turn valves, man the hose lines, rescue things. Cops look for trouble, make quick decisions, get in people's faces, sometimes kill things. Firemen never really think like cops. Cops never really think like firemen."

The cynicism of law-enforcement professionals had caused a great deal of anxiety for Marv Casey and Steve Patterson, who had nevertheless stubbornly followed their intuition as far as they could. Marv Casey's hunch had been right. Steve Patterson's had not, but no one could say it had been a bad thing for a cruelly murdered girl to have had a zealous champion struggle so long to find justice for her, and, as he put it, a "tiny bit of comfort" for her family. It didn't seem in the end to have been a failure, that Quixotic mission. That quest.

In fact, it seemed most fitting that arson sleuths Marv Casey and Steve Patterson were not police officers, as John Orr had always longed to be. They were firefighters, a vocation that John Orr had only settled for, and one for which he may have been ill suited. If he was what every member of the task force said he was—a classic psychopath—then clinically speaking, the firefighter's ultimate reward was of little value and beyond his grasp. And he may have known it.

John Orr himself had often set it forth in his writings, sometimes sardonically, but perhaps a touch wistfully: everybody *loves* a fireman.